TELL THEM, SUCH IS GOD

TELL THEM, SUCH IS GOD

Rose Mathias

 ABBEY PRESS

St. Meinrad, Indiana 47577

Cover Illustration:
Glen Hansen

Library of Congress Catalog Number
87-72435

ISBN 0-87029-210-2

Go about Zion, make the round;
  count her towers.
Consider her ramparts,
  examine her castles,
That you may tell the next generation
  that such is God,
Our God forever and ever;
  he will guide us.

Ps. 48:13-15

Author Rose (Chasin) Mathias, a youthful octogenarian, has spent "half a lifetime" in the field of radio and television, including many years as story consultant, editor, and writer for the famed television series, "Lassie." A widow, she has received numerous professional and community service awards. Among these are recognition from Pioneer Broadcasters, the Southern California Motion Picture Council, D.O.V.E.S. (Dedicated Older Volunteers in Educational Services), and Build Rehabilitation Industries (for handicapped teenagers). She makes her home in Sherman Oaks, California.

Tell Them, Such is God is based on the author's recollections and experiences. It takes place in the early 1900s.

CONTENTS

BOOK ONE

Woods End

~ 1 ~

Fr. O'Neil, pastor of St. Mary's Catholic Church in Woods End, had reached the age when a little rotundity around the middle can be expected. His face, under a balding head with silver-rimmed spectacles down low on the bridge of his nose, bespoke a man who believed in following ritual. Such softness as might have been expected in the cherubic contour of his countenance had long ago given way to a firm demeanor which left no doubt about his intention to fulfill a purpose.

He knew that children quavered when they appeared before him, but it concerned him not. This was the value of discipline.

As young Fr. Francis Xavier Malachi looked at his superior with questioning eyes, Fr. O'Neil wasted no time in coming to the point. "I haven't seen Mike McGrority back in church . . . " There was a tone of accusation in the comment.

Fr. Malachi nodded. "I'm aware of that, Father. I've discussed it with his wife. She's equally distressed, good Catholic that she is, and we're both going to keep working on him."

Mike McGrority was more than an ordinary stray. He was the financial backbone of St. Mary's parish. Since his defection, people had almost stopped wondering if St. Mary's would ever build a church to replace the basement that served them. They longed for a worthy structure such as Holy Cross, the neighboring parish, had already built.

In Fr. O'Neil's estimation, it put St. Mary's to shame. He sighed as he shook his head, thinking that life was full of the sweetness of ripe fruit for Mike. *How could he have lost sight of the Lord?* he wondered.

Fr. Malachi watched the emotional conflict apparent behind Fr. O'Neil's spectacles, but he made no comment, aware that it is sometimes wiser to be silent.

Then, as though to break the trend of thought, Fr. O'Neil inquired, "How is the old lady?"

Fr. Malachi shook his head. "I'm afraid she's not long for this world."

The pause before Fr. O'Neil's comment was significant. "You could have hallow'd her soul." Abruptly, Fr. O'Neil walked to the door and closed it behind him, leaving Fr. Malachi motionless with the sting of the rebuke—and the consequent self-scrutiny: *Could I have in the beginning? Could I even now? And more important, would I even if I could?*

Fr. Malachi moved to the window and surveyed the scene before him, so like a picture on a Christmas greeting card: pure and serene. He prayed, *Our Father, who art in heaven, have I failed thee?* And then he remembered it was Saturday. He would be hearing confessions, and the serenity of Woods End would be found only in the beautiful snow scene before him, and he would have to make his own peace with God.

~ 2 ~

Woods End was awake.

The milkman, with the cuff of his wool cap rolled down over his ears, moved his scarf around to cover his nose and mouth while snapping the reins to get his horse moving, the clop-clopping of its hooves dulled by the snow. Reaching a street of row houses, he reined the horse to a stop and grabbed a rack of milk bottles—the frozen cream extended like white corks from the bottles' mouths. His steady customers had year-round deliveries, but it was nice to pocket an extra dollar or two from those who found it too cold to walk to the dairy farm where one could have fresh milk squirted right into your milk tin for less.

The milkman swung his arms to stimulate warmth as he hopped back onto the truck.

The coal dealer's horse and wagon made virgin tracks in the soft white powder. This was weather he, too, liked. The kitchen stoves would be kept hotter than usual to push as much heat as possible into the dining rooms and the bedrooms, and extra coal would be needed for the pot-bellied stoves in the parlors, should company be expected. He click-clicked to his horse. He was sorry that much of the territory of Woods End was a waste of energy for the beast and for himself: the meadows, the woods, and the frozen brook were not things of beauty when there was no dollar to be made.

As he passed St. Mary's, he made the sign of the cross with

his mittened hand and wondered when a church would be built—
a real church like Holy Cross in the adjacent neighborhood. Now
that was a growing community. He felt a twinge of envy. Sup-
plying coal there, a dealer might earn better than a fair living for
his family.

He snapped the reins to stir up the horse. He was approaching
the McGrority place where, he comforted himself, there would
be the usual large order to heat their big barn of a house, the
envy of the "ordinary" folks in town.

~ *3* ~

Mike McGrority was awake with a hangover. He'd tossed the
night through, thrashing in the brass bed until Bridget had
slapped his rump to keep him still.

He stumbled from the bed, his body swathed in long-sleeved,
woolen underwear, and fumbling around, finally got his legs
into a pair of pants. Leaving his suspenders hanging loose, he
staggered toward the kitchen sink.

"A tirrible night . . . tirrible," he muttered. He splashed and
snorted until his eyes could focus, then gave Bridget a hangdog
look in hopes of evoking some sympathy for his aching head.

Mike was a redheaded bull of an Irishman who took his liquor
like he thought a man should—standing up until he was blind
and then still being able to find his way home. It was a man's
right, Mike insisted, to enjoy a bit of spirits with his friends—
and damned be those who thought otherwise.

Rather, Bridget contended, damnation would surely be *his*
end. She, a churchgoing, God-fearing woman who made a habit
of going to confession, was ashamed of him. And young Mike,
she feared, was the spitting image of his father, swaggering
about and giving her the lip. Many's the back of her hand she
had had to land on him. And why, Bridget wanted to know, was
Mike always using the kitchen sink to wash in like any immigrant when there was a fancy bathroom with a tub and basin
which he himself had installed in the house.

"Sure is a sad state of affairs," Mike grumbled, "when a man
can't be himself and wash where he wants to! Just tend to your
business, woman, which right now is preparin' a proper breakfast for a workin' man, so that I can be nourished enough to get
to the barber where I can rest my head under a hot towel an' not

listen to the jabberin' of a wife who's supposed to have a proper respect for her husband and provider!"

Bridget stirred up the coals in the stove, whispering a prayer for patience. She would have to talk to the good Father about Mike, for the devil was bound to take him if he kept up this way. She sighed—a deep, heart-heavy sigh. *The divil already has his eyes on us,* she thought, *what with Kathryn gone from home in disgrace, marryin' a Jewboy . . . and only the Lord himself can prevent young Mike from headin' toward perdition, playin' hookey from school until the teacher has to send for me . . . and there's no point in tellin' the mister because he'd answer, "Schoolin's not for everyone. I've had none nor my sainted father, and am I not your devoted husband and the most important man in Woods End?"* To the latter, Bridget had to agree.

An Irishman and the son of a bricklayer, Mike had learned to hold a hammer and strike a nail head-on before he was out of knee pants. With pride, old Jim McGrority had set a sign above his little shop declaring "McGrority & Son, Bricklaying & Building." Jim continued to be a bricklayer, but Mike cast his sights farther. The sign also said "Building," and a builder he would be. Together, father and son had scraped and saved every spare penny—and even those they could not spare—until there was enough for a down payment on a piece of land. Later, they managed to borrow enough to build a house that was the last word in comfort in the late eighteen hundreds. It was sold before they had a chance to polish the doorknobs. Mike prided himself on this, his first major accomplishment. The buyer, a Swiss watchmaker, knew the value of a handmade house in the same way Mike knew the value of a handmade watch.

Mike became a builder of custom homes and the legend of his prosperity grew. With prosperity came power. Mike boasted that he had made his money the hard way and that if he could do it, anyone could.

Mothers set traps to introduce this most eligible bachelor to their marriageable daughters, but it was Bridget Monahan, an orphan come lately to America, who caught his eye and heart. Mike built his bride the finest house in Woods End, with bedrooms to spare for the young ones who would come in due course.

Though Mike would have preferred a namesake to be the first, it was Kathryn, brown-eyed and dark-haired, who squalled her way into their hearts—a "black-Irish" lass who should have been a boy by the will of her!

And then there was a wait for the next wee one. "Where are the babies we were supposed to have to fill this cavern of a house?" Mike complained to Bridget. He was becoming the butt of jokes at Sweeney's Saloon. It was a reflection on his manhood: a big hulk of an Irishman who couldn't ram a baby into his wife's belly. Mike took her with viciousness and with lust, but to no avail. Their doctor knew neither the cause nor the cure. Mike doubled his intake at Sweeney's, and his bruised and swollen knuckles were mute testimony to the defense of his manhood.

Bridget prayed for Mike and for a baby. Fr. Malachi shook his head as he counseled the distraught Bridget. "You must not pray for *things*—even for a baby. Prayer is for faith in God's will, in his judgment."

But six years after Kathryn, the miracle occurred. Bridget was delivered of young Mike. The proud father celebrated by going on a brawling binge that lasted a week, all the while boasting that the young sprig would be a chip off the old block, and that from then on, he'd father a string of young ones.

But to Mike's chagrin, no more babies came—and Bridget knew she was a disappointment to her husband and to her church.

She also knew it was Mike to whom St. Mary's parish was looking to complete its dream of a church. But for each year Bridget did not deliver another child, Mike became increasingly bitter. And if Bridget was a disappointment to her husband, Mike in turn believed the church had failed him.

Fr. O'Neil sighed as he shook his head, thinking that life was full of the sweetness of ripe fruit for Mike. How could Mike McGrority have lost sight of the Lord?

~ 4 ~

Goldie lay quietly as she listened for the whistle of the locomotive with its train of coal-laden cars that shuttled and rumbled and left a trail of droppings alongside the tracks.

Ach, ach, ach, she thought sadly. There would be no more of that for her—bending to scoop up coal fragments until her back ached. Who would say it was a pleasure to get up while it was still dark and sneak out into a cold that hit like needles against one's face? Joey, who always got angry that his baba didn't wake him, would rush into his clothes to go with her. He knew a pail full of coal was a gift when the coal box showed it would soon be empty and money was in short supply. Often, they would have to tell the coal man to delay a few days before bringing up their weekly heap.

Goldie snickered to herself. It had been a game they played, outwitting Manya, who always seemed to be asleep the mornings she and Joey sneaked out. Ah, but then there was the argument afterwards, the same as before: "How does it look in a new neighborhood for a Jewish old lady to be going along like a ragpicker, scooping up pieces of coal?"

A ragpicker should only look so good, Goldie mused, recalling herself covered from head to knees in a woolen shawl over a sweater, both of which she had knitted. She would follow the tracks and, spotting lumps of coal, stoop and scoop the black nuggets into a sack, all the while reminding Joey to keep his stocking cap pulled down over his ears.

Later, as they sat sipping hot tea, Manya would insist further, "Even if we're poor, we don't have to advertise it."

Goldie would argue back, "We get there before anybody else, that way we get the best pieces of coal. We fill our bucket and leave, so we don't see anybody and nobody sees us. And," Goldie added with pride, "Joey watches out for me."

But Manya never gave in easily. "It's undignified for a grandmother. I don't even want Joey doing it. And now Veeza wants to go; she wants to prove she can do it, too."

Goldie had countered, "The children have to learn to face life."

"Not yet," Manya had protested. "Not while I can spare them."

Now, from her bed, Goldie heard the whoo-whoo of the diesel. No one would miss her along the tracks except maybe the engineer who always waved his hand as the train rumbled by. Yes, maybe he would miss her.

She lay watching the candles flicker in the gray winter dawn. *It must be the Sabbath,* she thought. Lighting the Sabbath candles had never attracted Manya. To Goldie, however, it was a pleasure to welcome the Sabbath princess on the Sabbath eve—Friday night. *How sad it is to be deprived of such a simple pleasure—but life offers no guarantees as to length or quality of years.* Then she snickered to herself. *Since when have I become a philosopher? With a burden such as myself on Manya's hands, it's a wonder she can remember she has a head.*

Goldie knew she was dying, and she wasn't the only one who knew it: the dog knew it, too. Where was it she'd heard that an animal senses death more readily than a human? Joey had brought the whimpering and half-starved mongrel home one day, its eyes closed with pus.

"We need another mouth to feed like we need a hole in the head," Manya had complained. But the dog remained and grew fat from the tidbits off their plates. And although Joey and Veeza had accepted responsibility for its care, the dog attached itself to Manya. You could see the sadness in its eyes when Manya left for work, and you could tell the time of day by the sight of the dog sitting near the door waiting for her to return.

Now the dog no longer took its place at the foot of Manya and Leon's bed, but kept vigil close to Goldie instead. For the dog knew and Goldie knew. Maybe not today or tomorrow, but for sure the angel of death was coming. Goldie recalled an old wives' tale. *Just how did it go? Oh yes, the job of being the angel of death was vacant, but no one had applied for it. Every angel knew it was a hated job. Then one angel said, "For all the people who hate the angel of death, think of how many more love her when she passes them by!"* But, Goldie thought, *that is before a person is ready to go. I am ready. I know and the dog knows.*

From the next room, Goldie could hear Leon's and Manya's breathing, and she longed for the little hall room where she'd slept with Veeza. Sharing a bed with a little ten-year-old girl was like recapturing a slice of time and life, with the future still a mystery, its path to be played like a game.

But Goldie knew it was more practical to have her in the bedroom next to the dining room where Manya could watch her from the kitchen. Unfortunately, Joey had to be moved from his bed to the parlor couch, which is not the most comfortable place for a growing boy.

Disrupting a household is not a comfortable feeling either, thought Goldie. *Feeling! Ach! What a word, feeling.* She could only feel her mind stretching the word out like a rubber band; she felt nothing else.

The snow formed delicate, lacy patterns on the window, and the flakes made tippy-toe noises as they danced against the windowpane. Imagine being able to see and hear across the length of a room! But then, not too long ago, Goldie had prided herself on being able, without glasses, to thread a needle faster than Manya could, and it seemed to her that even now her hearing was surely better than ever.

She felt her eyes closing. She would go back to sleep. But sleep escaped her and her mind inquired, *How long has it really been since I became like a prisoner, locked in the cell of my own body?* Time had drifted and she had lost all sense of it. Suddenly she felt an indefinable terror that time was endless.

"Oh God, why hast thou forsaken me?" she screamed. But the only sound which came from her was an eerie, "Aaeerree," and the pitch rose until it pierced the air like a stiletto.

In the adjoining room, Manya awoke with a start.

Why is it that my blood turns to water when she cries out like that? her mind questioned. She cast a quick look at Leon who lay staring at the ceiling, his face a mask of distress.

"Manya, it's too much . . . every night . . . all day . . ."

Manya looked at him, a world of thoughts unspoken. *Is it too much,* she wanted to ask, *for the years she has given to me—to us?*

But then a fleeting, guilt-ridden thought flashed through her mind. Were it not for Goldie, would things really have been different? Not that anything was Goldie's fault. After all, it was she, Manya, who had insisted that her mother live with them. Papa was dead and her brother, Sidney, couldn't include an immigrant mother in his life-style, and so Manya came as a bride to Leon, and with her came Goldie, Leon's shviger—his mother-in-law. *But,* Manya reminded herself, *Mama earned her keep. After all, who would have been our mainstay through the years while I went out to work?*

Leon sensed the words which were left unsaid between them: always another job, always another place, the letters he sent without money and the letters he should have sent. Would it have been any different without Goldie? He wondered. Why would it have been? She got along better with him than she did with her own son. But it was too late for him to ever know.

As Manya reached for her wrapper, she cast a quick glance toward the parlor where Joey lay sprawled on the couch, hunched up in the blankets, one leg hanging over the side. *A growing boy should have stretching room. Perhaps we could get a cot to set up in the dining room where it would be warmer, too.*

As she stood to tie the wrapper closed, Manya's eyes came to rest on the little Christmas tree sitting on the parlor table. Someone had asked if it was a Chanukah tree. Manya had never heard of such a thing, but then, who knows. Maybe somewhere there is such a custom. Meantime, there it stood, bare of its needles, like a spectre with bony arms outstretched. A few ornaments still hung forlornly on its dead frame.

Why couldn't she bring herself to get rid of it? Manya felt the blood surging through her body until, even in the chill of the room, she felt the sweat seeping out of her pores. Was she waiting for Goldie to die? She shivered as with the thought came another piercing protest—"Aaarrruuu"—which brought her to Goldie's bedside. She struck a match, turned the gas jet, and lit a low, flickering flame.

Goldie lay exactly as Manya had left her the night before, immobile as a log. She held her eyes closed to block out her feelings of indignity as Manya slipped the covers from her, rolled her to one side, and deftly slid the slip sheet toward the middle of the bed. Manya removed the diaper, expertly cleaned and powdered the sunken buttocks, and took a fresh diaper from the pile on the bureau. She knew the mechanics with her eyes half-shut. Then she replaced the blankets, tucking them close around Goldie's chin.

"Sleep a little more, Mama. You want something? a drink of water? some hot tea?"

Goldie lay quietly, her eyes now open wide, tiny pools of blue concentrating on Manya. *I will say it real slow,* she thought, *so it comes out just as I'm thinking it: "No thank you, daughter. Go back to bed, you need your rest."* But instead Goldie only heard herself say, "Aarree!" Her eyes darkened with fury. *No, No, No,* her mind protested, *it isn't coming out as I'm saying it!* She looked pleadingly at Manya, who stood waiting, praying for some miracle to take place.

Was it as hopeless as the doctor had said—that Goldie could last for days or weeks or months, that her mind was functioning, her hearing acute, and her eyesight better than his, but she would never speak or move again? He'd shaken his head. "She belongs in a hospital—if there is one that would take her in this condition." Manya recalled straightening herself up and saying, "Never will I let that happen. My mother took care of me and my children when I needed her, and I'll take care of her now." The doctor had shrugged as if to say, "If that's your choice, there's nothing I can do about it."

Manya now stood and watched her mother struggle with nature's punishment. "Oh God," she murmured, "what has she done to deserve this? She buried eleven small children who died from the plague in Europe. She watched me bury two babies of my own. Isn't that enough?" She watched Goldie attempt to speak and finally give up.

They looked at each other, mother and daughter, eyes full of love—and full of embarrassment from their shared helplessness. Then Goldie's eyes closed slowly, trying to block out the sight of Manya's heartache. As if exhausted, she slept.

Manya remained at the bedside for a few seconds. How pretty her mother still appeared—how smooth her skin and her hair with only a touch of gray at the temples. She looked like a delicate, fading flower which one hates to part with and yet which nature will wither anyway.

Manya then shook herself into reality and bent to pat the dog as he raised his head and yawned, now accustomed to these nocturnal sessions. The mutt barely moved as Manya rolled the soiled laundry into a bundle and carried it into the kitchen to ready the washboiler. As she shook up the stove, Manya grunted with satisfaction. *I'd like to see a hospital keep Mama as clean as I do.*

Then she went back to bed. She would get up again before the water in the washboiler started to cook, but there was time yet for a little sleep.

Leon's arms awaited her. As she felt the heat of his body, her own desire rose within her and, with it, the guilt: the conflict between her hunger for him and her contempt for his weaknesses, her need to punish herself for not being able to release him and her inability to forgive him. Manya knew that she—her strength to cope—was the rock which lay between them and which periodically drove him away. Leon often left home "to find himself," only to return unfulfilled.

On his make-shift bed in the parlor, Joey lay scrunched up,

trying not to hear the goings-on in his grandmother's bed. He put the pillow over his head, trying to block out the sounds, but he knew what was happening. *Even if I am a boy, Mama should let me help,* he thought, while admitting to himself that tending to Baba was an ugly sight.

In the hall bedroom, ten-year-old Veeza had awakened, but did not get up. She knew Mama would only shuffle her back to bed as she had when it all began. She didn't see Mama cry anymore. Maybe tears get used up. Veeza tried to figure out where all the tears come from because she and Mama had surely cried plenty when it first happened.

Once, Mama had fallen asleep from sheer exhaustion and hadn't heard Baba's whimper. Veeza thought she would take care of Baba so Mama could sleep. If Baba needed changing, the diapers were close by on the dresser where they could be reached easily. Veeza knew the procedure.

Baba looked at Veeza that time with a questioning glare. Veeza had explained that Mama was sleeping and that after the diaper was changed, Baba should go back to sleep.

The shock of seeing her grandmother's sunken thighs and thin gray pubic hairs brought waves of nausea to Veeza. *I don't want hairs on me like that,* her mind had protested. And she didn't want the curse like her friend Irene had told her about. She had asked Mama if it was true, and Mama had turned away saying it wasn't nice to talk about such things. "But is it true, Mama?" she had demanded. "Does every girl get a curse like Irene says, where you get all bloody?" She remembered Mama dropping her eyes and saying, "It is true. It's a curse on all women, and you will be a woman some day."

"No, no, no!" Veeza had screamed. "I won't let it happen to me!" But she knew it would happen and that some day she would look as disgusting as Baba.

Now, as she heard her mother get back into bed, Veeza whimpered into her pillow, "Oh, Baba, I miss you so much, and it's all my fault. God, wherever you are up there, why did you punish her? You ought to strike me dead, right now. And if you do, I'll surely go to hell."

Then she remembered what Irene had said—and Irene knew everything, being so churchgoing and all: "No one goes to hell right away. You go to purgatory first, wherever that is, and hang by your heels until hell is ready to accept you. And there you roast!" Veeza remembered the day she had lit a match and held its flame to her skin to find out how much burning she could stand. She had quickly pulled the match away.

"But you have to suffer something in order to get in to heaven," Irene had insisted. "Even Jesus says, 'Suffer, little children, to come unto me,' and if you look at pictures of Jesus with his hands out calling, you know he loves children."

With her head buried in the pillow as if to hide, Veeza rocked back and forth and moaned, "Oh God, even if Jesus says children have to suffer, I don't want to."

Veeza thought of the night she and Baba had lain quietly in bed watching the full face of the moon looking in at them through the window. "Is there really a man in the moon?" she had asked. "He looks so real, and he's got a little bit of smile—like he's pleased with what he is seeing."

Goldie had answered, "He's pleased because all the good people are sleeping as they should be, excepting one old grandmother and one little girl who'll be very tired in the morning."

"But I'm not sleepy. I feel like talking."

"So talk . . . maybe I'll sleep."

"Baba, are you ever going to learn to speak English?"

"Is it so important?"

"Sure, then you'd be able to call me by my real name—Louisa."

Goldie pursed her lips, "L . . . veeza."

"Say it with me: Loo-wee-za."

Goldie chuckled, "Loo . . . schmooo. Veeza, your mama wanted a fancy American name, so you got it. You mean you don't understand when I call you?"

"Yes, but if you learn English, you can talk with everyone."

"Sometimes it is better to keep quiet; you don't get into much trouble that way."

Veeza had wondered then how an old grandmother who couldn't speak English could be so smart. She wished she'd asked Baba about everything before she got herself into trouble.

That night, they had lain side by side, an old lady and a ten-year-old girl. Veeza thought, *Grandmothers are for loving and talking*.

"I think the man in the moon is God's watchman," Veeza had concluded.

"Oh, you think God needs a watchman?"

Veeza nodded seriously.

"And what else do you think?"

"I think the stars are really angels holding torches—no, not torches, sparklers like we have on the Fourth of July. And I think all the angels are good because they're the good people who died and went to heaven and they light up the sky like we turn on the gaslight."

"And what happens when the sun comes out?"

Veeza had a ready answer. "The moon and the angels go up to bed, and the sun is the daytime watchman. And when any of the angels are bad, all of the angels cry and that makes the rain, and the rain makes the flowers grow, so nothing is wasted. Didn't God figure that out good?"

Goldie smiled. "He has to be pretty smart because it took him only seven days to make the world, and that was a big job."

"Baba?"

"Yes, child?"

"How many gods are there?"

"Only one."

"Is he the same God the Catholics have?"

Goldie was definite in her answer. "There is only one God."

"But how do you know?"

"Because the Lord said it himself. It is written that when God spoke the words, 'I am the Lord, thy God,' the whole earth stood still. Not a bird sang, not a leaf moved, and he didn't mention about any other God but himself."

"So, no matter how anyone prays, it all goes up to the same God?"

Goldie nodded. "That is how we believe."

She moved the pillows back into place. Veeza's small head made a dimple in the broad expanse of the pillowcase, made even larger by Manya's crocheted edging. "That's enough talk for one night. You won't be able to get up for school tomorrow."

Veeza remembered snuggling close to Goldie and sighing deeply, "Good night, Baba. I love you so much."

As Veeza closed her eyes, a smile had lingered on her lips as she thought, *Now I can keep on going to the Catholic church and not worry anymore, because all the prayers go up to the same God.* Then, quickly, she had opened her eyes and looked at the moon's benign face. "Good night, God's watchman."

The night slowly ticked itself away. Veeza turned and twisted. It must have been the moon. He had heard all she'd told Goldie—and all she had not told Goldie—and he had reported it all to God, as a good watchman should, especially in heaven.

She looked fearfully toward the gray dawn where there was no sign of the moon. Nevertheless, she put her head under the pillow to hide herself from view.

~ 5 ~

Later that morning, the winter sun beamed and the snow shone like a network of tiny crystals. By afternoon there would be little rivulets rolling down the hillocks, leaving a lacy drape across the crusty ground, the projecting clumps of dirt and rock looking like fat buns with sugar icing.

It was a perfect day for drying sheets and pillowcases and nightgowns and diapers which Manya pinned across the yard on the clothesline. Clothespin in mouth, she yanked at the line, the pulley screeching as it turned. Stretching the sheet smooth and flat, she clamped the pin close to the edge. The sun was a blessing. She would not have to string the wash across the kitchen, shifting each piece from time to time so each would get the benefit of the heat from the stove—and how much fresher they would smell. Goldie might not know the difference, but she would. When the laundry filled the line from window to pole, Manya shut the window and turned to ready the washboiler for its next batch.

She moved the half-burned candles flickering in the Sabbath daylight to the sideboard on which stood a cut-glass bowl holding a few letters and other small items to be taken care of later. She pushed aside the mission-style dining table. Hearing the men's voices, Manya turned to open the hall door for Leon and their upstairs neighbor, Mr. Murphy, who maneuvered a folding cot through the doorway.

"My missus says to excuse her—she's down with a touch of her asthma—but she says to tell you not to worry about using the cot. Take your time. We don't use it unless we have company." Mr. Murphy wiped his florid face with a red kerchief and continued, "Gotta get some of this lard offa me. Too much beer, I guess. My missus says that's what comes of livin' on a block with a saloon at spittin' distance and free lunch to boot." He guffawed at his own joke, then turned to look toward the bedroom where Goldie lay. "Excuse me," he said, lowering his voice to a whisper. "I'm soundin' like a bullhorn. I hope I didn't disturb the old lady. How is she?"

As Leon moved the cot to a corner of the dining room, Manya answered Mr. Murphy, "The same, thank you," all the while thinking, *How can you tell someone how she is when you don't know yourself.* "Today she slept some, but who knows what the night will bring if she's slept out. Tell Mrs. Murphy we're so grateful you had the cot to spare. At first, we thought the couch in the parlor would be all right, but . . . " She hesitated, stopping herself from saying what she was thinking—*but we didn't know it would be so long . . .* "If I get a few minutes, I'll go up to see Mrs. Murphy—a little chicken soup, maybe?"

"Lord love you, Mrs. Picker," Mr. Murphy grinned. "I'll tell her, but you've got enough on your hands already. Remember, there's no need to hurry about the cot." Then he quietly added, "Not that anyone wants to think about it, but the boy might not want to sleep in the room—or the bed—right after . . . so, don't hurry 'im."

As Mr. Murphy left, Manya reached for a spread which was hung across the back of a chair. She handed it to Leon who hung it like a throw over the folded cot in the corner. He watched Manya out of the corner of his eye to evaluate her mood. How yielding she had been last night, clinging until he felt the fire leave her. But there was no sign of it as he watched her adjust the throw so it hung just right.

Manya's face gave no evidence that she likewise surveyed her husband. But she was practical. Last night was then. Today there was work to be done before Leon napped and went to work on the night shift. His eyes were still blue as larkspur, his face taut and youthful, his figure far better than that of her own brother, Sidney, who was younger. Yes, Leon was still handsome, one to whom many a woman would be attracted. *But,* she thought, *he isn't a man. He doesn't take life by the horns and force it to meet his demands. He lets his friends influence him—convincing him that cards will work for him, that he will be the one to take home the pot.*

Yes, Leon was a dreamer. Always, for Leon, success would be just around the corner. And sadly, he really never would understand why his dreams had not come true.

Manya was the realist; she had the backbone to stand up and accept the burdens. Yet, Manya despised herself because she was able to do what Leon was not. Ah, how much she would have preferred to be the weak one, like Paula, her brother's wife, who took to her bed with a cold, wet cloth across her forehead, when her wishes were ignored. Sidney knew he had to provide the very best for Paula because she expected it, and he worked like a horse to do it.

Not that Manya had anything against her sister-in-law. Indeed, Paula was kind and thoughtful to Veeza and Joey and sympathetic to Manya's plight, but she couldn't resolve it. Sidney had not visited Goldie for weeks. Later, he would say he was busy, but Manya knew he found the sight of his mother's condition distasteful.

If Sidney had failed his mother, Manya, conversely, knew she had failed her children. She recalled the days Joey or Veeza had pleaded, "Mama, let's do something. We could just go for a ride on the trolley car and see things, even only from the window. We won't have to pay an extra fare if we just stay on." Counting the carfare, Manya had concluded, "If you promise to take care of each other, both of you can go."

"But Mama," they had pleaded, "we want you to go, too."

Manya had answered, "Five cents will buy a pair of socks for one of you, and that's more important than my going along." Her strength was her weakness. She deprived herself of the little joys of life and thus also deprived her children.

Still, she protected Leon—and the children's pride. Their papa, she told them, had a "condition" and couldn't work steady. He had to be away for a change of climate every so often. Manya was happy that the children really loved Leon. He still romped with them as he had when they were tiny. When he made up outrageous adventure stories, all of them would laugh. The children loved him with total abandon.

~ *6* ~

Goldie found herself waking up. *Ach,* she thought, *how good it would feel to stretch a little—not too much, though. Old bones don't like to be pushed around. But a little stretching would feel so good.* She snickered to herself. *It's a marvel my mind can remember what my body has forgotten; what a mechaieh it is to wake up and s–t–r–e–t–c–h to get the blood stirred up. But on whose calendar does it state what day or month or year the devil is going to stick his nose in and say it's his turn to play tricks?*

Now her eyes focused. Standing beside the bed was not the devil but, happily, the good priest—her special friend—with Veeza.

"Aaarruh," Goldie greeted them.

Fr. Malachi looked helplessly at Veeza as the weird noise rolled from Goldie's throat. "I wish I could help her—or at least understand some little thing she's trying to say."

"She's trying to say hello," Veeza pointed out, turning to Goldie. "Aren't you trying to say hello, Baba?"

Goldie's eyes blinked three times.

"She only blinks twice if she means no. She's always glad to see you, Father."

Fr. Malachi pulled a chair up to the side of the bed, trying to disguise the look of pain on his face. "Guten Welt," he said, patting Goldie's motionless hand—so cold to his touch, almost like the touch of death. "Lord, have mercy on her soul," he whispered. Cupping her hand between his two warm palms as if to squeeze life from his flesh into hers, he turned to Veeza. "Tell her I pray for her every day, the same as I do for all who are sick. Tell her that I say an extra prayer for her because she's become like my own grandmother."

"Aahh, aahh," Goldie responded, blinking again and again as Veeza translated. Goldie's eyes were alight with pleasure.

As they stood listening to Baba's weird voicing, Veeza thought again of the sins she had committed.

Fr. Malachi had come to their door one Saturday, intending to make a call on the previous tenants who had been members of the parish but who had apparently not notified the church of their moving. Baba answered his knock in her Sabbath outfit: her sheitel brushed until it shone like golden bronze and pinned carefully in place on her head with the bun sitting just so at the nape of her neck, her taffeta waist and her full skirt, with only the tips of her laced shoes peeking out from underneath.

She had called Veeza to find out what this distinguished-looking stranger wanted. Thus, Veeza came face to face with the priest. Her misdoing rose like a ghost to confront her.

New to the neighborhood and anxious to conform, Veeza had

taken to joining her new walking-to-school friend, Irene, as she slipped into St. Mary's church to make a hurried prayer every morning. Along with her friend, Veeza would dip her fingers into the holy water font and sign herself, praying silently, "Dear God, forgive me, but if she finds out I'm a Jew, she might not want to be my friend, and the other girls won't either. So you understand, God, that I'm only pretending to be a Catholic."

One day, she saw Fr. Malachi, so handsome even in his black cassock. He had patted this newcomer on the head, and Veeza immediately fell madly in love with him. Nothing, nothing could stop her from going into the church to receive his blessing.

Fr. O'Neil, on the other hand, because of his stern face, would send her scurrying. None of the girls liked Fr. O'Neil. He stood for no nonsense—such as little girls giggling in the holy environs of the church.

Veeza had a special secret she had told no one. She once had dreamed she was to marry Fr. Malachi, but when she went to order a long, white wedding gown, the dressmaker said that what she wanted was like the gowns new nuns wear to marry Christ, with a wedding ring and all. So, if Veeza was going to marry into the Church, it would have to be to Jesus, not to Fr. Malachi!

Veeza recalled waking from this dream in a fright. She couldn't marry Jesus. He was dead and nailed to a cross because he was a Jew and the Jews did it. His name was Jesus Christ and that's why the Jews are called Christ killers, which Veeza didn't believe, even though Irene, her best going-to-school chum, said it was printed as plain as can be in their catechism—and Veeza should know that! Veeza didn't even know what a catechism was, but she didn't tell that to Irene. Still, if it was printed, then it must have been Jews as mean as those in "Little Jewtown"—they'd be the kind that would do it.

As Veeza said good-bye to Fr. Malachi now, she thought again about how strange it was that her misdoing had created a dear friend for Baba. Fr. Malachi stood there saying good-bye, and thought the same thing. So, there'd been a grievous error, a misguided child of a different faith who'd confessed her transgression. That should have ended the incident. But it hadn't.

The fact that he had to pass their floor to go upstairs to the Murphys was a feeble reason to stop to see an old lady with whom he could hardly communicate. Yet, by some weird visualizing on his part, she reminded him of his grandmother in Ireland. He argued with himself, saying there are old ladies everywhere. What and why did this one have that special something which made him return?

As he looked down at Goldie's face now, her eyes looked back up at him with a secret smile in them. Sad as her condition was, Fr. Malachi knew she was thinking of that same day, and the times following.

Ach, thought Goldie, *the days we spent sitting, not like I am now, a pitiful clod not as good as the earth which produces something—if only a weed—but when he came to have a glass of tea with an old woman he couldn't exchange a word with.* She smiled to herself and warm blood coursed through her motionless body. To think even her own son didn't come to see her as often as this young Gallich who had more important things to do—he found time to stop, even just to rest. Goldie knew he could have rested in the quiet of his room or enjoyed nature's handiwork by taking a walk in the park.

She smiled to herself. God chooses who shall match with whom, and he matched an old Jewish grandmother with a handsome young Gallich to bring softness into her life—a substitute for her own son.

Fr. Malachi stood above Goldie and understood the affection in her eyes. He knew there was total communion between himself and this gentle woman. With it came the vision of Fr. O'Neil's rebuke earlier that morning, "You could have hallow'd her soul . . . "

"May I pray?" he asked Veeza, and as Veeza nodded, she sensed the aura of that moment.

Fr. Malachi placed the tips of his fingers on Goldie's forehead and murmured, "Merciful Father, bless and give peace to this, thy ailing servant. Amen."

"Amen," whispered Veeza.

Fr. Malachi laid a comforting hand on Goldie's hand and noticed that her eyes were closing. In a fraction of a moment, she was asleep, her face in total relaxation, the barest hint of a smile on her lips.

He turned, and Veeza led the way to the parlor door. The withered little Christmas tree stood on the table in mute testimony to the vagaries of fate.

BOOK TWO
Manya's Heartaches

~ *1* ~

Goldie lay quietly. She would think a little about the past. After all, there was no longer a future.

How many years had passed since she and Yussel stood at the foot of the eleven tiny mounds in the village burying ground, dry eyed with silent grief. Two and three in a day, the little ones had died in their arms from the plague which nearly wiped out their small Russian village. How strange that a heartache can stay buried for so long, only to come burning to life like coals that have been banked and then suddenly flare into a bed of fire.

For years, letters had come from cousin Laban describing the wonders of "the land of milk and honey"—America. Laban wrote of how rich he had become as a manufacturer of men's shirts and of how he lived in a house with an inside water closet. His success was certainly a surprise. Everyone knew Laban hadn't a brain in his addled head when he was a growing youth, the blame for which had been placed on his mother, may she now rest in peace. She had been too lazy to let him suckle until he was tired of her breast, and everyone knows some children nurse until they are three years old—or at least until another baby comes to need the milk.

So the villagers marveled. If Laban could become a rich man in America, surely it must be a land of wonders, at least for the young. The oldsters shook their heads; for them, thank God, it was a good life in their village.

Yussel had standing in the village. Not only was he the melamed—the teacher, thinker, and spokesman for the villagers—but he was also an artisan. The poritz, or count, making his rounds of the village, had been so impressed with Yussel's skill that he commissioned Yussel to design parchment lamp shades for his new home. With this came Yussel's acceptance as a gentleman of talent, invited into the homes of the aristrocrats.

Later, Manya, still quite young, was invited to teach these noblemen's daughters to do exquisite embroidery for which Yussel drew the designs. Like a lady, Manya would sit in the gardens with members of the family and drink tea served by maids.

Then a devil came into their midst when Avrum arrived to visit his Tante Sophie. Sophie's sister, Avrum's sainted mother, had long since gone to her heavenly rest, and Sophie had not seen Avrum since he was a young boy. How was Sophie to know that he'd become a silver–tongued rogue? A black-haired, dark-eyed gypsy, Avrum rode into the village and swept Manya off her feet. She became bewitched—putty in his hands.

The wedding contract was decided upon and the bride-to-be properly attended at the mikvah—the purification bath—where ministering women admired the whiteness of her body. They comforted Manya as they snipped off her hair, a traditional ritual which would make a frau unattractive to other men. On holy days or the Sabbath, wives wore a perücke—a wig—and otherwise a babushka—the head shawl.

The dowry was set and paid and the wedding took place. Everyone danced to the tunes of the fiddlers—Manya happiest of all as Avrum swung her around until her petticoats ballooned out. In all, it was a wedding to remember. Was not Yussel the most respected man in the village, and was his only daughter, who had survived the plague, not entitled to such a wedding?

The following morning all knew, in the traditional ritual, that Manya had delivered her virginity to her husband. The women predicted it would be a happy time nine months hence when Manya would present Yussel and Goldie with a grandson, please God.

The dancing and celebrating lasted for three days. Those who came from distances slept in the alcoves over the fireplace or in the haystacks. No one hurried to leave for home; after all, one seldom had the opportunity to visit and discuss and learn with this melamed. When the women and children had been put to bed, there were little glassfuls of schnapps to be sipped and savored—and one learned much.

Then one night, Avrum disappeared, leaving his bride the laughingstock of the village! How fortunate, the village women consoled Goldie, that Manya had not conceived on her wedding night and that Yussel, with his influence, could obtain the aid and consent of the high rabbi from a nearby city to dissolve the marriage. The marriage wig was put aside, and Manya's hair grew back. But who could give Manya back her virginity, Goldie lamented. None of the young men in the village would be interested in a girl who was, in fact, a woman, when all over the villages were young girls just blossoming.

Then letters came from cousin Laban. Not only would Yussel make out in America, but surely a husband could be found there for Manya. After all, Manya was the shana—the pretty one—with skin like pure cream and a laugh that trilled like happy music.

What was there to discuss?

"But my babies! How can I leave them?" was Goldie's heart-rending cry.

Yussel turned his face from her misery. "They are no longer ours," he told Goldie. "Their souls are with God, and we must turn to the living. Sidney is a boy—he'll manage in life. We must think of Manya."

So they stood together, tears finally falling like silver droplets while they whispered good-bye to their children sleeping side by side in the ground.

~ 2 ~

It was a long and tortuous journey by foot and by rail. They met others who came from far distances, all destined to take a ship to "the land of milk and honey."

How did we carry so much? Goldie wondered. Pots and pans and featherbeds and pillows, precious samovars in knotted sheets, paper packages and cardboard suitcases held together by whatever means as the wear and tear took its toll. It was a wonder they were even let into a country, so weary and disheveled they were, the women trailing behind the men and weary children dragging their feet.

In Hamburg, Goldie noted the number of men on the streets and the large buildings and how clean the city looked. If there were as many men in America as there were in Hamburg, Goldie was sure Manya would soon be a bride again.

But the wonder of the city soon faded. Huddled like pigeons in a coop, they waited for passage on a ship, everyone sailing to the golden land, each family clamoring and pushing, no one daring to leave the premises lest they lose their place.

Yussel tried to comfort his family. "After all, are we the only ones in search of happiness? A small inconvenience must be overlooked with understanding. Once on the ship, all of this will pass like a bad dream." Goldie relayed this logic to Manya and Sidney.

Like fruit in a jar, they were crowded into the steerage. Anticipation overcame inconvenience, however, as the ship slipped away from its moor and into the expanse of the ocean.

Days passed into weeks. The ship rolled like dough in the hands of a baker, while the heat grew intense. The black bread and salted herring spoiled, but no one noticed when the pangs of hunger set in. Then, stomachs rebelled as dysentery followed, joined by the stench of seasickness.

Goldie held Manya's head until she could no longer keep her own upright, and Sidney, already white and limp, lay on the bench beside Yussel. All the while, the ocean vented its fury as if in defiance of anyone's predictions.

Finally, like all nightmares, this one came to an end.

~ 3 ~

No whistles blew, no bands played, and no crowds applauded the arrival of the shipload of greenhorns that day in August in the late eighteen hundreds. The heat hung like vapor, the air lifeless as the wet wash which dangled limply from the lines and the windowsills of the tenements nearby. The only sound seemed to come from the clop-clop of the horses' hooves which stirred little clouds of dust into the air as they pulled the streetcars and carriages. Inspectors, awaiting the onslaught of new arrivals, wiped their faces with clammy handkerchiefs and watched as the ship disgorged its load into the New World. The passengers would come swarming like ants from under a rock—sweaty, rumpled, stinking.

It was an old story to the inspectors. All those greenies were alike: they couldn't write their names and wouldn't make a cross because it was against their religion. Instead, they would make a circle—a kikel they called it. The inspectors would point to the paper and say, "If you can't write your name, just make a kikel," and the Jews would laboriously and precisely make the circle instead of the cross. When the inspectors could not understand or spell an individual's name, they interpreted it to suit themselves—the greenies wouldn't know the difference. And whatever was written on the paper was who they became.

Thus Yussel Berinovkowich became Joseph Berron, and

Goldina quickly became Goldie; and so they remained. With papers in hand, they made their entrance into the New World.

They were in America.

~ 4 ~

Outside Castle Garden, the parklike point of debarkation, the immigrants waited in little groups while one by one, relatives came to lead them away. Goldie and Manya waited by their bundles as Yussel and Sidney looked everywhere for a sight of someone who might be Laban looking for them. Soon, they were the last ones remaining.

A kindly policeman walking his beat asked, "You got no one coming for you?" but no matter how they gestured and chattered in Russian and Yiddish, they could not make him understand.

Then Yussel remembered the letter. He went through his papers hopefully, fearfully, until he remembered just where he'd put it for such an emergency.

Ah, that Yussel, Goldie thought, *always papers in his pockets.* "Put it away carefully," she'd cautioned him, "not mixed up with the others." But Yussel said he knew exactly where it would be and besides, cousin Laban would surely be there and he wouldn't need the letter anyway. Feverishly but with relief, Yussel read the letter. He turned to Goldie. "Cousin Laban says that if he is not here to meet us, we are to go to this address and wait until tomorrow." Yussel showed the letter to the policeman who then showed them where the horsecar would stop. Yussel was to show the letter to the driver who would tell them where to get off.

Goldie was disappointed that Laban was not there to meet them. After all, he should know they would be tired after such a long journey, and coming to a strange land besides. But Yussel consoled her: "There must be a good reason, and when we reach this address, we will have a chance to rest and perhaps make some new friends. Meantime," Yussel continued, "take a look around. This is America—'the land of milk and honey!' "

But what Goldie saw was a row of old buildings four or five stories high with lines of wash hanging from poles to windows.

Sidney said disdainfully, "Hamburg was nicer," and Manya thought of the tea tables in the gardens of the count's home.

As the horsecar clop-clopped along, Goldie voiced her first

impression. "Yussel, Laban surely doesn't live here—or even near here. He said he was rich!"

Goldie, in her bed now—thinking, thinking—recalled Manya's turning in distress to Yussel. "Papa, this can't be America!"

~ 5 ~

"Aaarrr!" Goldie lay, her mind zigzagging, trying to put the pieces of that day together. She remembered thinking that maybe Sidney was right; perhaps they should have stayed in Hamburg. There were so many fine men on the streets there. Here, where in God's name would they find a husband for Manya?

The horsecar finally came to a stop and the driver called out, "You . . . you . . . off here," indicating they had arrived at the address Laban had given them.

Goldie remembered Manya's face, pale from the voyage but paler still at the sight before her: the screaming of the peddlers as they shouted their wares; the women pushing their way to pull a fish, a chicken, or a piece of meat from the pushcarts; everywhere herring, hot knishes, carrots, onions, and potatoes; bagels stuck on a stick protruding through the holes in the center; clothes slung on racks. Surrounding all of this activity were brick buildings seven stories high, wall to wall and back to back. The streets were hidden by an endless stream of Jews with children running helter-skelter in between the carts and into the middle of the street—and nearly into the paths of the horsecars. The poorest peasant in the village they'd left behind lived better than this.

"Don't worry," Yussel had reassured them. "After all, it's a marketplace. Didn't we have a marketplace in our village? Our village was small; this is a big city, so it has to be noisier."

Sidney had not been impressed with Yussel's reasoning. "It's not as clean as Hamburg, and that was a big city."

Goldie had pointed to the tenements walled up to form a blockade. She bent her head back to look up toward the sky, to see the rooftops. Instead she saw bedding hanging from windows and people watching the scene or screaming down to their children.

"God in heaven, where have we come?" Goldie asked.

She heard Sidney reply, "I wish we'd never come to America," and as she looked at Manya, she felt for the young girl who knew why her parents had torn themselves away from their beloved village.

"We're here, and things will be better when cousin Laban comes, and there's no going back," Goldie reprimanded Sidney. "One day when you're rich like cousin Laban, you'll tell your children about how you came to America and what you saw first."

As they stood in confusion among their bundles, afraid to move a step from them, a woman inquired, "You're looking for someone?" Yussel showed her the letter.

"I don't know how to read, but we will ask somebody," she told Yussel. One by one they inquired until finally they found someone who could read the letter and point out the place.

"Sure . . . Moishe Gorilic—who doesn't know Moishe? You walk up till you can't go up any more—the first door . . . you'll find him."

The man laughed. "You got lotsa company there."

Step by step, flight after flight, they lugged their bundles to the top floor, then knocked at the first door. As they waited, they saw an endless expanse of hallway—and doors leading to other flats.

The door opened and a bearded giant greeted them. "Come in, come in," and from inside the smoke-filled rooms came his wife to greet them. "Welcome to America!" Her tired face was lined with tiny wrinkles, her head was wrapped in a babushka, and her cotton shirtwaist and skirt were partially hidden by an apron.

"Meyer, bring them inside. My name is Gittel. What do they call you?"

Goldie introduced her family and then added, "We were supposed to be met by Laban Goldfarb, Yussel's cousin."

Gittel nodded as she led the way into the flat. "We know—he wrote us. Don't worry. He'll be here. We're friends for a long time."

They followed Meyer and Gittel into the parlor, a room filled with immigrants like themselves who seemed to have been there for a long time. "Meet Michel. He's a Frenchman who can't speak one word of Yiddish. And here's a Galitzianer, and here's a Litvak, and how we dare to bring a Litvak and a Galitzianer together in the same room, I don't know. A war could start any minute."

While the men either nodded or didn't even look up from their study of the Scriptures, Gittel led Goldie and Manya to the bedroom. "The boy," she said, "can stay with the men, yes?" And not waiting for a reply, she opened the door to where the women and young children were congregated. "This is where you will sleep." Gittel's arm waved toward the crowd of bodies already using up all available space.

~ 6 ~

Ja, ja, ja, a body which remembers nothing about motion and a mind which is as sharp as the point of a needle. Goldie continued to reflect: Was this the America with gold in the streets and even in the rocks? She had looked at Manya who sat stone-faced on the edge of a chair which some kind person had vacated for the newcomer. With one sweeping glance, Manya had noted the sleeping mats, old mattresses, and featherbeds, with the traditional mountain-sized pillows laid out on the floor.

"We'll make you a place," Gittel assured them, moving a featherbed aside and readjusting the sleeping pads. "At least you will be gone tomorrow. Some others here have no place to go until they can find something—or somebody who has a bed to take them in until they can find work."

For a fleeting moment, Gittel's guard dropped as she sighed, "You come to America to take the world in your hands, but what God portions out, you learn to accept." And then, with a cautious, evaluating look, she quickly added, "We charge ten cents a night for a person to sleep."

Goldie watched Manya's face turn from white to green. Manya's hands went to her mouth, and Gittel rushed with her apron outspread to catch the vomit as it spurted like a geyser.

With Gittel's quick guidance, Goldie directed Manya's steps to the water closet down the hall. There, the filth and stench turned Goldie's stomach, too, and together she and Manya hung over the bowl to retch.

Finally, Gittel led them back out.

"We charge two cents for cleaning up," she told the sickened women guilelessly. As Goldie and Manya looked at her with disbelief, Gittel shrugged her shoulders. "In America, everything costs money."

Supper was a community affair. Gittel's food was plain but palatable, and Goldie found to her surprise that they could eat.

She dug into her cache, which hung like a pendulous tumor under her skirt, for the kopecks to be exchanged to pay the ten cents per person for the meal.

As Gittel predicted, they found pads on which to sleep.

How Goldie prayed that night that all the confusion would stop—just long enough to calm the ache in her heart which kept asking what hapless pattern their lives were taking.

As she lay there on her mat, sleepless with unhappiness, her eyes concentrated on a splash of moonlight which filtered through the grimy window and danced on the walk—perhaps it was to be seen as a ray of hope.

Then she became fascinated by the movement of the pattern on the wall. *Surely it must be caused by a kopfwetig—a headache,* she thought. But the bizarre pattern was moving and Goldie watched in horror. Slowly, the pattern scattered and reassembled itself, and other pattern parts came out of nowhere and joined. Bugs! Bedbugs! As if on cue to sample the new blood which had arrived, they crawled about.

Goldie lay frozen in disgust; she thought that never in her life had there been a bedbug in her house. Perhaps a little lizard from the outside, but a bedbug—God forbid! Her name would have been shamed forever in their village.

As she watched their march with disgusted fascination, she heard a new sound. She lay still and listened, and then sat up in terror. Mice! Quietly, though, she lay back down so as not to disturb Manya who lay in a sleep of total exhaustion.

Finally, the dawn's early light brought an end to the horror of the long night, and Manya and Goldie joined the seemingly endless line from the four flats to the only water closet.

"Welcome to America!"

"Danke, danke."

Weariness was etched in every face.

~ 7 ~

Upon his arrival to claim his mishpocheh—his relatives—Laban was apologetic. He'd had a rush order of shirts to finish and deliver, but he knew Meyer and Gittel would take care of his family in case of such an emergency.

Goldie and her family looked with amazement at the horse

and wagon which Laban had waiting for them, and at the people who stood admiring it. A horse and wagon with no wares on it to peddle was indeed a luxury. Laban helped Yussel and Sidney load their belongings onto the back, and Goldie and Manya were given the seat of honor in front with Laban. "In America," Laban pointed out, "ladies come first, not like in Europe where the women walk behind the men."

Yussel and Sidney sat in the bed of the wagon surrounded by their bundles, an unlikely place for a man with a professorial beard and a frock coat, albeit rumpled.

Goldie sat prim and proper holding Manya's hand as the horse threaded its way through the yelling peddlers. Then, impulsively, Laban reined the horse to a stop and, digging into his pocket, leaned over and dropped a few coins into a peddler's outstretched hand in exchange for knishes, still hot and fragrantly savory from the fat in which they had been cooked. Urging the beast to move forward, he guided it with one hand holding the reins as he bit into the juicy knish. Goldie and Manya followed suit.

"No place in America has food like they have here. A knish like this," Laban commented while licking his lips, "is a marvel."

"You don't have knishes at home?" Goldie asked in surprise, as if to say, "Who doesn't have good, savory knishes at home, with potato dough rolled out so thin it crackles when eaten?"

"My wife makes bacon."

Goldie looked questioningly. "Bacon? What is bacon?"

Laban click-clicked to the horse, then answered, "Pork—chozzer."

Goldie drew in her breath. *Chozzer? Pig? God in heaven, only the goyim eat pig! Could Laban be married to a shikseh?* Goldie looked at Manya, but Manya's mind was a thousand miles away, in the peace and beauty of the gardens with the count's children. She had not told Yussel and Goldie that she could have gone to live with the count's family. The countess had hoped Manya would remain with them as the children's companion and governess. She and her husband did not regard her as a Jewess; they respected her as a young lady of good manners whom their daughters enjoyed. The marriage? They considered it an unfortunate incident not unknown in their society. They said that, in time, Manya would find a nice young Russian, perhaps even a junior officer, with whom she would fall in love and marry. But Manya felt she could not desert her parents.

From the wagon, Manya watched the passing terrain and wondered if her life would ever again be as serene as it had been in that garden.

Laban chattered agreeably. He lived an hour's ride away, in a small town not unlike the village they'd left behind. The children would have good schools with lady teachers.

Goldie asked how many children Laban and his wife had, and Laban shook his head. There were no children to bless his life.

Goldie sympathized. "A sadness, indeed, but life must be accepted. It is God's will." Then she inquired, "Is there a school—a cheder—for learning the home language, for learning Hebrew? a place where Yussel can teach?"

Laban shook his head. "Only English. Today, the first thing is to learn English. What the children learn afterwards is up to them. No one has time to do more than make a living."

God in heaven, what will become of us, Goldie moaned to herself. *A shikseh wife who will despise us, and no way for Yussel to earn a dollar to support us.* Woe ran cold in her blood.

They rode along in silence, caught up in their own thoughts. Then, timidly, Goldie asked, "Laban, a shul?"

Laban wiped his face with a kerchief, and Goldie felt the knish settle in her stomach. She didn't need for Laban to answer.

"No shul. You want to pray, you pray at home. First, you make a living."

Goldie asked quietly, "Your wife, she's . . . she's . . . "

Laban laughed heartily. "You don't have to be bashful. She's a shikseh, a Svenska—a Swedish girl."

Goldie looked back at Yussel. His friendly relationship with the aristocrats had never interfered with his religious beliefs. Everyone knew that she and Yussel could trace their family histories in that little village back four hundred years. Among their relatives had been rabbis, melameds, intellectuals—all Jews to the bone and marrow. A person could hold his head up.

Before Goldie had time to think further, her eyes were drawn in horror to a moving spot. A bedbug was crawling out from the folds of the bedding. As though hypnotized, Goldie's eyes followed its path back into a crevice of the bedding where it was lost from view.

A fine way to enter a woman's home! Goldie thought. A shikseh yet—a Svenska. Goldie had never met a Svenska. What would she think of Laban's relatives arriving with bedbugs in their bedding? She had to restrain herself from telling Laban to stop immediately so she could shake everything out—because only God knew how many others were tucked inside.

The ride continued, but from that moment on, Goldie squirmed, restraining herself from telling Manya, who sat with her mind closed to everything but her own misery.

~ 8 ~

"Aaarrraeee!" Goldie replied when Veeza popped in to ask if she was thirsty or hungry. Goldie didn't want anything. She was anxious to get back to her memories of the arrival of Veeza's mama in America when she was a young girl.

The sun's rays seemed to sear as the heat of the morning rose. Laban stopped to cool and water the horse. He helped the family down from the wagon and indicated that they could go into the woods to relieve themselves. Then he opened a box of sandwiches his wife had prepared for them, and Goldie made a short prayer—adding to herself that whatever it was, it not be from chozzer.

Laban told them about his shirt factory and how he started with one machine on borrowed money. "The way to get along in America is to operate on borrowed money," he explained.

Yussel and Goldie were bewildered. In their village, to borrow money was an admission of failure. Besides, you would be putting yourself in the hands of a moneylender who could rob you blind, put you in jail, or take your possessions. A villager they knew had had that experience.

Laban quickly continued. "It takes courage, good cousin. You look the lender in the eye as if you are demanding that he prove you cannot pay it back, and you keep looking until his eyes drop. Then you know that he knows that if you can face him that way, your integrity is as good as his word. In that way you establish credit. You pay back the first loan and then you borrow more—soon you can borrow whatever you need to put into your business."

Goldie stared at Laban in fascination; his confidence was contagious. *Ah, there is hope then for Yussel. But what business will*

*Yussel go into? Who will lend money to a melamed? And if there
are no Jews, who will need a Hebrew teacher?*

Goldie looked at Manya, who barely nibbled on the sandwich.
Not one word had she uttered since they started out that morning. *If only she could find a man like Laban—a man with ideas
as to how to start a factory—what a blessing that would be.*

Then Goldie looked at Sidney, and for the first time the boy
had a spark of interest in his eyes. *Sidney will learn; a boy in
America can learn to be smart. Laban is a perfect example.*

The journey continued. Here and there they passed small
frame stores and barns, a few houses, fields with wildflowers,
yellow and green patches of grass—and always there was the in-
ferno of heat. Finally, Laban drove up to a small store and reined
his horse to a halt.

"So, we're here," Laban pointed proudly. Goldie and Manya
looked with uncertainty and some disappointment. When Laban
had described his factory, they envisioned Hamburg's city-size
stores and factories. How could Laban be a rich manufacturer in
such a small store? Sidney looked disgustedly disappointed, but
Yussel was most polite.

"A very nice place," he complimented Laban, who grinned
from ear to ear.

Greta, the Svenska, came bustling from the store, a jellyroll
figure with a voice like little chimes tinkling in the breeze. Laban gave her a fast swat on the behind while he encircled her
roundness with his arms.

"Meshuggener, you," she laughed at him. Laban turned to his
relatives. "You see, my Svenska talks Yiddish like a Yid." Goldie heaved a sigh of relief.

As Greta's folds of flesh rolled toward them, her moon-
shaped face aglow with a smile of welcome, the couple's happiness brought a pang of envy to Goldie. She looked toward Manya and read her eyes; she was thinking the same thing. Then
Goldie was swallowed up in the fat of Greta's arms, letting herself be hugged until her bonnet and her wig were askew.

Next, Greta hugged Manya, stood off to look at her, and commented, "Here's a pretty one." She quickly kissed Sidney's
cheek and observed, "a gontser mensh—a young man." Finally,
she turned to Yussel and with a little tweak at his chin said,
"Like a doctor, with such a pretty beard. Welcome to America."

As Laban started to unload their things, Goldie rushed to restrain him. "We'll go inside first. After all, there's no hurry. You want to show us your house—and your factory—no?"

"Of course, of course," Laban agreed.

Goldie heaved a sigh of relief as they followed Laban and Greta into the store. Laban stood proudly in the doorway and pointed to his six machines. A man hunched over each machine and busily sewed shirts; not one raised his head to look in their direction.

"If I had gone in to get you yesterday, I would have lost a day." He pointed to one machine without an operator. "That's my machine."

Greta nodded and beamed. "Ja, ja! He's the gontser macher here—the big boss. From gurnicht—nothing—he makes himself a baleboss—a big boss."

Laban roared heartily. "You hear? You hear? Soon you'll be talking English and she'll be talking Yiddish, and between all, we'll get along!"

The workmen were introduced. "You think they worked machines before I came here? No! They learned. You want to make a living? You learn."

Goldie looked a little fearfully toward Yussel, who was now much interested in the surroundings. He asked about the shirts, who made the patterns, who did the cutting.

"Everything comes from New York," Laban told him as he showed Yussel the huge scissors used to cut the multiple layers of cloth. "The big manufacturer portions out to the small one and," Laban predicted, "in time, I too will be big enough to do the same."

Greta took them into the rooms behind the store and to the rooms above. Yussel and his family would live upstairs. The rooms were small, Greta admitted, but until they got settled, they could be their home—pots and pans and bedding they had.

Bedding! The bedding with the bedbugs was still outside. Goldie had no choice but to try to convey to Greta that the bedding had to be thoroughly aired and baked out in the sun before it could be brought into the house. But try as she did, Greta was unable to comprehend. Her Yiddish was limited to the essentials. She comforted Goldie and suggested that perhaps Laban would be able to understand the problem.

Lying helpless and motionless in her bed, Goldie recalled how Laban had exploded. His voice shook the ceiling. "That vershtunkena—that slob! I should have known. But one lives in hope. I haven't been there for a long time." Then he shrugged, "Her place is no worse than others there. Bringing over greenhorns and making a few pennies off each one every day, they haven't the time to spread the walls with poison. And what would be the use of traps for the mice—for every mouse caught, half a dozen are born. Someday, they'll have to get rid of those buildings, but I'm afraid they'll be there longer than we are. You saw the peddlers? Where would they go?" He hugged Greta. "How lucky we are to live in the countryside out here—and you, also, my cousin Yussel, with your family."

Goldie thought, *It's one thing to be married and living happily in the countryside like you, cousin, with or without Jews. But how will it be for Manya? Where are the men?*

Sidney went with Yussel and Laban to lay out all their belongings; every pillow, quilt, the clothes, even the pots and pans were spread out. Laban predicted that by dusk every bug would perish.

~ 9 ~

That evening, the plans were made. Goldie and her family listened as Laban explained. "Sidney will go to school. As soon as his English is good enough, he can run errands or do any odd jobs he can find. Yussel, you can learn to work one of the machines and become a shirtmaker. And until you get settled, you can live here, rent free."

Goldie could see Yussel's thought waves, and finally Yussel spoke up. "But I am not a shirtmaker. I am a melamed—a teacher of philosophy, a teacher of Hebrew. I want to teach children the history of our life and prepare them for bar mitzva."

Laban was a kindly man. He could offer them shelter and Greta would do what she could to make the family comfortable. But Yussel had to understand how things are in America. "A teacher of Hebrew? Forget it, good cousin; the only teaching here is done in the schools and the only education necessary is to speak English and learn a trade. Believe me, I speak from my heart. As for Hebrew—who reads it? This isn't the old country. Hebrew is the old language, and this is the New World. You live with the times. And if you find a Jew who has a boy to prepare for bar mitzva, you teach him the words, you have a little schnapps and honey cake—and he's a man."

Greta patted Goldie comfortingly. Laban's Yiddish was far beyond her, but she knew that her husband was explaining things to Yussel and that it was all for their good.

"Why do you think I married a shikseh?" Laban asked. "I needed a wife, and who had time to go looking for a Yiddisheh maidel. A dollar came first." He gave Greta's cheek a pinch. "I wouldn't change her for five Yiddisheh maidlach!"

Goldie remembered how Manya's face had blanched. She knew that Laban had meant it as no reflection, but Manya was not at her best right then, whatever that might have been. Laban had gone on, unaware that a mother sat there with a mother's aching heart, watching her daughter's unhappiness and pain.

"I was lucky. One of my customers brought Greta over from the old country. She couldn't speak a word of English, and I couldn't speak a word of Svenska—but we got along, eh dumpling? . . . No, no, cousin Yussel, forget the Hebrew. And as for Goldie, a good midwife can always make a few kopecks."

Greta poked Laban, "Not kopecks—cents, dollars."

Goldie recalled Laban's burst of laughter. "A good midwife," Laban went on, "can make a bit to help out. Once in a while in an emergency, they need to have a doctor, but it is the midwife they call first."

Then, having settled Goldie's future, he turned to Manya. "And you, young woman, what are your accomplishments?"

Goldie felt a little stab at her heart—*no, no there is no feeling now, not even an imagined stab—but then, ach, there was a stab at the heart.* She wondered why Laban didn't like Manya, their cherished only flower. Manya had replied in straightforward fashion, "I embroider. I do fine embroidery."

Laban looked uncertainly toward Greta. "Who needs fine embroidery?" He was genuinely puzzled.

Why should he look so puzzled? Manya thought to herself. And then the cold fingers of doubt entered. *Does no one need fine embroidery? Where are the homes of the aristocrats with their ladies who wear chemises with stitching so fine the eye can barely detect them? And cutwork designs drawn by Father? Oh, take me home. Take me home,* her heart cried. *Avrum, Avrum, love of my life. How could you have done this to me?* The years rolled back and the scars lay raw and searing, and with anguish Manya knew there was no turning back. She smiled politely at

Laban, "I also teach embroidery to the children of aristocrats."

Laban looked at this girl who'd literally uttered no words since they'd met, and who now held his eyes until his dropped. Then with a hearty bellow, he slapped his knee. "Well then, I'll take you over to Market Street where the fine stores are and see if they need a fine young woman to do fine embroidery for the fine ladies who buy there."

Goldie looked proudly at her daughter. Already Manya had learned from Laban's lesson to Yussel: You look the loaner in the eyes and when his eyes drop, you know you've won. Goldie wasn't sure about Yussel, though. His brow was a picture of furrows in a newly planted field.

Their destiny settled, Greta led them to rest awhile in the clean beds upstairs.

Goldie moaned a little as her mind swung back into focus. Her back itched. It would be good when Manya came to rub her with alcohol and dust her with cornstarch. Goldie grimaced; her mouth was dry and she wished for a few sips of cold water. Can thinking back so many years dry the mouth—but not the mind?

True to his word, Laban had taken Manya and samples of her embroidery to the fine stores. Later, Manya told Goldie that Laban was surprised at their appraisal of her work. Manya was immediately hired to do custom work on the sheerest of batiste corset covers. "Only the finest embroiderers who can compete with the work done in France or Belgium are hired," Laban had been told.

At home, Laban looked at the quiet Manya with considerable respect.

~ 10 ~

Goldie remembered how her heart had ached for Yussel. He would sit, pale and exhausted, unable to eat. Laban, not unkindly, tried to explain that it takes time. "After all, working a machine is not reading from books. The legs have to get used to pushing the pedals."

Ach, Goldie recalled, the nights she had rubbed Yussel's back and legs with a rough towel to stimulate the circulation, but in her heart, she had known it was a lost cause.

"How is it," Yussel had asked, "that I could study over a book for hours without so much as an ache in my back. Soon my chest will be as hollow as the other machine operators'. And my legs! If pushing those pedals is like walking, then I must be walking miles every day. Yet, my legs aren't getting stronger; they seem to be getting weaker—and the pain greater." Yussel couldn't understand it—but Goldie could.

Day by day Yussel's heart longed for the traditional past. He needed his books and his teaching as a thirsty man needs water. Laban meant well, but he was an intellectual vacuum. Laban was concerned only with how much money his shirts brought in.

Sidney, on the other hand, was impressed with Laban's business "kopf"—his shrewd head. Sidney picked up English quickly and his ambition was to become an American as soon as possible and make as much money as his papa's cousin, Laban. But he was not interested in learning to run the sewing machine—not that Laban would let him experiment. Machines cost too much for a boy to fool around with.

But no matter, Sidney was not going to become a prisoner of a sewing machine. He was cocky in his independence—he took on any odd job. Goldie would shudder when she saw him rub the horse down and clean out the stable.

How ironic, came to Goldie's mind now as she thought of Sidney's well-cared-for nails and the softening creams he used to keep his hands smooth. *Sometimes a little dirt is necessary to remind us that dust is the leveler of all people, my son.*

It hurts that you turn your head away from me who represent the full cycle of life. And where will you hide, God forbid, when your time comes? Her heart wept.

When Yussel's coughing started, Goldie had begun to worry. He would cough all night long until she and Manya were haggard from lack of sleep. Finally, Yussel agreed to have the doctor look him over, and Laban took off an hour to go with Yussel.

The doctor, Goldie learned, had shaken his head. Yussel's lungs were badly affected. He would have to go to the country where he could rest and have fresh air and eggs and milk.

But where? There was no place to go—and so he remained with his family at Laban and Greta's.

With winter came the first hardship of snow, and the rooms

were hard to heat. Yussel caught cold. In three days, despite all the remedies, Yussel's weak lungs exploded in a hemorrhage—and he was gone.

Goldie's memory blacked out the following days. Somewhere, there'd been a burying ground, the renting of their clothes, a slash made to signify a parting, and the five of them riding in Laban's wagon back to the house to sit shivah—the days of mourning.

But even this could not be proper. Laban had to oversee the shop, Manya could take no chances on losing her job, and Greta, kindly, had to make food for them all. So Goldie sat alone and remembered what Yussel had once told her: "Man loses his hold on life as a leaf from the bough, when his time has come. It is written in the Book of Life: the date you are born and the date you will die." Goldie sighed; eleven little jewels lay in their graves, and Yussel had been the diamond in the crown of her life. Now, he was gone too. Where were the tears that refused to flow? Her heart wept.

~ *11* ~

Manya, then, became the breadwinner. Here and there, Goldie would help to bring a baby into the world or would care for the new mother's house should it be necessary. Manya protested that her mother worked like a servant, but Goldie shrugged, "Pride is a false image. A tiny baby needs me and so does its mother."

Ach! In her bed, Goldie sighed and tried to strain her body, hoping to feel one pinpoint of pain. *How one struggles through life against a pain here, a pinch of a nerve there, never realizing the pain of feeling no pain at all.*

She recalled that the loneliness had been the hardest to bear. She missed the mama-loshen—the chitchat in the mother tongue. She missed the busyness of being the wife of the village melamed.

And then came a beautiful ray of hope. Laban introduced a sewing machine salesman to Manya. His name was Leon Picker and he was a few years younger than Manya, but he was so taken with her that age made no difference. She showed him an embroidered velvet case with an intricate design and an ink drawing of a beautiful synagogue, both drawn by her father. She pulled out Yussel's correspondence with the high rabbis in large European cities. Not only was Leon impressed with Manya's cultural background, but he was unconcerned that there was no dowry. He considered it an honor to get such a girl. And Manya was wildly in love with Leon. Goldie had thought she would never see such a glow in her daughter's face again. There would be a wedding, after all!

Manya and Goldie worked for days on the dress: yellow satin with a small crown of matching net for a head covering. Together they baked the honey cakes and strudel for the sweet table to be enjoyed by the few "goyish" neighbors who came to wish the bride happiness.

Goldie glowed at Manya's radiant face as the couple stood under the canopy held by Laban and Greta in the little parlor of their rooms. Leon and Manya pledged their vows before a rabbi Laban had brought from the city to marry them.

Ach! A happy day. If only Yussel had lived to see it.

And soon after the wedding, how delighted they were with the news that Manya was in the family way. To Laban and Greta the child would be like their own. Greta insisted that when Manya's time came, a doctor should attend her—not that she didn't have faith in Goldie's midwifery.

When the time came, Laban went to alert the doctor while Greta traipsed back and forth from Manya's bed to the lower floor. When finally she came downstairs and noticed the doctor's coat draped over the back of a chair, and the doctor himself seated with his shirtsleeves rolled up, she became upset.

"There's no hurry," the doctor reassured Greta as he removed a deck of cards from his pocket. Motioning to Laban to sit, he shuffled the deck. "We'll play some pinochle to pass the time." Laban wanted to protest that he could use the time in his shop, but the doctor was already dealing the cards.

The hours passed. Greta served coffee and Swedish twist, and suffered with Manya and Goldie. Finally, Laban protested to the doctor, "Can't you do something?"

The doctor responded, "When she calls on God to help her, I'll know the time is near. Somehow, it's then that the awareness of God is in its truest form."

Finally, Manya was delivered of a son.

Laban again traveled to the city, this time to bring a mohel so the new boy could be properly circumcised. Again, Goldie baked honey cake and cookies to serve with the schnapps.

Goldie now had a grandson, named to perpetuate Yussel's memory: Joseph.

~ *12* ~

No, Goldie thought now, *I cannot complain about Laban. If my dear Yussel was not cut out to become a sewing machine operator, it was not Laban's fault. Nor was it Laban's fault that Leon was not a moneymaker. Leon was a gentle, loving husband, but he wasn't a Laban.*

Sidney had taken off to find work in the city. "If I'm going to get rich," he told them, "I want to get started early." Laban had approved. "Where would I be now if I hadn't left to go to America? Don't tie him to your petticoats, Goldie."

For sure, Leon wasn't a Sidney, Goldie reflected. *But he was a husband—a good husband—for Manya. Our leaving the village was not in vain, God be thanked.*

Manya had continued to work as an embroiderer while Goldie and Greta shared the joys of Yussel's namesake—Joey, American style.

The second year brought Louisa.

"Mama," Manya would tell Goldie, "say Loo-ee-za. You should try to learn English. After all, the children are Americans and you can't speak a word of English yet!"

But try as she would, Goldie was tongue-tied with the language. Louisa became Veeza. Goldie would roll the name around her tongue and was satisfied with what she heard. More so, she was satisfied with the cuddling she and Veeza enjoyed in the bed they came to share.

After Manya discovered that she was pregnant again, they moved from Laban's place. The little flat was already overrun with people, and it was time that Leon and Manya be on their own. Laban and Greta cried when they said good-bye to the little family, which included Goldie, of course. After all, what would Manya do without Goldie when the new baby came?

Shimon, the new baby—with blond curls and the face of an

angel—was a darling child and no trouble at all.

The new flat was on a lower floor separated by a vestibule. Their neighbors were a quiet couple with a daughter Veeza's age. On the street was a fire station, a special attraction to Joey and Veeza. Close by was a school and—just in case, God forbid, someone needed a medicine—a druggist.

That, Goldie lay thinking, *was a place to forget, and yet not to forget. That place served as a reminder that life runs a path like in the woods back home, where it takes blind turns and not until you are there do you realize that it was a wrong turn. But who knows? Do we sit in judgment on God's will?*

This unforgettable day was hot. Manya was sitting on the steps fanning herself when Joey and Veeza asked, "Mama, can we go across to see the firehouse?" Goldie had quickly piped up, "Tell the fireman I didn't bake any cookies this week, but next week, I'll send cake for them, too."

"Hold on to your little brother," Manya cautioned as little Shimon joined them, and the children skipped along to the curb.

Suddenly, just as the three children reached the middle of the road, an oncoming carriage drawn by two prancing horses appeared. As Manya watched in split-second horror, Shimon loosed his hands from Joey and Veeza and ran directly into the path of the oncoming carriage, frightening one of the steeds which rose on its hind legs and struck out at Shimon. Within seconds, the small child lay dead in the street. One bloody blow to his forehead had crushed out the candle of life in his third year.

Manya was inconsolable. She refused to accept Leon's comforting, she ignored the needs of her two other children, and Goldie's recalling the little graves left in Europe brought small comfort. She refused to leave the house, not able to bear passing the scene of the tragedy. The doctor advised moving—a new neighborhood, and perhaps in time, a new baby would help.

Sidney came and sympathized, then broke the news that he had married a lovely young lady. She was spending a few weeks in the country to avoid the heat. He agreed that Goldie was essential to Manya's welfare at this time.

"And, after that?" Goldie asked him.

Sidney brushed a bit of dust from his sleeve as if preoccupied with it—as if he had not heard her. Then, leaving a dollar bill tucked under the sugar bowl, he wished them well and left.

All soon learned that Manya was pregnant again. The family

moved—and Goldie moved with them. Even if she had another place to go, could she, with a mother's heart, have left Manya then?

Goldie lay thinking. *Too much, too much to relive.* She could almost feel the pain now as she had felt it then—the headaches and the heartaches. She watched the Sabbath candles flickering in their pool of wax. *Soon they'll burn themselves out.* She envied them. A low moan escaped from deep inside her.

BOOK THREE
A Pretty Holiday

~ 1 ~

In the kitchen, Veeza nudged Joey. "Joey, you feed Baba. You haven't seen her all day. Tell her Mama's upstairs to see how Mrs. Murphy is."

Goldie watched Joey come into the room and turn on the gaslight. *How tall he is growing, a strong face—he'll be a man soon.* No, no, she wouldn't think of that. A boy needs a bar mitzva to become a man. Goldie shut her eyes, and Joey tiptoed out. He rejoined Veeza in the kitchen.

"Joey?" Veeza's voice was hesitant—if Joey jumped at her, then she would truly have no one to ask.

"Whaaat?"

"I want to talk to you about something."

"Well then, go ahead and talk. But don't waste my time just standing there. I'm working on something important."

"Like what?" Veeza knew that was a silly question. Joey was always working on something important. After all, he was older than she was, and the teacher once told Mama that Joey would amount to something, but Veeza couldn't figure out what amount it was supposed to be in—nickels or dimes, or even dollars. And if it was dollars, where would they come from? But then, she reasoned, why worry. No one would say that about her. Joey's marks were always A+ , which she knew meant better than A. And she'd always wondered how they could mark something better than A, which was the best. The teacher had once told her, "Veeza, you could get an A if you really tried." Oh, well.

She studied Joey a moment. He was growing tall and skinny and his nose was bony. Is it a Jewish nose? She remembered Irene's sister's beau once saying he could tell a Jew a block away by his nose and his hair: "They got eyes like 'Eyetalians,' Jews have, and black hair—and those noses!" All that afternoon, Veeza had kept feeling her nose. Was her nose different from other Jews' noses? She was sorry that she didn't know any "Eyetalians" so she could compare, but she was sure about her hair. Now that she thought about it, Joey's hair was almost black, and she had to admit that Joey's nose was bony. She didn't know what kind of eyes were "Eyetalian," but Joey's eyes were real blue.

"Joey?"

"Whaat?"

"Have you got a Jewish nose?"

Joey looked at his sister with eyes of azure blue. "What's a Jewish nose?"

For want of a better reply, Veeza shrugged, "That's what I'm asking you."

Joey shrugged, "I guess if you're a Jew, you have a Jewish nose. If you're Irish, you got a nose like a mick, and if you're 'Eyetalian,' you have a nose like a wop."

"Joey Picker, those are dirty names and it's a good thing Mama isn't home to hear you say them!"

"That," Joey told her, "is why I said them. Besides, your questions are stupid. A nose is a nose."

Veeza shrugged, realizing that it was only one of the questions she wanted to ask him. But she knew there was no point in pushing further because Joey never wanted the Christmas tree in the first place, or that's what he said anyway.

Veeza heard Goldie moan. "Baba is probably dreaming—or maybe she's hungry, or wet." She hoped she'd never live to be as old as her baba. Once they had asked their mama how old she was and she had said she was thirty-eight. Veeza and Joey had cried because at thirty-eight Mama was already so old; they were sure Mama would die soon. So Baba must be very, very old. But even if she wasn't that very, very old, Veeza didn't want to ever be paralyzed and have to lay like that, not being able to talk or move. Veeza felt the tears coming to her eyes. *Oh, Baba,* she thought, *please don't die!* But in her heart she knew that it would have to happen. And dying would not be too bad for Baba because she surely would go to heaven.

The doubt pierced Veeza like the puncture from a needle threading its way through her flesh. If Baba did not go to heaven to be an angel to look down on her every night, would it be because of the tree? And why wouldn't Mama let them take the tree down? Every day, Mama brushed the dropped needles from the table and carefully dusted the ornaments, but she would not allow the tree to be taken down and thrown away.

Oh, God, Veeza thought, *why did you punish Baba, when from the beginning it started with me—long before I even went into that church! That letter started it!*

~ 2 ~

The letter had come addressed to Miss Louisa Picker. How important it had sounded. It was the first letter Veeza had ever received and it took several minutes before she realized that it was indeed addressed to her. Wanting to savor the mystery of its contents, she had held it delicately in her hand until Joey spoiled the enjoyment of it by grabbing it and holding it aloft.

"If you don't open it, I will," he teased, running around the room with it.

Finally, Manya put a stop to his nonsense. "Give your sister her letter and let her open it and read it." Manya shook her head like she couldn't understand Joey's behavior.

Veeza opened her letter and mouthed it to herself, not believing what she was reading.

"Who is it from?" Manya asked.

Veeza didn't want to see who it was from. Half the fun was reading it through and then discovering who wrote it. She turned the page over reluctantly and found it was from Ida Young.

"That dopey girl over where we used to live?" Joey scoffed.

Manya shook her head. *You'd think he had not a bit of bringing up, that boy . . .*

If there was one thing Manya believed in, it was proper behavior. If not for your own pride, she would tell the children, then for others. People judge your upbringing by your good manners. Veeza knew that Joey had good manners, but he just had to tease her.

"All right, let Veeza read her letter. But wait! Let Baba hear it, too. After all, the Youngs were her friends there. So Veeza waited until Mama called Baba into the dining room, and they all seated themselves around the table. Then, Veeza started to read again: *"Dear Louisa . . ."* Joey interrupted to say she read that before, and Manya scolded, "Joey, behave!"

"All right, all right . . . "

Veeza waited a moment to make sure she had everyone's attention, and then continued aloud:

"Dear Louisa . . . Mama says she hopes you and your family

are in good health. We would like you all to come to our tree-trimming party on Christmas Eve. You are to come for supper and, afterwards, we will have more refreshments. I miss you since you moved away, so please come ... Your friend, Ida.

P.S. My mama says I should not have put that in about refreshments because everyone knows that, specially it being Christmas Eve."

Veeza sat with the letter in her hand, a glow of happiness permeating her whole body. She had never been to a party, and she had never received a written invitation. Holding the letter in her hand, she danced around the table, tingling with excitement.

"Mama, Mama," she turned to Manya. "I have to write an answer so they'll know we're coming!"

Manya and Goldie looked at each other, then Manya said she'd have to think about it first.

Veeza felt her world crashing. What was there to think about? *Well,* she admitted to herself, *there are some things, like Papa. Would he want to go now that he has lost his job again?* Veeza knew he wouldn't be able to talk about what a good job he had and how he had gotten a raise—like Uncle Sidney did when he came to visit. *After Uncle Sidney leaves, Papa always goes out and doesn't come home until very late. Then there's Mama who is in the family way again—not very much, but the doctor says she must be very careful because it is so soon after the last new baby died, right next door to where the party is going to be—and that would make Mama sad again. And Joey has been sick with a cold and fever and maybe he won't be well enough to go out at night.* Veeza knew that night air was unhealthy.

Yes, Veeza had to admit that there were many things for her mother to think about. So she settled herself to doing homework, but with ears almost flapping to catch every word that Manya and Goldie would say.

Goldie said it would be bad manners not to go, especially since the Youngs had been so kind when little Shimon died.

~ *3* ~

Ja, ja, ja, Goldie lay thinking, *it was a pleasant flat on a street with a firehouse and a vacant factory where it was rumored that bats flew at night. Of course, who was out at night to prove if it was so?*

Veeza and Joey and Ida, the neighbor-girl, would watch the horses pull the hook-and-ladder trucks. They loved to watch the spotted fire dogs race alongside, barking happily like they enjoyed the activity. When there was no fire, the firemen would sit around in their red flannel undershirts with their suspenders showing, playing cards or shining up the fire engine. If the kids were real quiet and didn't bother them much, the firemen would let them slide down the fire pole which came through a hole in the ceiling. Goldie would bake cookies and send them over to the firemen so they could have a little nosh while waiting for fires.

But the bats that were supposed to be in the factory disappointed them. Try as they would, they never saw a bat, and no one had the nerve to go into the factory through the broken windows to see if bats were really in there.

It was a pleasant place to live, Goldie reminisced. But she did have one complaint: there were no Jews in the area.

"Shviger," Leon said, trying to be patient. "Shviger, none of us can have everything like we want, so we make the best of it. Do like you did at Laban's: sprinkle salt on the meat and make a prayer—a broche—and the meat will be as good as kosher, and the same with chicken. Thank God fish comes from the water so it's koshered for you by nature, so that takes care of that!"

Finally, Goldie admitted it was better than when they stayed with Meyer and Gittel. Not that Meyer and Gittel were not kind and willing, but this, at least, was living like menshen—not imposing, but living like people who know their life has to take its own path in its own time.

The neighbors would smile and Goldie would smile back, and Veeza learned to share with Ida, the well-behaved only child of the neighbors. God indeed had smiled on them there, and Goldie had shown her appreciation by sharing portions of her gefilte fish with the Youngs, who learned to eat it with the horseradish Goldie herself would grate.

Goldie, still recollecting, gurgled to herself in amusement as she recalled how the Youngs had helped themselves liberally to the freshly grated horseradish and how they had almost lifted themselves out of their chairs as the strength of it reached up into their nostrils and made their eyes water.

Joey and Veeza had attended the nearby school. It was so easy for one to bring a lunch the other had forgotten and take it right to the classroom—so comforting to Manya, not having to worry about either of her children being deprived of lunch.

Ah, yes, Goldie recalled, *it was a place of comfort from every direction.*

The happiest moment of all came when Manya discovered she was with child again. For a little while, life seemed to have taken its best turn. Leon was working at something which Goldie could not recall—but after all, one loses count if things take a turn for the better, please God. The household had an air of glowing life.

But when there is a devil lurking, there is no way of knowing where he will lay a curse.

Manya glowed like a young woman during the months before the new baby—Margaret—was born with Goldie attending. Goldie washed the little body with olive oil and wrapped her in warm blankets heated with hot bricks. But cold chills ran down Goldie's spine as she saw that the baby's skin did not have a pink tone. Her heart told her that Manya had given birth to a blue baby—a death sign.

That was a sad time. Manya paced the floor with the baby wrapped in its blanket, hoping to hear even the tiniest whimpering, but no sound came. Leon tried to tell Manya that baby Margaret had simply slept away.

The Youngs, their good neighbors, took care of Joey and Veeza while the baby was laid to rest somewhere.

But the family had to move again. The heartache was too much to bear.

~ *4* ~

"Weeeumph, weeumph." Goldie heard the sound issue from her throat. To anyone listening, the noise would have no meaning; she knew that, because there was nothing wrong with her hearing. *No matter what anyone thinks, an idiot I am not. I can hear what I am saying, and it is not what I am thinking.* All she could hope for was for someone to understand just one word, one little word.

Goldie recalled once seeing a deaf and dumb person—*now was it a man or a woman? . . . ah, a young man . . . trying to say something and trying to explain that he couldn't hear.* She had felt for him because she could speak but no one could understand her Yiddish. Now this was worse—no one understood her at all.

Do they think my brain is not working also?—someone, say, like Sidney, whose face always looks like he is smelling something bad when he sits next to me, though he rarely comes at all. If one thinks about it, who would dare say that God should have given preference to me over a nice young man who still has a life to live in a speaking and hearing world.

Goldie returned to her reflections: the party at the Youngs.

"It is a duty to go to the tree-trimming party," Goldie had said. "Not so much because it is their holiday, but because it is a tribute to us—of our friendship." And Manya agreed, even though her face was full of sadness.

Then came the question of a dress. Manya insisted that Veeza couldn't go to the party looking like a poor child.

That Manya, Goldie recalled, *her proud head up always. And her expression: "Having no money is a misfortune of circumstance, but admitting to being 'poor' is a lowering of your own respect."*

Goldie recalled the day—*when was it? Oh, yes, just before Thanksgiving one year*—when there was a knock at the door. When Manya answered it, there stood a man with a basket. He asked if their name was Picker and Manya said yes. The man then explained that someone had sent a food basket to them.

Manya had stood in the doorway listening to the man, and then explained in her proud voice, "There must be some mistake! We don't need any food basket here!" Manya hadn't seen the children standing behind her, their eyes glued to the turkey and all the mysterious packets tucked in the basket.

The man asked again, "Your name *is* Picker?" Manya answered, "You must have the wrong family, but thank whoever sent it anyway." The man went away with the basket, and Joey and Veeza somehow knew that it was not the right time to say they had never had a turkey, and especially at Thanksgiving when all the kids were talking about how big their turkey was going to be. Irene's mother was already baking pies. No, it was not the right time to say anything.

That same Thanksgiving, Leon came home with the happy news that he had bought a raffle ticket and had won the prize—and guess what! It was a turkey!

Manya had smiled. "You see, children. God takes care of everyone. Now some other poor family has a turkey, too."

The turkey had kept Goldie busy as if she were readying for the High Holidays. The only difference was that instead of chicken, she boiled the turkey. She used the usual soup greens, a couple of carrots, and whatever else came to mind to make the soup taste like chicken soup, only it should taste better than usual because it was a turkey—and twice as large as a chicken. But no matter what she did, somehow the soup was not as good as she had expected it to be.

Yayaya, her mind said. *Did anyone tell me that a turkey is really not an oversized chicken and that it has a different taste?* So she had to admit that the big surprise that Leon brought home was not really as good as her plain ordinary chicken soup.

Goldie came up with a brilliant idea, however. If the soup wasn't tasty, then the turkey meat would not be tasty either. So, like a mensh does with meat, she decided to take the meat from the bones and grind it up for latkes. What could go wrong with that? She would add an egg or two, a chopped onion, some matzo meal, and it would be a feast that isn't so fancy, but is nourishing—and nothing would be wasted.

And so it was.

Goldie, in her bed, prided herself; she could make something from nothing. *Such a skill kept the family fed in the hardest of times, glory be to God.*

~ 5 ~

Veeza needed a dress.

It was morning and Goldie noticed that Manya's face was drawn and her eyes were red. Manya had been crying—again—and when Manya cried, you could be sure there was a serious reason.

Then Goldie saw the reason. Across the back of a chair lay a butter-yellow dress—for Veeza. Obviously, Manya had stayed up most of the night to make Veeza a party dress. For material, Manya had cut up her own cherished wedding gown. "What good is a wedding dress packed away to rot? I want my daughter to remember that life has moments of beauty to enjoy while they are there."

Veeza tried on her dress, and they watched as she danced

around in admiration of herself. It was when Veeza looked for Leon to show him the dress that she discovered her papa had not come home—again.

Manya's eyes dropped as Veeza looked questioningly at her.

How the children loved Leon—so handsome and so playful. He was the lovingest papa. He never minded when they crawled all over him or begged him to read the funny papers to them. He was a papa to be proud of, Manya admitted, but she wished he would have a steady job like Mr. Young or the landlord downstairs who went to his tailor shop every day. Goldie knew that Manya was always worried about rent day—and about having people know. Manya was fussy about keeping their private affairs very private.

But despite it all, Manya forgave Leon. She would explain to Goldie that it was his friends who were at fault. After all, they knew he could not afford to play cards, but they invited him anyway. Goldie always wanted to respond that there's no friendship in card playing, but instead she just listened, knowing the hurt Manya was trying to hide.

Ja, ja, ja, Goldie lay in her bed, thinking. *Those were times like life: no guarantees. Every day to be lived however God portions out. Still, life has its moments, to be played with like a game. Cards? God forbid—to compare God's judgment to cards. But it is the mind that juggles the brain—or is it the brain that juggles the mind? And who appointed me the philosopher?* Perhaps she had inherited something from her Yussel, of sainted memory. How many times, in their village—*God Almighty, so many years ago*—Yussel would discuss the yes and the no of situations that came up between people, within families. As he would talk out loud to himself, Goldie would hear and wonder how anyone could be that smart. *Well, no, not smart, better than smart, intelligent—with such a sense of the problems of life and humanity—and of God's judgment.* Of course, in the end God's judgment is what the solution would be—God's own judgment of how one handles life and what life portions out.

So, here I am, Goldie's mind continued, *remembering those sad days and recalling the worry about a dress for a child so she could go to a Christmas party like a mensh.*

Once the dress was readied, they wondered what to do for a present. Presents cost money, and Goldie knew that Manya, having good manners, would not send anything that was not worthy of their friends who were so kind to invite them.

Goldie snickered to herself in bed. *God Almighty, how can anyone snicker? But then what is a snicker? A sound that has no real meaning. You make a noise, and whatever the other person hears is what they judge. So, I'm snickering. Why? Am I less miserable than I was a few minutes ago? No . . . it is the remembering of how brilliant I was. And that is enough to make anyone snicker!*

They needed a gift. After Leon came home later that evening, Manya explained that Goldie and Veeza would go to the party, and proper excuses would be made for everyone else. But they couldn't go with empty hands; there had to be a nice present. In each of their minds, there weighed heavy the same thought: a nice present costs money. Then, after some reflection, Goldie said that she would take care of the present.

Veeza noticed that no one questioned Goldie about where she would get a present without money. Besides, supper was ready and it seemed natural to drop the subject for the time being.

Later, no amount of coaxing on Veeza's part could get Goldie to reveal her secret.

As the days went by, Veeza was consumed with curiosity. Cuddling up to Goldie in bed at night—Goldie's body was so soft and warm, and her skin smooth as a rose petal—Veeza would beg Goldie to tell her what the present was. But Goldie said that little girls ask too many questions. "When the time comes, there will be a present."

~ 6 ~

Christmas Eve, the day of the party, finally arrived. While Manya brushed and braided Veeza's hair, Veeza admitted to praying for fat curls like her twin cousins had. Manya had told her that girls should be satisfied with what the good Lord sees fit to bestow upon them. As Veeza looked at her skinny braids, though, she still wished they could be fat curls.

The party dress shone like fresh butter. Manya had Veeza turn around and around to make sure no threads were hanging and that the sash was straight and the ruffles in place.

Goldie's wig was brushed until it shone like burnished copper. Her many petticoats were washed and starched, and her skirt ballooned out over them. She wore a plaid taffeta shirtwaist which Manya had made for her years ago; Goldie had first worn it to Manya and Leon's wedding. Now, she wore it only for company or Sabbath, so it was expected to last many years. Manya always said, "If you're going to use your eyes for sewing, always get the best material so that what you make will last."

Finally, atop Goldie's wig went a bonnet. Then she wrapped herself in a woolen shawl, over which she wore a capelet of fur which she had brought with her from Europe.

Veeza was bundled into a winter coat—a little short but still good for another year if the hem were taken down—then mittens and a warm stocking hat.

The two twirled around for Leon to admire—and then they were ready.

"Ah, not yet!" Goldie reminded them. "The present!"

As Manya stood, her arms akimbo, admiring her handiwork, Goldie went into the kitchen. Leon was busy writing down directions to show the trolley car conductor, and Joey was busy drawing, as if he didn't care that he wasn't going.

When Goldie came back from the kitchen with a package sitting across her outstretched arms, Veeza asked happily, "What is it? What is it? Such a big present! What is it, Baba?"

Manya carefully lifted the package from Goldie's arms and placed it on the dining room table. As her mother lifted the paper off the top, Veeza stood aghast! The present they were taking to the party was a giant-sized challeh—an egg bread. It's hot buttery fragrance wafted around the room. "Look how perfect it came out," Goldie declared proudly, pointing to the braided top, shiny and golden. Not even a bubble marred its smooth crust.

"A work of art," Manya agreed.

To Veeza, it was only an oversized bread.

Ach, kinder! Why do we expect them to be like grown ups? Goldie pondered. She remembered how Veeza had turned on her.

"You said you were going to think of a present—a special present! How can we go to the party bringing a bread?"

Manya took Veeza by the shoulders. "You're acting like a spoiled, ungrateful child!" Silent, head bent down, Veeza knew her mother was right. Still she was unable to change her feelings.

It was Leon who finally took a firm stand. "I've never spanked you before, Veeza, but if there was ever a time when I was tempted to, it is now." His blue eyes were steel cold. "Do you realize what it meant to your mother to cut up her wedding dress so you could go to this party?" All the pride and pain of a man's distress crossed Leon's face. He turned away for a moment to regain his composure, and then continued. "It took a lot of effort for your grandmother to make such a bread."

As they all stood watching, Leon cupped Veeza's face in his hands and looking his wonderful loving way into her eyes, he said, "I bet it will be the nicest present they have. You wait and see—and you'll be the prettiest girl there!" Veeza forced a smile as Leon patted her on the head, and Manya once again made sure she was snug and warm.

With Veeza carrying the directions and the pocketbook to pay the fare, the two started out. "The cookies," Goldie suddenly remembered. "I forgot the cookies—for the firemen to have a little nosh . . ."

~ 7 ~

Ja, ja, ja. Goldie wanted to snuggle under her bedcovers as if she were still feeling the nippy cold of that Christmas Eve night. *Feeling? Who remembers what feeling is? Ach!* What she wouldn't give to feel cold again. *But miracles are in storybooks, and maybe one or two in the Holy Book. But there are no miracles today.*

So back to yesterday. Yesterday—an expression. I can't even remember an hour ago, but I'll keep on trying. What better have I got to do with what is left of my mind? No, no, my mind is still sharp. It's where I put it that confuses me. But I can still remember that night.

Riding through the streets on the trolley car, Goldie and Veeza were glad to be out of the cold. As the bread and cookies gave off mouth-watering aromas, Veeza sniffed and Goldie smiled knowingly. Reaching into her pocket, Goldie dug out a small, paper-wrapped packet.

"There's something about fresh-baked challeh which stirs up the juices in the stomach, so I made a little nosh for us. A person should never go to a party so hungry that they can't wait to be served."

From the little packet she brought out two palm-sized loaves, crumbly and fragrant. Goldie's one tooth knew how to chomp at the bread until it was soaked and soft, and so they chewed, savoring each piece. Finally, Goldie nodded approvingly. She could tell by the feel of the dough that it would be a good challeh.

The two of them enjoyed the ride. Along the streets, windows were showing tiny candles lit on decorated trees—curtains were drawn back so they could be seen from the street. People got off and on the trolley car, loaded with packages or carrying Christmas trees. Everyone was smiling.

"Merry Christmas," they would greet Goldie cheerfully, and she would nod happily while nudging Veeza to say "Merry Christmas" in return.

At last, the conductor called out their street, and Goldie and Veeza hurried off, careful not to injure the challeh or to drop the bag of cookies. They stood for a minute, looking around the familiar neighborhood.

"There's our old school," Veeza pointed out. "I remember the first day I ever went into it, and I wasn't really in school yet because I wasn't old enough. But Joey forgot his lunch so Mama sent me to give it to him. They had a big sliding door between the classrooms, and I got into the wrong class, and the teacher slid the door open so I could go through it into Joey's room. I always liked that school when I got to go there. I liked this neighborhood," she said as she gave a reminiscent sigh.

They walked along comfortably snug against the cold.

"I remember your Uncle Sidney picked this neighborhood for us after your little brother was killed—he should rest in peace—and it made your papa angry because he said Uncle Sidney made him feel like a gurnicht—a nothing—who can't even pick out a flat for his family to move to. I'm afraid your papa doesn't like Uncle Sidney because he's always made a living for his family," Goldie spoke proudly. "The first day, he stood right there on

Castle Garden where the greenhorns come from the ship and said, 'I'm going to be a rich man in America.' "

"Is Uncle Sidney real rich?"

"Well," shrugged Goldie, "who knows how rich is real or how real is rich. Your dear Tante Pessie—excuse me, *Tante Paula* . . ." Goldie mimicked Sidney's admonition, "We don't use the Jewish name any more; Pessie is Pauline, and we've shortened it to Paula." Goldie continued without a break in her thought, ". . . but—God forbid!—if Sidney didn't provide her and the children with the things she wants, I don't think she'd stay with Sidney. Now your mama is different. She loves your papa in a different way. Maybe she loves him too much for his own good, but she is the kind who will stand when others fall."

They passed the ink factory, and Veeza wondered if anyone ever did see the bats which were supposed to be there.

Then they came to the fire station. Veeza knocked at the door which was shut to keep out the cold. A fireman opened the door; he was wearing a red flannel shirt and suspenders just as she remembered. And then he recognized them.

"Well look who's here! The little Jew lady who used to send us cookies. Where ya been? We heard you moved away."

Speaking properly, Veeza replied, "We did move, but we're going to a party across the street and my grandmother wanted you to have some cookies like she used to send over."

The other firemen left their game of cards and came to the door to thank them for the cookies. Goldie bobbed her head, smiled, and pretended to understand every word they said.

It had been a happy neighborhood for them until the tragedy of baby Margaret dying. This time Leon insisted that he would find a place for them. "Let Sidney take care of his family, and I will take care of my own."

"If we have to move," Goldie urged, "find us a place with tradition. We need to be among Jews. After all, the children are getting to an age where they should have some feeling for their own people, for their heritage."

Manya, however, said it made no difference to her where they lived; two parts of her heart were already buried elsewhere.

"And how did I feel leaving eleven small graves behind to come to America?" Goldie had retorted. "How did I feel when I left your papa's grave, may he rest in peace. You have to take courage in your hands and heal your heart, Manya. We came to America to make a new life for you, and you are moving now to make a new life for yourself and your children. You don't forget the past—you just move it aside to make room for the present."

When Leon found a flat, even Goldie could not complain about the lack of tradition in the neighborhood. For blocks around, there were only Jews and Jewish stores. To Goldie's delight, there was a live chicken market where a customer could feel between the slats to find out if the chicken's crop was stuffed with pebbles or grain, which was how the grower would sometimes make a few pennies more on the weight. There was also a fish market where the fish swam in tanks and were swept up by a net, clopped on the head, and sold. There was also a grocer who sold all kosher goods, milk, butter, eggs and all kinds of sweet and sour appetizers. The butcher had fresh cuts of meat that would make tasty dishes for little money—like stew thick with potatoes, carrots, prunes, yams, and chunks of meat which would be put on the back of the stove to simmer all night. Oh, and how tender was that meat. And one could buy yards of entrail casings which could be washed until they were transparent and then stuffed with mashed potatoes, browned onions, and bits of fat.

Ah, eating fit for a . . . rabbi. Goldie couldn't think of anyone better than a king, so she settled for a rabbi.

The neighborhood they were moving to was in Woods End, and Goldie rejoiced. At last, a home with her own people—good Jews.

Veeza remembered her first friends in Woods End. She remembered Jakey Jacobson, whose real name was Melvin, sitting on the brownstone steps alongside her and sending little kissing noises up her arm.

"Don't let him kiss you like that," Joey had warned. "You can get a baby from being kissed by a boy."

But Jakey scoffed at that. "You can only get a baby if I kiss you on the mouth. How can you give a baby through your arm?"

Of course, that sounded logical to Veeza. But she had to admit that she didn't care much for Jakey anyway; he was pale and thin and sneaky looking.

It was her best friend, Isabella, who told Veeza that she heard Jakey's mother tell her mother that Veeza's mother was in the family way again. Veeza wondered how this could be. She had never seen mama and papa kissing.

Goldie was happy in Woods End. This was how Jews should live, like in the village back home. The grandmothers dressed alike with their babushkas or their wigs and their shawls on Sabbath. And none of them spoke English in or out of the home; English was for the schools. In the home, the children spoke their mama-loshen—the mother language.

But Manya gained little from their Jewish environment; she would not socialize. She could not compete with the women who bragged in the stores about their husbands getting raises or how hard their husbands worked.

Goldie explained to the neighborhood women that Manya's reluctance to socialize was a result of the recent tragedies, but they offered no sympathy. They merely clucked their tongues and shook their heads and spat three times over their shoulders to ward off the evil eye.

~ *8* ~

Goldie opened her eyes, lost and feeling frightened. *God in heaven, where am I? Where is the fire station and the streetcar and the big challeh I baked so carefully . . . and where is Veeza?*

The howl of terror which escaped her lips echoed through the rooms and brought Veeza and Joey running to her bedside.

"Baba, Baba! Are you dreaming? Are you hurting?" Veeza turned to Joey. "What shall we do? I never heard her scream like that before!"

In his typical and practical way, Joey responded, "You don't do anything. She probably just had a bad dream. Besides, I've heard her scream like that before." He leaned over close to Goldie's face. "Baba, you had a bad dream?"

As the children came into focus, Goldie felt a deep sense of relief. *All is well, thanks be to God.*

When Joey and Veeza tiptoed out of the room, Goldie felt herself dozing again. *Ah,* she thought, *if this is dying . . .*

Then, as if she had turned a page of life backwards, Goldie remembered the Christmas party: she and Veeza, the lovely challeh, and the cookies for the firemen. She felt a giggle permeate

her numb and dying body as though she still had feeling in it.
The kopf—the head—ach, it is still alive, thanks be to God.

Goldie remembered every minute of that evening. As they
reached the flat where the Youngs lived, she and Veeza could
hear the buzz of conversation from the parlor windows. They
walked up the steps into the vestibule, and Veeza pushed the bell
button. The buzzer released the latch to open the door just as Ida
came out to greet them.

Veeza's first thought was, "My dress is prettier than hers."
Then they hugged and kissed, and Goldie found it difficult to
hold the bread. As her mother had instructed her, Veeza explained that Joey had a cold and Papa had not wanted to leave
them alone. While Goldie handed Mrs. Young their package,
Veeza quickly explained, "It's only a bread, but my grandmother baked it special for you." When they removed the wrapping,
the fresh, buttery fragrance filled the air.

The parlor was full of company and, as they admired the
bread, someone whimsically sang out "A loaf of bread and a jug
of wine." Everyone laughed as another said, "Bring out the
bottle," and the party went on.

Goldie sat down and watched all the people enjoying themselves. She nodded to those who smiled at her and admired some
of the presents already opened and displayed at the foot of the
tree. As if it were her holiday too, Goldie's face lit with excited
anticipation when she realized that the tree stood waiting to be
trimmed with all its brightly colored ornaments.

But first, the guests must eat. Mr. Young honed the knife until it was razor sharp, and then sliced the ham and turkey. Mrs.
Young scooped out large servings of vegetables and mashed potatoes with gravy.

When everyone had filled their plates, Goldie's bread was
sliced and served. What a fuss everyone made over it. Many said
they'd never tasted Jew bread before; how good it was. When
Veeza translated that to Goldie, she beamed and nodded and told
everybody, "Danke schön."

Goldie ate everything, including the ham and the turkey. Nibbling with her one tooth, she ate until there was nothing left on
her plate. She sipped her wine, rolling it around in her mouth,
tasting it carefully. She whispered to Veeza, "It's not as good as
the cherry wine your mother makes."

When the meal was finished, the men loosened their vest buttons and took off their coats, showing their striped silk or cotton shirts and brightly colored suspenders. They all settled back to smoke their cigars and to talk "men talk."

Chattering, the women washed up in the kitchen. Veeza and Ida made their own "girl talk," and Goldie sat contentedly full of food and wine.

Then came time to trim the tree. Its boughs were draped with yards of strung popcorn and garlands of raw cranberries. Tiny Christmas balls and ornaments shaped like teapots or birds with shiny tailfeathers were clipped onto the branches with delight. Everyone took turns putting things on the tree; the children decorated the lower branches. Mr. Young had to stand on a chair to do the upper part of the tree. At the very top, he placed one shiny star—and the tree was finished. Everyone admired it. When Goldie put one last Christmas ball on the tip of a branch, everyone applauded.

The tiny candleholders had been placed just right so they wouldn't be too close to the lace curtains. With the trimming finished, everyone helped light them, and one by one, the wicks caught. The little flames flickered uncertainly at first, and then seemed to decide that tonight was their night to glow. Each small flame took hold and burned steadily.

Everyone said it was the nicest tree the Youngs had ever had. "This year's trees are fuller than last year's, don't you think?"

"No, they're skinnier than before."

"Well, they're certainly shorter."

"No, they're taller."

But everyone agreed that this tree was the nicest of all.

Mr. Young took out his harmonica and played "Silent Night," and everyone sang quietly or hummed. Then the tunes got livelier. Goldie surprised everyone by singing a Russian song and then, as everyone applauded, she raised her skirts above her laced shoes and danced a little jig. Her eyes glowed with gay abandon, and Veeza thought she had never seen her grandmother so happy. "But then," Veeza thought, "that's what parties are for—to sing and dance and clap hands to the music." Veeza wondered why Jews didn't do this, too. All the Jews she knew were sad-like, although she didn't know many Jews at all, come to think of it.

Finally, the party came to an end. Everyone began to talk

about going to church early, and others just talked about getting to sleep in late. The brandy bottle was passed around to warm the blood before going out into the cold. This time Goldie didn't comment about whether or not the brandy was as good as Manya's cherry wine. Veeza figured it must have been because Goldie took a good mouthful before they wished everyone merry Christmas and left.

~ *9* ~

The late-night air crackled with the cold, and the stars hung low in the blue-black sky. Veeza felt that she could almost reach up and bring them down, one by one. The moon's pumpkin face smiled down at their happiness.

As they waited for the trolley car, Goldie and Veeza huddled for warmth in a little recess at the front door of a liquor store. Seeing them, the owner came out, his scarf around his neck and the earmuffs on his cap pulled down over his ears.

"You wanna tree?" he asked, pointing to two huge trees standing against a rope barricade.

Veeza shook her head no, but Goldie pointed to a lone little scrub at the far end. Its little wooden crosspiece lay somewhat lopsided. The man was sharp enough to see the glimmer in Goldie's eyes; she didn't have to ask him anything.

"Five cents," he answered Goldie's pointing mitten.

Goldie looked at Veeza questioningly when the man asked, "Italiano?"

Veeza shook her head. "Jewish."

The man stopped for a second, then shook his head, "Y'get all kinds—but *Yids?*" Then he chuckled, "G'wan. Y'can have it for a souvenir."

When Veeza translated the store owner's comments, Goldie wouldn't hear of it. "Business is business," she said. "He's entitled to his money."

She dug into her pocketbook, took out change, and counted out the pennies one by one. Proudly, she lifted the tree from its place, and it became hers by right of purchase.

The man went back into the store to warm himself near the potbellied stove, and Goldie and Veeza went on their way. The trolley car came down the line and picked them up, sparking along the cable above like sparklers on the Fourth of July.

The motorman, stomping his cold feet to put life back into them, greeted his new passengers with a cheerful "Merry Christmas." Other passengers, huddling in their coats and scarves, smiled, sharing the mutual enjoyment at the sight of the old lady, the child, and the tree. The conductor helped them get firmly seated before he gave the two pulls to the starting bell.

While Goldie paid the fare, Veeza held on to the treasure, wanting to shout her happiness to the whole car as it rumbled along the tracks.

Now as they passed houses, they noted more closely front parlor windows which had trees in them with the flickering little lights on the branches. Goldie then dozed a little, but Veeza was too excited. She wanted to get up and dance with happiness.

When they got off at their proper stop, the cold air hit like hot needles. Goldie put her hand over Veeza's mouth to keep the icy air out and held her close as they hurried along the dark street. The flames in the gas-lit street lamps danced a little ballet in time to the humming of the wind as the two scurried along, hugging their little tree close.

There remained with them remnants of the party's gaiety: the warmth of their reception and the total pleasure of being with other friends of the Youngs. It would be good to relate all of it to Manya and Joey and maybe even Leon—if, please God, he should be home.

~ 10 ~

"Lookit what they brought home!" had been Joey's greeting. Manya and Leon looked at the tree before they saw Veeza and Goldie. It was as though all motion was suspended for the moment.

Puzzled, Veeza looked at Goldie and then to the others. The heavenly moment was suddenly gone, vanishing like frosty breath. Goldie's face lost its cherubic smile, and the light behind her eyes went off. What had a short time before been a thing of beauty, unadorned but lovely, suddenly became a bare little scrub.

"We only paid five cents for it," Veeza said timidly.

Leon scoffed unbelievingly. "You mean you bought it? In heaven's name, why?"

Why? For a minute, Goldie and Veeza stared at the tree; they couldn't answer why. Then Goldie's spirit seemed to rekindle itself. The smallest of smiles played across her face as though suddenly she was being renewed by the recollection of the evening's gaiety.

"It's such a pretty holiday. I wanted us all to have some enjoyment out of it."

"But we're Jews! You wanted to be with Jews so we found you a Jewish neighborhood—and this is a goyish holiday."

"Beauty doesn't know religion," Goldie answered.

"Go tell that to the old rebs down the street," Leon snapped. He turned to Manya. "Your mother is going to be the spreader of beauty—with a Christmas tree in a Jewish neighborhood!"

Manya shook her head in equal wonder. "Mama, were you shikker? Did you drink too much? You wanted to live with Jews; you wanted the children to absorb their heritage here in a traditional neighborhood. Yet you buy a Christmas tree? In Europe, in your village, you would be stoned! Papa was a melamed—" Then, calmer, Manya continued, "You can put it down. It isn't going to walk away while you take off your things. Come on, both of you. I'll make some tea to take the chill out of your bones."

As they sipped their tea, Manya suggested that they put the tree in the stove and burn it. "At least we'd be putting it to good use." Then her superstitions arose: the tree had been cut, its life in the forest brought to an untimely end. *It's not the tree's fault, after all,* she reflected. But she didn't voice her afterthoughts.

Veeza piped up, "Mama, you and Papa are missing something. The tree doesn't know that Jews bought it. Anybody can buy a tree if it's pretty. It isn't the tree's fault if it really wasn't the prettiest and so didn't get bought. There were two others that didn't get bought either. This one happened to be cut for Christmas, but the tree doesn't know that. And it's not the tree's fault that we know why it was cut. So, it's not the tree's fault that we bought it. You see? It's not a Christian tree or a Jewish tree—it's just a tree!"

"The child's logic is what I was trying to tell you," Goldie added. "God made the tree, but he didn't put a sign on it to say what or who it was for. It just happens that tonight—their holiday—was the night we bought it."

The five sat thinking. Eventually Joey concluded, "Well, what good's a tree anyway, without decorations?"

With that, Goldie's face sank. They'd forgotten all about decorations. For a brief time, the only sound was the hiss of the kettle on the stove. Then, Goldie had an idea. She took a sip of her tea, pushed back the saucer, and went to the hall closet.

From the top shelf, she pulled down a carton and brought it to the table. It was her left-over wool holder. A myriad of colored yarn ends, little rolls and larger rolls, were stashed in this holder to be made into something later on. Goldie smiled, pleased with her idea. "We'll make little balls out of yarn . . . "

Veeza piped up, "Pompoms! Big ones and little ones! And we can string some yarn just like it was a popcorn chain!"

Goldie was suddenly as bright as a summer dawn, her eyes alight, and as she looked at Manya, Goldie saw that there was a softness in her expression.

Excitedly, Veeza continued. "It's going to be such a different tree. It won't be Christian because it'll be made by Jews for our Jewish house. And it'll be so pretty, Papa. Please don't be angry anymore."

Leon took Veeza in his arms. "I'm not angry, pigeon. Papas just lose their tempers sometimes, you know. We worry about one thing and then lose our temper over something else."

"It's such a pretty holiday, Papa. Baba just wanted for us all to have some prettiness out if it, too."

Leon hugged his daughter. "It will be."

They cut and twisted lengths of yarn until Joey and Veeza fell asleep at the table.

When Veeza awoke, she found herself undressed and in her bed, but Goldie was not there beside her. The room was icy cold, but Veeza slid into her slippers, wrapped herself in a flannel robe, and went to look for her grandmother.

The flat was dark and spooky as she felt her way into the kitchen. There seemed to be no one there. When she lit a match to turn on the gas jet, she saw that everything from their tree trimming was put away—the scissors, the yarn carton, even the tree was gone from where it had been standing.

It was as if the whole thing had been a dream, but Veeza knew it wasn't. She tiptoed on into the parlor. There, standing on the parlor table, was the tree, festive with its colored pompoms and chain of yarn strung around the scrawny branches. Then, Veeza saw Goldie huddled in a chair. She squeezed in next to her and together they looked at their tree. Goldie sighed deeply.

"Baba, was it wrong to get the tree—really wrong, like a sin?"

Goldie held Veeza close. "To my mind, it wasn't."

"Were you shikker like Mama said?"

"You think your grandmother can't drink some wine and have a little brandy without getting shikker? Your mama was just excited. But now we have the tree so we're going to enjoy it."

~ *11* ~

It was Jakey Jacobson who awakened them bright and early that Christmas morning. Manya quickly pushed her hair together with a hairpin and tossed a wrapper around herself as she hurried to see who was at the door so early.

"My goodness, Jakey, Veeza's not up yet. None of us are. What are you doing here so early?"

Jakey came right to the point. "Is it true that you have a Christmas tree?"

One by one, the family came: Leon in his pants with the suspenders hanging, and Joey in his nightshirt. Veeza and Goldie followed.

Veeza spoke up. "You've got some nerve, Jakey Jacobson, waking us up to ask us that!"

"I always wake up real early anyway," Jakey stated matter-of-factly. "My whole family believes in getting up early. I just wanted to know if it's true you have a Christmas tree?"

"It's none of your business," Veeza told him sharply, and started to shut the door in his face.

"That means you have one," Jakey retorted.

Joey moved closer to the doorway. "Who told you? Tell us that, and then maybe we'll tell you if . . . "

"Children," Manya intervened, "let's come away from the door. You're letting the cold air in." But Jakey stood firm.

"Herbie from the fish store, that's who—the one who's married. He was on the trolley car last night when Veeza and the baba got on, and he said Veeza was carrying a Christmas tree. So his mother told my mother and my mother told her that Herbie must be meshugge because no frummeh alte baba would bring a goyish tree into a Jewish house. So there!"

The family, a disheveled group, stood listening to the arrogance of this young boy who was unafraid to stand his ground. He *knew*, so there was no shaking his self-confidence.

Goldie finally acted. Taking Jakey by the arm, she led him into the parlor. "Come and see. Then you'll know what to tell your mama."

In the shimmering frosty sunlight, the little tree stood on the parlor table, festooned with the pompoms and wool chains. Jakey's eyes bugged out and his mouth fell open. As he turned and ran, he hollered, "Wait till I tell my mama!"

As Leon shook up the fire in the coal stove and put the kettle of water on, Manya remembered what she had once said about Mrs. Jacobson: "If anybody gets into her mouth, I pity them. You go into a store, and if she's there and she says hello first, then she says you're stuck up. If you don't stand and mama-loshen, then again you're stuck up. So big mouth or little mouth, you're in her mouth. Now we'll all be in her mouth for sure."

Goldie answered spiritedly, "So let her talk about us. Do we owe something to her? Let her take care of her business, and we'll take care of ours."

"But a Christian tree in a Jewish neighborhood, Mama? That's everybody's business!"

Gloom fell on the household. The specter, not wholly unexpected, had arisen, and no one knew how to get rid of it. Manya prepared a breakfast of thick oatmeal and slices of challeh and butter, and cocoa to drink.

Joey turned up his nose. "If we're gonna have Christmas, we ought to have something good! We have oatmeal or farina all the time."

Leon spoke up. "We're not having Christmas! We have a tree because your grandmother drank too much at a party and lost her senses."

Manya looked at Leon with the kind of black look which the children knew meant someone was driving her temper too far. "Just because I said that last night without meaning it doesn't mean you have to believe it, Leon."

Goldie snorted as she sipped her tea from the saucer. "You think a person has to be shikker because they have a couple of glasses of wine or a little glass of brandy to warm the bones? I remember once at Sarah's wedding in Europe, I drank twice as much. They tried to make me shikker, and they couldn't. And I danced at Sarah's wedding, too—like a feather my feet were!"

Manya felt her face getting red. She didn't like Leon to argue with Goldie in front of the children—or at all. She had to admit that Leon really was not an arguer, and he was far more polite to his shviger than many other husbands were to their mothers-in-law. But then, the other men were making money and could afford to establish who was boss in the house.

Whatever else Manya had intended to say was interrupted by another knock on the door. She turned pale as she started to get up from her chair, but Goldie motioned for her to sit.

"Let me go," Goldie said. Leon went on eating, making believe he was out of the whole mess, but the children sat still, waiting to see who was at the door.

Manya had expected it to be Mrs. Jacobson, but it was Mrs. Sylvester from across the street. She planted herself in the middle of the threshold and held out a cup.

"Suddenly, just today," Mrs. Sylvester said, "I'm out of sugar. I'm baking a noodle charlotte with raisins and pot cheese, and how such a thing could happen, to be out of sugar, I don't know. I stopped first by Mrs. Jacobson and by a strange how-do-you-do, she is also out of sugar."

Goldie took the cup and walked back toward the cupboard. Mrs. Sylvester moved toward the dining room and smiled innocently as she saw the family at breakfast.

"Guten Appetit," she greeted them.

Manya turned to face the woman. Always be polite, she had taught the children, and never turn your back when someone is talking. She answered Mrs. Sylvester with a thank you.

As she moved further into the dining room, Mrs. Sylvester was obviously not seeing what she had come to see. Leon asked her if she was looking for something.

"What should I be looking for?" Mrs. Sylvester questioned in return. She smiled and asked Manya how she was feeling, and Manya answered that she was feeling fine. Then Mrs. Sylvester said that she'd heard Manya was in a nervous condition. "I know what it is to be in the family way. Why, with my fifth child—it should rest in peace—I felt nervous, too, like the black angel was hovering overhead."

Leon jumped up from his chair as he saw Manya put her hand to her stomach. "Mrs. Sylvester," he contained himself, "you came for sugar and my shviger has it for you." Goldie came into the dining room carrying the cup. Leon's eyes bristled as he escorted Mrs. Sylvester to the door. "And don't bother to return the sugar," he told her. "You can accept it as a present."

Mrs. Sylvester's face gleamed. "A Christmas present?"

As Leon tried to control himself, Goldie pushed Mrs. Sylvester toward the door. "Christmas, Chanukah, Pesach—a cup of sugar has to have a name yet?"

With Mrs. Sylvester out the door, Goldie came back to the table and spat over her shoulder three times. Manya, feeling faint, shuddered and moaned, "She'll put the evil eye on me, that Mrs. Sylvester." Suddenly she ran to the toilet to vomit.

Joey turned on Veeza, shouting, "You did it, you did it with that rotten little tree!"

"I did not!" Veeza screamed. "Baba bought it!"

Later, Manya noticed Veeza put her arms around Goldie and beg forgiveness. "We bought the tree together, didn't we, Baba?"

Patting Veeza tenderly, Goldie said, "No, *I* bought it. If there is a sin, it's mine alone."

Later in the morning, Manya rested with a cold towel on her head while Leon washed the breakfast dishes, Goldie made up the beds, and Joey and Veeza dusted. Suddenly, there was another knock at the door. "Oh my God, not Mrs. Jacobson," Manya moaned. But it was only Isabella, Veeza's friend.

"How come you're here so early?" Veeza asked. "You always have to help your mother even when I don't have to help mine. I'm helping today because my mama isn't feeling so good."

"I know," Manya heard Isabella say.

"But how could you know it ahead of my telling you?"

"Mrs. Sylvester told my mama that your mama is nervous. And she said that your papa gave her a Christmas present. Of course, it was only a cup of sugar, but it's more than you gave me, and I'm your best friend."

Veeza tried to explain that she hadn't given anybody a Christmas present—not even her teacher in school. And besides, Isabella hadn't given her one either.

"We don't give Christmas presents to anybody—not even cups of sugar. *We're Jews!*"

"We're Jews, too," Veeza shouted, "and don't you dare say we're not, Isabella Gitelson!"

"Then how is it you've got a Christmas tree? Jews don't have Christmas trees. That belongs to Jesus. His last name is Christ, and that's how they got the name for the tree. Christ people tell everybody the Jews killed him on a cross, and that's why they hate the Jews. So how come a Jew has a Christ tree if she's a Jew?"

"We got it because it is such a lovely holiday. My grandmother said so, and she knows more than you do, even if you are my best friend."

Manya moved from the bed toward the door as the two girls stood looking at each other with heated stares.

"Don't be mad, Isabella," Veeza finally said sadly. "Everybody is mad at us today. Please be my friend again."

But Isabella turned her back. "My mother will not allow me to be friends with anyone who is turning into a goy."

With tears in her eyes, Veeza watched Isabella turn to leave. "Could I see the Christmas tree?" Isabella asked hesitantly.

Manya wanted to speak up and say no, but the two girls went into the parlor. Isabella looked for a second without saying a word, while Manya watched Veeza's eyes glow. Then Isabella said with a shrug, "It's not much of a tree. After all, it has no shiny things on it like they have at school."

Manya watched proudly as Veeza's dander rose. "It's a very special tree," Veeza countered. "It's got handmade ornaments on it, and my mama always says anything handmade is better than store-bought—that's why this tree is better."

But Isabella wasn't convinced. As they said good-bye, Isabella added, "I'll write in my diary about our friendship and our parting, and I hope you all won't get punished for having a sin in your house. My mama says you will."

Manya had to retch again.

Later, Leon answered another knock on the door. It was Mrs. Katzman, the landlady. Manya knew that Leon probably wondered whether the rent was past due. Then, when he remembered that the rent had been paid, he invited Mrs. Katzman to come in and sit down. He spoke pleasantly. "I'm glad to see you. I had intended to stop in at your flat and ask to have our flat painted. Now that you are here, this is as good a time as any to speak about it." Leon showed Mrs. Katzman the dining room walls so she could see for herself that they needed painting—and the kitchen also.

"Whoever lived in this flat before," Leon continued, "obviously didn't take good care of it." He knew full well that it was Mrs. Katzman and her family who had lived in the flat before his family had moved in. Leon went on, "If we had not needed a flat so badly, we would not have moved into this one in this condition. After all, my wife is a very particular housekeeper, and it offends her." He asked Mrs. Katzman if she would like to see the bedrooms.

Mrs. Katzman was equally uppity. "I'm sorry you're not happy with the flat. As a matter of fact," she offered, "I have a cousin who'd gladly take it just as it is if you want to move."

Aghast, Manya listened. Leon had no steady job, and moving was expensive. Where would they find a place as convenient as this for Goldie? But Leon smiled at Mrs. Katzman and in his most charming manner said, "I would not think to make such a decision alone. After all, the children are in school and it is close to the stores for my shviger." Then, changing the subject abruptly, Leon looked inquiringly at Mrs. Katzman and said in his most charming manner, "What can I do for you?"

Mrs. Katzman hemmed and hawed. Finally, Manya heard her say that she was sure what she'd heard was not true, but it was all over the street that the Pickers were really not Jews at all, but were goyim. Not that Mrs. Katzman believed them, but after all, the Pickers had lived there only a short time. If it were true, she wanted to know who the Christian was in the family who brought home the Christmas tree—not that she had anything against Christians.

Leon smiled the same charming smile that had won Manya's heart when he was courting her. How proud she had been to go out with him. "What a handsome young man is courting your cousin's daughter," people commented to Laban. A beautiful couple they made on their wedding day. "Such a smile that man has; Manya will have to be careful some rich woman doesn't steal him."

"The tree?" Leon was saying ever so pleasantly to Mrs. Katzman. "Well, if you must know the truth, and I would not tell you anything but the truth—a good, respectable woman like you should always be told the truth—the truth is that it was my shviger, a good Yiddisheh frummeh baba, who bought the tree."

Mrs. Katzman stood erect, her eyes snapping. "Mr. Picker, from you I don't have to be made a fool."

"It's true," Leon answered. "Here she is. Ask her yourself."

Mrs. Katzman turned to Goldie who just then came into the room. "Your son-in-law is playing games with me. He says that you, a good religious Jewish baba, brought home the Christmas tree. What kind of a man would blame his poor old shviger for such a sin?" she snorted contemptuously.

Manya watched Goldie look Mrs. Katzman straight in the eye and say, "But it is true. I am the guilty one."

Dramatically, Mrs. Katzman grabbed the back of the chair as if this news was too much to bear. "Oy vay! I can't believe it."

Goldie answered Mrs. Katzman innocently. "Veeza and I went to a Christmas party to help trim the tree, and it was such a lovely time—a tree decorating. I wanted that my family should enjoy doing the same thing."

Mrs. Katzman stepped back as if not to be contaminated. "If you want to disgrace your family, that's your business. But to disgrace my house, that's *my* business." Without further delay, Mrs. Katzman took herself off, leaving Manya wretchedly watching Leon and Goldie looking at each other in bewilderment.

"Leon," Goldie asked, "what are we going to do?"

"Don't excite yourself, shviger, it will blow over."

~ *12* ~

The following morning, the streets were blanketed with snow. Goldie said she would go early to bring in the Sabbath groceries and whatever else they needed. Manya sent Veeza along to help and to make sure that Goldie did not slip in the snow.

Not a soul was on the streets. But at the fish market, they found all the women there as usual for their Friday fish.

The market woman, her voluminous fish-bloodied apron tied around her waist, was degutting a fish, her diamond-ringed fingers slithering in and out of its belly. As Goldie and Veeza came into the store, the women suddenly stopped talking. Goldie stood for a moment, not sure what was going on. Herbie, the market man, stopped weighing a fish because of the silence. Then Veeza saw Jakey's mother. Mrs. Jacobson addressed the group.

"The frummeh piroshka is here—the religious dumpling, the hypocrite—to get a fish for the Sabbath." Then turning toward

Goldie, Mrs. Jacobson spat at her. "Real spit," Veeza told her mother later, "not like Baba does when she spits to ward off the 'evil eye.' "

Goldie opened her pocketbook, took out her handkerchief, and wiped her face. But then all the other women repeated Mrs. Jacobson's insult.

When Veeza lashed out and hit Mrs. Jacobson, Herbie banged on the counter with his large fish knife. "Weiber, weiber!" he shouted over their cursing, "this is a place of business. I make a living selling fish. If you want fish, you come in here, tell me what you want, pay for it, and go! I don't care who buys my fish, so long as they pay my price. If you frummeh damas want to spit, spit outside. It's not sanitary inside. Mrs. Jacobson, you got your fish, now pay for it and go home."

The women quieted down. Goldie and Veeza waited for their turn which meant that they were the last ones. When Goldie told Herbie what kind of fish she wanted and how much, he didn't say a word. He wrapped the fish in newspaper, told them how much to pay, and made change. Goldie had always liked Herbie; he always gave her an extra head or tail that was left over. This time he didn't.

As they left, Herbie's wife spit after them.

Their next stop was the butcher.

Moishe, the butcher, had a wasp's nest of a beard, gray and black. His apron was as gory as a surgeon's. As Goldie and Veeza entered the shop, he greeted them. "And what can we do for you today? Maybe you'd like a nice ham?" Before Goldie could figure out what a ham was, Moishe continued, "I'm all sold out of hams," and laughed like it was a big joke. Veeza wasn't sure what it was that he was laughing at. The ham they had at the party was very good, and Goldie had enjoyed it.

When Goldie and Veeza didn't laugh, Moishe stopped laughing, too. He waited on them, took their money, and shrugged as he quipped, "Business is business; you want to be a goy, it's your sin, not mine."

There were no old rebs sitting outside because of the cold, so they did not have to pass them to go to the chicken market.

Veeza knew the procedure there: you walk through the aisle separating the coops holding the chickens; you feel the chickens until you find the one you like. You pay the shochet a penny to slit its throat to make sure it is killed in a real kosher way. Then, if you want to spend another penny, the old woman sitting there will pluck its feathers and will swing the chicken over a flame to singe the pinfeathers.

Goldie picked out a chicken, but the shochet turned his head away from Goldie when he slit the chicken's throat. The old woman plucking the feathers kept her head down and muttered to herself, "I'm a poor woman; every penny counts."

It was like a council of war when they returned to the flat and reported it all. Manya wrung her hands and said in a whisper, "What shall we do?"

"What is there to do? In Europe when the mutchniks stirred up trouble in the villages, people kept to their homes until the mishegoss was over. But those were Russians, not Jews."

"I hate Jews!" Veeza cried. "I hate all those Jews!"

Leon slapped her across the mouth. As Manya ran for a cold, damp towel to keep the lip from swelling, Leon and Goldie glared at each other.

Then came another knock on the door. "My God in heaven, not again," Goldie sighed. "Don't answer it."

"What are we going to do, hide under the bed forever?" Leon shouted as they all stood fearfully wondering who this caller was.

Leon finally opened the door to find three old rebs standing in the doorway, their white socks showing above their slippers, their hats pushed down low against the cold, all three bundled in long coats.

Leon invited them in; after all, they were scholars of the old country and had to be treated with respect. They marched in, one after the other, properly leaving their hats on and greeting everyone.

Leon started to lead them into the parlor, then thought of the tree, and directed them instead to sit in the dining room. Manya offered to make tea, but the rebs sat stony-faced and unresponsive. They had come, they said, to talk to Mrs. Berron—God forbid they should drink tea in a goyisha house.

Goldie banged her fist on the table. "There are no converts in this house," she insisted. "If you want to talk, you had better mind your manners."

The rebs remained there, imperturbable. Following Goldie's

outburst, they leaned toward each other, disregarding the family, and held a small conference. Reb Herschel, the patriarch, nodded his head, adjusted his squirrelly hat, and pulled at the fringes of his prayer shawl which peeked out from under his coat. Then he started. He began a dissertation about what the Jews went through for hundreds of years—how they were persecuted in every country, how they all came to America so they could remain Jews, and how they finally moved with their sons and daughters and daughters-in-law and grandchildren to Woods End, to lead a pleasant, quiet life. "Thanks be to God," he said, "who helped provide all this. Such goyim as there are send their cooks to pick fat geese for their tables, and even those who don't have cooks come for chickens. Where else can they find poultry like in a kosher market? Thanks be to God, the goyim don't bother us, and we don't bother them."

"But," the reb continued, drawing out the "but" for emphasis, "bring one dissenter—one hypocrite—who poses as a frummeh alte baba, but who believes as a goy, and this could disrupt our whole peace, God forbid, exposing others to contamination."

The other two rebs listened, nodding their heads and muttering forebodings under their breath.

Finally, Goldie spoke up. "No one is going to call us dissenters or hypocrites or converts! The hypocrites are all of those women—the gossips, or even you—passing judgment!"

Reb Herschel shrugged. "Let's not argue over words," he said. "If not a hypocrite, then one possessed by a demon—the dybbuk." At this, the rebs spat over their shoulders and murmured warding-off prayers. This, they said, brought them to their next point. They declared that the guilty one who brought the Christmas tree into a religious Jewish household must be cleansed before appearing again in Reb Herschel's house for religious study or services. It is the reb's duty to cleanse that person's soul to save her from perdition.

"And if she doesn't get cleansed?" Goldie asked.

"Her soul will be left to wander between heaven and hell . . . a soul possessed which will have no resting place," the reb replied with a threatening and fearful expression.

"You can't do that to my grandmother!" Veeza cried out.

"Show them the tree to see how pretty she made it," Joey added.

The children started to grab at the rebs' coats with hysterical frenzy, but Manya held them back. Goldie raised her head high, her blue eyes stormy, and said, "If I am not afraid, you needn't be afraid for me. There is no dybbuk in me, and I will not agree to being cleansed." With that, she started for the kitchen saying that she had to start her cooking.

The old rebs stood up and, without a word, walked toward the door. "Your mother is accursed," Reb Herschel declared to Manya as they left.

~ *13* ~

"Aarrggruu," Goldie moaned and remembered. *That was a day!*

The ensuing argument between Manya and Leon had been fierce. Sometimes Goldie couldn't make out the words, sometimes she could hear their raised voices, and sometimes they argued with her.

"What would it have hurt," Leon asked, "if you'd said you are—or had been possessed? It wouldn't mean that you really are, but it would satisfy the rebs. You could be cleansed and everything would be forgiven."

"But," Manya interrupted, "how would it look for all of us, and for Veeza especially, to admit that the only reason we have the tree is because the demon prodded Mama into it?"

Leon looked at Manya in astonishment. "Do you really believe all of Goldie's story? Maybe the old rebs were right; for one short spell maybe your mother was possessed to do something no other old Jewish religious baba has ever done."

"But you like my mother," Manya insisted. "You're not like men who resent their shvigers! It's not that I agree the tree should have been bought, but who are we to tell Mama what she must do now. Just looking at her trying to defend herself gives me a heartache."

In the end they agreed it was Goldie's decision to make on her own.

Joey and Veeza had their own disagreement. Joey blamed Veeza. She should have known better than to let Baba bring a Christmas tree. Christmas was for Christians. He insisted that even if the Youngs invited them, it wasn't a party for Jews; they really shouldn't have gone. If Veeza hadn't wanted so much to go, none of this would have happened.

That night, Sabbath Eve, Goldie lit the candles as was her custom, covered her head with her little lace headpiece, and said the prayers.

The challeh was cut, and the supper started in silence. However, the pleasure of eating the gefilte fish, the chicken soup with the matzo balls, and the succulent chicken was missing.

Goldie ended up carrying most of the food back to the pots on the stove. Shortly afterward, Manya started her pains and Leon ran to get the doctor.

~ 14 ~

It was late morning when Manya awoke, a feeling of vagueness about her as though she'd been very ill. Her mind seemed to have disconnected from her body, and she was afraid to think. Yet, she had to pinpoint what she feared to know. In her innermost consciousness, she somehow sensed that the baby was no longer within her.

Suddenly, all her contained tension burst out in hysteria. Leon pinned her down forcefully, while Joey and Veeza stood watching, crying out for their mama not to die.

Then came the knock at the door.

Leon stood rigid, fearful of who it was this time and what further consequences were yet to develop. Goldie went to answer.

It was Mrs. Jacobson. "Was it not the doctor I saw leaving? Someone is sick?"

Goldie stood in the doorway, at first unable to speak. Finally she explained that Manya had had a miscarriage.

Mrs. Jacobson shook her head, an expression of fear yet smugness crossing her face. "It's retribution," she murmured. "Retribution!"

"You are an evil woman," Goldie flared with anger. "Now go down and pray to God that he doesn't punish you, too."

Having vented her anger, frustration, and grief, Goldie slammed the door in Mrs. Jacobson's face and stood white and shaking, her back against the door. Gradually, she calmed herself.

"Jjjiiidddssrr!" Goldie lying paralyzed in her bed screeched, and Veeza came running with Joey behind her.

"Baba, are you hurting? Where does it hurt?" But Veeza knew

it was useless to ask. She consoled herself by thinking that maybe Baba was having a bad dream like she would have once in awhile before all this happened. Her grandmother had explained that sometimes the past and all the things that made her unhappy would come back, as real as could be. Since there was nothing one can do about the past, she added, it was better that these things be forgotten. "But it's hard to forget," she lamented. "When the mind takes something in, it is like a hot iron—it burns the soul."

Veeza understood what her baba meant. There were so many things she wished she hadn't done and could forget. *How much worse it must be for Baba who is so old—and now can't even talk about it.*

As they left Goldie's bedside, Joey commented that he wasn't sure he wanted to be a doctor. "What good is knowing all about sicknesses and stuff if you can't help somebody like Baba, even if she is old?"

"Joey," Veeza asked, "how old do you have to be to be *real* old?"

"About forty," Joey said.

"Wow!" Veeza responded, wondering if Baba was as old as some of the mummies in the pictures she once saw in the school library.

She went in to take another look at her grandmother. Goldie lay there, eyes wide open, staring at the past.

Ah, thought Goldie, *what strength I had then—the strength of life and power to cope. Now I haven't the strength to raise my finger. Ah yes, that New Year's Eve and New Year's beginning were unheralded. It only meant a change of calendars for us. There was no change in our isolation.*

One day Leon came home with the happy news that he had found a steady job. It wasn't much yet, but he was told that he could do very well selling insurance. He was to collect weekly payments, but first had to sell a big policy. He was so enthusiastic that Manya did not have the heart to ask him where and to whom he was going to sell this big policy.

"Maybe Sidney will take out a big policy to give me a start," Leon wondered.

"Sidney?" Goldie had snorted. "If Sidney takes out a big policy from anyone, it will be from someone who can return the favor and do him some good." But Goldie congratulated Leon and wished him the best—for the sake of all.

As the days of the new year marched on, the little tree was all but forgotten in the pressures of their daily life. When the needles started to drop, Goldie finally faced the fact that they had to dispose of the tree. She put the pompoms in a little box.

"Why are we saving them, Baba?" Veeza had asked.

Goldie looked at Veeza in surprise. "You didn't like them? They weren't pretty?"

"Oh no, Baba," Veeza protested. "They were beautiful."

"Oh, I don't know," Goldie teased. "The knots were not tied so good, and the colors could have been more mixed. And the chain . . . well, I must say, I guess children like popcorn better, but then you can't save popcorn chains like you can yarn ones like this."

"But that's what I mean, Baba. What are we saving them for? We're not going to have another tree, are we?"

Goldie looked at Veeza. "You don't want one?"

"Oh, but I do! I'm always going to have a tree because, like you said, it's such a pretty holiday. But all the trouble came because of it."

Goldie shook her head. "The tree was only a symbol. Your grandfather, he should rest in peace, was a student of philosophy. He believed in freedom of thought, of the mind. Maybe he was ahead of his time, and that is probably why he and the poritz of the town, from our village—he, too, had a mind that your grandfather could relate to—that's why they were friends. And the poritz was a goy!"

"But Baba," Veeza protested, "it's Jews who are doing this to us—Mrs. Jacobson, Mrs. Katzman, Mrs. Gitelson. Isabella isn't even allowed to be my friend anymore, and Jakey turns his head away when I pass."

Goldie snorted, "They're sheep."

"But if they're sheep, then all the people around us are sheep, too, and we're the different ones. Why did we turn out to be different?"

Goldie looked at Veeza, a small frown settling across her forehead. *I'm talking too much,* she thought. *I don't want this child to be so sharp—not right now, anyway, because I don't have the answers. I lived in a small village where my people and my people's people were raised. Yussel, bless his name, came from a nearby town, and he was learned and circumspect in his way of life. Never did I do anything that would bring disrespect to him, and our children were examples of what a melamed's children should be. So, how did it come that at this time in my life, something happened to make me different—a Christmas tree! In our village, too, I would have been spat on. So, it's a pretty holiday—it's their holiday. Why am I butting in? Yet, if they wanted to enjoy our holiday, would I have said no? It's said, for every joy, one must expect a little heartache. As for me, it doesn't matter.*

Then Goldie felt herself sighing. *Who am I fooling? It does matter that we can't walk down the street without the women spitting or turning their faces away or the store people ignoring us as though we are worse than a goy.*

The truth of it was that Goldie missed going to Reb Herschel's house on the Sabbath Eve when he allowed the women to attend. Dressed in her sheitel and blouse and skirt and fur cape, Goldie enjoyed sitting with the women in the rear of the room, screened off by a curtain so as not to distract the rebs. She enjoyed saying her prayers and listening to the elders, all wrapped in their prayer shawls and swaying and chanting. It had been the reb's wife who had insisted that the frummeh weiber be allowed to attend. At first, Reb Herschel had protested that the women were a nuisance, and in fact had no business there. After all, in his village in Russia, no women were allowed to interfere with a man's praying or his discussion of the Law of the Torah. The reb's wife had countered that if a woman wants to pray, she should pray under the same roof as her husband. Besides, the prayer room was in their home. And so, one by one, the weiber came.

Missing her prayer opportunity, Goldie shrugged. *So the old man is a grouch. It doesn't matter.* She relived her years with Yussel and his gentle soul, and she prayed, unseen, along with the other women.

Goldie and Veeza finished stripping the tree in silence. Each little branch resisted as if defying destruction, until only the thin trunk remained, standing on the crossbars.

The yawning gap under the stove lid accepted and quickly devoured the dismembered remains of nature's handiwork. Goldie and Veeza watched their first Christmas tree—such a thing of beauty—come to a useful end in the stove.

BOOK FOUR
Goldie's Exile

~ 1 ~

Mrs. Katzman sat across the table from Manya, her teacup and plate of cookies left untouched.

"After all," Mrs. Katzman said, "it wouldn't be proper to drink tea and have a nosh with somebody I am asking to move."

Manya didn't understand. "Isn't the rent paid?"

Mrs. Katzman folded her arms across her bosom and snapped, "The family, I cannot complain about. Better children I could not ask for. But after much thought, I've decided I don't want make-believe Jews as tenants. If the old lady wants to be a goy, she can go and be a goy among the goyim."

Having delivered her dictate, she hefted herself from the chair and moved toward the door.

Manya sat stricken, recalling that their moves had always followed a tragedy. True, they would not have remained as long as they had at Laban's if Leon had got a steady job. And Shimon's death was really no one's fault; it was an accident. And who could understand why little Margaret was a blue baby, destined to die? Now this miscarriage and another move. Manya put her hands to her face and moaned, "Oh God, when will it stop?" Her mind briefly recaptured Leon mimicking Goldie: "Find us a place with tradition, where there are Jews and Jewish stores and the children can be raised with some understanding of the blood that is their heritage." Leon had finished by insisting, "Isn't that what she said? Isn't it?"

Manya had screamed back at him, "She said it, she said it!"

While they glared at each other, Joey had moved over to hold on to Manya, and Veeza had run to Goldie who was just coming into the room, as if to shield her from hearing what was being said.

Looking like an overgrown child, her face small, her babushka pushed back from her head, and her thin hair tousled like a little girl's, Goldie calmly asked, "What kind of a man are you, Leon, to fight with your wife on account of me? Am I not here to speak for myself should the need be?"

They stood, eye to eye, until Leon's shoulders drooped and he turned away.

That night, after Mrs. Katzman's icy visit, Leon and Manya talked. "After all," Leon asked, "why should we have the burden of keeping her? What Sidney drops off toward her keep, when he remembers or is reminded by Paula, you could put in your pocket and not even feel it. Why can't we send Goldie to Sidney and Paula for a change?"

The argument seesawed back and forth: Goldie was so accustomed to the family; she would not be happy with Sidney. But then, Sidney had some obligation for his mother. Would Paula take Goldie? After all, Paula was so social. What would an old woman who doesn't speak English do in her house? They'd have to hide her when they had company—all those fancy ladies who speak only English.

"But Paula is kind. She will be good to your mother."

"Yes, Paula is kind, and her children are well-behaved," Manya considered. "But they have seen their grandmother so seldom; they hardly know her. And they speak only English, so how will they talk with her?"

"Well that will be one good way for them to get to know their grandmother and learn to speak a little Yiddish," Leon asserted.

"But how about Goldie? How will she feel about it?"

"Manya, Manya," Leon pleaded. "For once, give us a little privacy—a feeling that our home is ours, that we can speak about family affairs without having to worry about leaving her out."

"But Mama is not like that. She has never interfered."

"No one said she interferes. It's just that a man likes to feel his wife and children belong to him."

In the end, Manya conceded. They would send Sidney a letter and ask him to come and talk about it.

While they waited for a response, Mrs. Katzman continued to pry. From time to time she would ask the children, "Did your papa find a place yet?" Each time they would shake their heads in the negative. "But he is looking?"

"Yes, he is looking."

Before long, Veeza found herself avoiding Mrs. Katzman in dread of her persistent question.

~ 2 ~

Sidney and Paula came. Beth and Barbara, their twins, also came dressed in white caracul coats with hats and muffs to match. Veeza looked at her cousins and felt her heart move right out of her body with envy. Never had she seen such beautiful outfits, and never, never, she knew, would she own one.

The girls sat, standoffishly pleasant, hands crossed in their laps, ankles properly crossed. They discussed the possibility of their getting a Shetland pony and a cart. The final stab to Veeza came with the realization that both of the girls had sausage-fat curls. Joey dared to pull a curl and Veeza watched it spring back into place, looking as untouched as if it had never moved. All her life, Veeza had longed for sausage-fat curls instead of her stringy straight hair.

Goldie came out of the parlor, her eyes brimming with tears. When she took down the cardboard suitcase, Veeza knew for real that Papa had won and that Goldie would go with Uncle Sidney and Tante Paula. She ran to Goldie, circled her body with her arms and cried, "You can't leave us! You can't leave us. I don't care if we never have another Christmas tree. Please stay with us!"

Sadly, Goldie held Veeza until the child's hysterical weeping quieted down. Unperturbed, the twins sat politely while Joey looked daggers at them.

"You better be good to her," he said, "or I'll come and get you myself."

The twins looked at him. "Why shouldn't we be good to her? She's our grandmother, too, isn't she?"

Veeza stood beside Joey. They were both surprised at their cousins' attitude. Maybe they were not as stuck-up as they looked.

Frozen-faced and maintaining control over her composure, Manya watched Paula help Goldie pack her few things.

"Just take enough to hold you over, shviger. Later, we'll buy you some new things."

"I don't need any new things," Goldie protested. "I have things here I don't even wear." She put back some of the odds and ends she had taken out, and finally the suitcase was packed. Goldie was bundled into her clothes, the sheitel a little askew on her head and the bonnet equally askew, then the shawl and cape.

"They're dressing me like I can't put on my own clothes," Goldie muttered to herself, but she made no protest. *In the hands of the enemy you move with caution.* But then she rebuked herself. *After all, Sidney is my son and Paula is a good woman.*

Finally, Goldie found herself being led out.

"Take care of yourself."

"Send a postcard right away."

"Don't worry; she'll be fine, and the twins will love her. We'll let you know how she is."

"How could everyone miss one baba so much?" Veeza had asked Manya.

Only Leon was happy. He had his family alone with him for the first time in their married life.

But Friday there was no fish. Manya did not feel up to chop-chopping, even if she could send Veeza to the fish man. Besides, she did not want to expose her daughter to what she herself was avoiding—the confrontations.

Leon ate a piece of store-bought bread without enjoyment. "You can say what you want, but if challeh isn't baked at home, it just isn't . . ." Then he realized that no one was really eating with enjoyment.

"Somehow," Manya said, "Friday isn't Friday without the chopping of the fish and the bentsh licht—the blessing over the candles. It was kinda nice to see her standing with her little piece of lace covering the sheitel . . ."

It was then that Leon grew angry. "So I said the bread from the store had no taste. So what? People learn to eat anything if they're hungry. And besides, Manya, keep in mind that you're not going to have your mother around forever. You'll have to learn to get used to being without her."

Manya flared, "I don't want to get used to it until I have to, and pray God, it shouldn't be for a long time yet!"

A few days later, Manya told Mrs. Katzman that Mr. Picker had found a place. "We are moving," Manya said, her head held proudly, "and to be very honest with you, Mrs. Katzman, we aren't sorry about leaving you."

The neighbors stood on the sidewalk as the truck backed up to the curb, and little by little their possessions were piled high and tied. As the driver flicked the whip, the horse snorted against the lash, and the move started.

The women stood watching, and Veeza could see them spitting over their shoulders three times to ward off any evil eye that the Pickers might have left behind.

~ *3* ~

Manya was pleased with Leon's selection. Their entry into a new section of Woods End caused no commotion. He had rented a railroad flat, one room leading into the other, with a little hallroom off the parlor and a bathroom off the hall.

It was a good neighborhood—stores for everything including yardage, and within walking distance of the school Veeza was already attending. The fact that a saloon was on the corner didn't bother Manya—Jews are not for saloons. Not that she thought that Jews don't drink, but she knew that when they do they drink at home. *But a saloon keeper has to make a living for his family,* thought Manya, and she didn't begrudge him his customers.

It was while they were settling in that Leon broke the news to Manya that there were no Jews in the area. "Thank God Mama is with Sidney and his family," she commented. "As for ourselves, it might take a little time for us to get acquainted and to show the neighbors that even Jews are nice."

Overhearing her mother, Veeza determined that she would tell no one she was a Jew, especially Irene Holihan, her new walking-to-school friend.

Before they had really settled in, a postcard came from Paula: *Dear Manya and Leon . . . You will have to take Goldie back. She sits and cries and misses your family. Sidney is not accustomed to her being here. It upsets him, and the twins are uncomfortable with someone who can't speak or understand English. We will bring her on Sunday. Regards . . . Paula.*

Manya cried with relief, and Leon, when he came home, was not angry. Manya knew he missed Goldie's cooking.

"Aaarrreee!" Goldie's body lay like a fallen tree. *Does the tree have a mind that eats at it like a worm burrowing into its fibers? If you walk along and pull a blossom from a branch— does it have pain? Pain. God Almighty, just to feel one little streak of pain. It would be like the miracle of life entering the world from its own cavern of survival. Ach, to feel the pain of a slap on its little tochis, fortunate, fortunate baby.*

Am I going out of my mind? No God, leave me just that remnant of a human being. Don't take my mind yet. I have a lot to think about. But first, I will rest a little.

When she awoke, Goldie's eyes fell upon Fr. Malachi. His hands were softly stroking hers, and Manya stood close.

"Aaaayyyrrr. Arhdknd." Goldie's eyes shown like little blue pools with the reflection of the sun in tiny crevices of pleasure.

"Mrs. Murphy, upstairs, has a bit of asthma, but she asked me to bring her regards to you." Fr. Malachi looked up at Manya, who translated to Goldie. "You understand, Mama?"

~ 4 ~

Goldie returned to the family, and Leon laid down the law to her himself, to make sure she understood. "There are no Jews and there will be no mama-loshen with the neighbors. The couple upstairs is Irish, and they go up and down the stairs minding their own business. So let it stay that way!"

"So lock me in a closet," Goldie retorted, "but you can't lock up the children!"

Veeza had sat, cringing as she listened, and then Joey stormed in and angrily tossed his cap at her.

"You've got a big mouth!" he accused her. "You told Johnny Burke we were Jews and Johnny told Tommy and Tommy's mother told him that now that we're here, half of Little Jewtown will probably be moving over! Now I haven't got any friends at all, and Tommy was gonna let me ride one of their horses. You and your big mouth!"

"I didn't tell him—he asked me, and I told him we got kicked out of Little Jewtown because they thought we were turning Christian, and Johnny said he'd tell his mother so she could tell Mike's mother, and then he ran home!"

Their dreams for peaceful living seemed shattered.

In the little hall bedroom, Goldie bemoaned her fate. Where was the joy she had anticipated in returning to her family? Not that Sidney was not her family—he was her son. Not that the twins, God bless them, were not nice, well-mannered little girls, and not that Paula was unkind. It was just not her home, and she was a stranger.

The breakaway from Manya and Leon had been a good idea—for once, they could be without a shviger under foot. After all, Leon was entitled to husband-and-wife privacy, and the children to being raised by their parents, even if she didn't butt in.

For sure, she was "home" again. But there was a difference now. Like a string broken and tied together again, the knot was firm but the smoothness was gone.

"Jajajaja!" Her mind returned to the priest. He had been up to see Mrs. Murphy who was having another asthma attack, Manya had just explained. *The mind is like a natural spring—it flows, emptying and refilling. I remember the priest, but how did he get here? A priest, yet!*

~ 5 ~

Goldie drifted off, remembering. Manya had found work with the dressmaker who sewed for the fine ladies from the other side of Woods End. The money was important, but Manya was especially happy that she had found a sewing job with someone who designed clothes from beautiful fabrics. Leftover pieces were always given to Manya, who used them one way or another for Veeza, to let her get the feel of good things.

One afternoon the quiet of their flat was disturbed by the sound of persistent coughing from above. Leon had told her to stay away from the neighbors, but does a mensh ignore someone in distress? So, Goldie had walked up the stairs and faced an open door.

There in the bedroom off the dining room lay Mrs. Murphy, her heavy chest struggling for breath in a coughing spasm.

Goldie remembered proudly how she had stoked up the fire under the coals and moved the kettle from the rear of the stove to the hot spot. Searching the icebox, she found a lemon and a small jar of honey. She worked with sureness as she located a large towel; soon she had Mrs. Murphy breathing the steam from the spout of a kettle under a towel-tent. Gradually, the tightness in her throat and chest was relieved. Goldie then fixed a mixture of hot water, lemon juice, and honey for Mrs. Murphy to sip.

Later, Mr. Murphy, red faced and heavy set, with a walrus mustache, came down to thank the new neighbors for the old lady's help.

With that kindness, the ice had been broken. The Murphys and the Pickers started saying, "Good morning" or "Good evening" to each other when they met. The Murphys knew the new tenants were Jews, but learned they didn't have horns! The Pickers gradually became more relaxed in their new neighborhood.

"Aaeeyaya." Goldie made a little welcoming sound and could see that Fr. Malachi was nodding that he understood. He smiled at the pixie-like expression which he had seen on Goldie's face in happier days. He knew she was pleased with herself about something. He patted her hand to concur.

Ah, she thought, *what a joy it is to see this servant of God, kind and warm to this wreck of a human being, this remnant of a life.* She made a little face as she reflected. *What is a well-lived life? Who could call my past life well lived? Lived to the fullest, maybe, but full of many heartaches—such as I see now with Manya and Leon.*

It seemed to Goldie, lying there, that it was only yesterday— or many yesterdays—since Leon had broken the news to Manya that he was going back to the little town where Laban had his factory, to work for him there. True, Goldie had argued with herself, Leon could not understand why such a good salesman as he had always been before he married Manya—as though to say Manya had something to do with it—could not sell even one big insurance policy. He would have to sell a second big policy, and then a bigger one. If he couldn't sell one, chances were he couldn't sell any. The logic was clear in Goldie's mind. A big insurance company could not exist on nickel-a-week policies.

So, if Leon could make a good living working for Laban, what would happen to Manya and the children? Never, Goldie knew, would Manya move back to the little town where Laban lived.

All through the night, Goldie had heard the murmur of their voices. In the morning as Goldie fixed breakfast, Manya, white-faced with fatigue and grief, watched Leon kiss the children good-bye. He promised to write. The children cried and asked who would read the funny papers to them, since Papa made them funnier.

When Leon left, suitcase in hand, Manya held her head high and went off to her sewing job—and the house was one person quieter. But Leon's going did not settle in their minds immediately. One can almost feel the presence of a person who is no longer there. But Manya remained staunch. "Leon," she said, "will make a very successful shirt salesman for Laban."

Goldie remembered feeling she was needed again.

BOOK FIVE

Veeza's Secret

~ 1 ~

It was a springlike day and Goldie thought it would be nice to go to the dairy farm for milk. Veeza said she would take her.

As they passed a cemetery, Goldie marveled at the size of it and Veeza explained that it wasn't a Jewish cemetery. Goldie remarked, "That explains it. In Europe, each family buries its own close by. Imagine being buried with strangers!" She spat three times over her shoulder to ward off the evil eye as they hurried past on their way to the dairy farm.

There, also carrying a jug for milk, was Irene Holihan and her mother. Veeza stood transfixed for a moment, wanting to run. Before she could steer Goldie in another direction, however, Irene caught sight of them. She greeted them warmly, then introduced her mother. Veeza, in turn, introduced Goldie, whose tiny face was almost hidden by the babushka.

"This is my grandmother," she said. Goldie stood nodding and smiling, an eager friend, unaware of Veeza's embarrassment. "Baba, this is my friend, Irene, and her mother, Mrs. Holihan."

Mrs. Holihan stood, head cocked questioningly as she struggled to understand Veeza's language. "Is it Polish you be speakin'? Some Catholic Polacks live on the other side of Holy Cross—they take their old folks to mass at one of them Polish churches, I heard tell."

Veeza shook her head. "It's Yiddish. We're Jews—Russian Jews." She stood with her eyes lowered, not looking at Irene and not seeing Goldie's friendly, unsuspecting face with its shining blue eyes. Goldie was pleased to be meeting Veeza's friends.

"Schön, schön," she bobbed her head in greeting.

"Well now, it's nice to have been meeting you. Jews, are you? Well, we hadn't heard of any Jews movin' over. An' all this time we've been thinkin' you're a Catholic child—an Irish lass livin' in St. Mary's Parish 'n' all that. Now it seems to me that my oldest girl, Lucy, once knew a Jew over in the city."

Goldie bobbed her head, her one tooth exposed in a disarming smile. She didn't understand a word of the conversation, but knew from the tone of voice that the woman was friendly.

Uncertain of this turn in events, Veeza wondered what she would say to Irene, who was standing there with questioning eyes. Just then the farmer arrived with Mrs. Holihan's jug of milk. She paid for it, and waving little good-byes, she and Irene left.

The next morning, Veeza waited fearfully for Irene, uncertain of Irene's reaction to the previous day's episode.

"You don't have to go in the church with me if you don't want to," Irene said. "Jews don't go to a Catholic church."

"But I want to," Veeza answered. "I feel happy in the church."

Irene smiled. "Mama said you'd be a good Catholic some day on account of you took to it so quick. Probably, you'll marry a fine Irish lad."

~ 2 ~

With Veeza seemingly destined to become a devout Catholic, the two young girls became inseparable friends. The Holihan household became a second home to Veeza.

Veeza would feel a twinge of distaste when she'd return home to find Manya on her knees scrubbing the kitchen floor. Never would her mama go to bed without knowing that should she die in the night, no one would be able to say a Jew had kept a dirty kitchen floor. The smell of yellow lye soap, the steaming water, and the sight of her mama's perspiring face made Veeza want to turn and run right back to the Holihans where there was laughter, piano playing, and the Holihan girls dancing with their beaus in the parlor. Veeza had never witnessed floor-scrubbing there.

One afternoon, Veeza was full of news for Goldie and Manya. Mrs. Holihan had predicted that there would be a letter from Leon the next day—with money in it, Veeza had emphasized.

Manya had sat back on her haunches in distress. "You didn't tell them about your papa, did you? I told you that if anyone asks why he isn't at home, you're to say he's gone to help his cousin who's a shirt manufacturer, because his cousin is sick and needs your papa's help." *Heaven help me,* Manya thought, *teaching a child to lie.*

"I didn't tell them anything, Mama. I did just as you told me—never to embarrass ourselves. But Mrs. Holihan reads cards. Sometimes she just gets a feeling. She reads the cards and then knows lots of things without anyone telling her! She told me about Papa—I didn't tell her!"

Manya was a proud woman. She knew that Jewish husbands had a reputation for being the best providers for their families. Hardly anyone ever heard of a Jewish wife taking in washing. As for drinking, Jewish husbands practically never drank. What's more, it was understood that Jewish husbands brought their wages home to their wives. Manya emphasized to her dressmaker that her husband, a devoted man, would never have left them except that he was so important to his sick cousin who could not pay him too much because doctor bills were so high. That was the reason she was helping out by doing some sewing.

That night, Veeza asked Goldie, "Baba, why is it Papa plays cards and loses his money?"

Goldie shrugged sadly, "Why does a moth play with a flame? Some kinds of power have a stronger will. That's how it is with your papa. He wants to be a winner, but he is destined to be a loser." And then Goldie quickly added, ". . . at cards, I mean."

To Veeza's delight, Mrs. Holihan's prediction came true the following day. A letter arrived. Instead of money, however, it held something flat and tightly wrapped in paper. Goldie watched Manya eagerly read the letter—and then saw her face drop.

Leon was apologetic. He had tried his luck at cards again and, this time, had won. But the loser could not pay in money. He paid his debt with a small diamond ring which Leon thought might fit Veeza's finger. It could be a birthday present for her.

Manya looked at the ring and then at Veeza. The child knew what her mama was thinking. "Mama, you could sell it, couldn't you?"

Manya carefully put the ring back in the paper and tucked it into the cupboard. "It's not mine to sell. The ring is your birthday present—it belongs to you."

Veeza put her arms around her mama. "I give it to you—for all of us."

The following day Manya had money, and Veeza ran to the cupboard to see if Mama had sold the ring. It was still there.

Close to the package, however, was a pawn ticket for a gold wedding band. Veeza had seen such tickets before.

In the middle of the night, Veeza slipped into bed to nestle with Manya. Though no sound came from her mama, Veeza noticed Manya's cheeks were wet with tears. Veeza knew then that she couldn't ask her mother for money to buy a ticket for the church social at St. Mary's. Besides, even if she had a ticket, she couldn't wear her pretty party dress with her old scuffed shoes—next week they would have a cardboard put in them to postpone resoling for a week or more.

All week long, Irene had talked about the social.

"Is it for kids?" Veeza asked.

"Of course not, silly; it's for grown-ups. But there are always people who bring their kids because it's a . . . well . . . a social—like a party. My sisters are going to take me, and I'm getting patent leather Mary Janes. They're party slippers, you know."

Veeza felt her world grow black. She remembered the caracul coats and matching hats and muffs which the twins wore that day Uncle Sidney and Aunt Paula came to get Baba. They wore Mary Janes, and there wasn't even a party. Veeza guessed that the twins could wear party slippers anytime they wanted to because Uncle Sidney was rich.

But the Holihans weren't rich, and Irene was going to get Mary Jane patent leather slippers. Veeza felt a special twinge of envy because Mama had said that patent leather doesn't hold up. One needed shoes that would take wear. *Some people,* Veeza thought, *have everything!* Right then, all she wanted was a pair of patent leather Mary Janes.

~ 3 ~

As she came out to the hall closet to fill the Sabbath wine jug from the keg of Manya's cherry wine aging there, Goldie spied Fr. Malachi coming up the stairs. Quickly, she opened the parlor door to welcome this distinguished visitor who had come by mistake the last time.

Taken by surprise with Goldie's obvious display of pleasure, the young priest followed her gesture, a bemused look on his face. The old lady smiled winningly. *How Yussel would have been pleased, like in our home village when the poritz brought a*

distinguished guest to meet the Jewish scholar and artisan.
Should this guest be treated with less courtesy? Goldie reasoned.

She tried anxiously to offer the guest hospitality. "Tay?" she asked, bustling out of the parlor toward the kitchen. Just then, Veeza came in. "Please tell the visitor in the parlor there will be tea and cookies in a moment," she directed.

Immediately, Fr. Malachi recognized Veeza as one of the little girls who regularly came into the church on their way to school. They sat for a moment without a word being spoken. Then Veeza said, "I only went into the church to be with my friends. I wanted to be like them because I am the only one of them who is Jewish."

"And you wanted to be a Catholic?"

"No, no! I just don't want to be different."

"You feel you need them, but they don't need you?"

Veeza nodded miserably.

"Do you think they might have accepted you just as you are, with your own faith, as a person—a nice little girl?"

She wanted to tell the priest about Little Jewtown, but she remembered Mama saying you should never talk about anyone unless you can say something good—and she couldn't say anything good about the Jews there.

Fr. Malachi continued, "If you don't think much of yourself, how can you expect it of others?"

It was getting too complicated. Veeza sat with her head down until the silence was too much to bear.

"Can't you give me a penance, Father, so I can wipe away my sin?"

"No, my child, I can't," he replied gravely.

"Are you going to tell my friends?"

Fr. Malachi smiled and shook his head. "I will leave that up to you."

When Goldie came in with a tray of cookies and cups of tea, she motioned for Veeza to join them.

"How honored we are," she said to Veeza who repeated it to Fr. Malachi. Goldie followed with, "Guten Welt," and Veeza translated, "It's a good world."

Fr. Malachi nodded and repeated, "Guten Welt."

When his tea was finished, Fr. Malachi rose to go. Goldie shook his hand and murmured, "Danke schön" and asked Veeza to invite him to come again. "Ah," she reflected with a deep sigh of satisfaction, "you are an honored visitor just like we would have at home in the village."

Before translating, Veeza protested that maybe the priest didn't want to know about that, but Goldie insisted. "A distinguished man like the priest will appreciate knowing about your grandfather's friends, just as I am appreciating his friendship with us."

Stumbling, Veeza repeated what Goldie had expressed and Fr. Malachi studied the woman's weathered face. Looking into those steady blue eyes full of extraordinary vitality, he felt a surge of emotion. *Holy Father,* he found himself thinking, *she's like my own grandmother—or am I bewitched?*

Goldie's face was aglow as she watched the priest leave.

When Manya arrived home, Goldie was full of the news about the priest's unexpected visit—"a beautiful young man." Manya reacted pointedly, "What did he want—to make us Catholics or something?"

Goldie's face fell. She tried to reason to herself: *Manya is tired. All day long she works with the Catholics and has to be careful how she speaks, not that she doesn't speak nice English—and never a word that anyone would be ashamed of. Manya learned early how to be a lady among people.*

Joey popped up, "I hope he keeps coming, then people will believe we're studying to become Catholics." Joey boasted that he hadn't told Tom that they weren't Catholic, so in case Tom's mother asked, Tom wouldn't be able to say yes or no. If Tom's father asked him, he could say that since the priest goes to their house, maybe they're becoming Catholics.

Veeza accused Joey of telling a lie, but Joey said he wasn't telling anything to anybody. "You can't be accused of lying if you're not saying anything."

It got so complicated that Manya turned on Goldie. "You see what you started, Mama? I won't have my children turning into liars."

Veeza listened, stricken, and wondered why everything has to get so mixed up. She knew Mama wouldn't let her go to the church social now, even if her shoes weren't so worn out.

Manya apologized to Goldie. "Mama, I didn't mean to yell at you, but remember that Leon said not to get involved with the goyim. We had enough trouble getting involved with the Jews."

~ 4 ~

Goldie was proud of the way Manya insisted that her children become good Americans by sending them to school to get a good education. "A person without an education," Manya would say, "is like a meal without salt. Something is missing to make the most of what you have." Even Manya practiced writing English words so she would be able to write as well as she spoke.

Manya didn't have anything against the Catholics; rather, she was reflecting her disappointment in the Jews. Goldie understood this, because in spite of their nice flat and the nice friends the children were making, they were being deprived of the homey—haimish—environment of their old neighborhood which had been their first exposure to who they were. Goldie had mused within herself: *Who cares who anybody is? And which comes first, decency and character, or where you come from?* Finally, she decided it was too complicated and concluded, *Whatever you make of yourself is who you are.* With a smirk of humor, Yussel, of sainted memory, would have been proud of her. *In our homeland, the weiber—the wives—were not expected to waste their time thinking. So how could they know if they even could think if they never had to do it?*

Still, Goldie found herself questioning. *Why can't my own kind in that haimish neighborhood understand me as a person— a mensh—whereas a young Catholic priest can. It's a puzzle.*

"So what did you use to talk with—sign language?" Joey asked.

"Smarty," Veeza retorted. "*I* was the translator, and I'm not even as old as you are!"

"And what did they talk about?" Manya asked.

"They talked about the world. Baba said it was a good world, and Fr. Malachi said it was a good world." Veeza laughed. "Say 'good world' like you said it, Baba."

"Guten Welt," Goldie answered seriously. "Are you making a joke? The Gallich is a man of God. So who cares which God is whose since there is only one God anyway? God made the world and he made it good. What more proper thing could I have said than that it is a good world because it is God's world?"

Having said her piece, Goldie snorted at their apparent derision and went into the kitchen to start supper.

Manya shook her head. "Your grandmother . . ." as if to say they might as well give up trying to outwit her—she's smarter than they thought. Manya opened the box she had brought home.

"Hang up this dress, Veeza. It's for Mrs. McGrorty, and I have to work on it tonight. She'll be wearing it at some church social, so be careful how you handle it."

Veeza wondered how Mama felt, working on those lovely dresses. She could not remember Mama ever having one new dress to wear to a social, but then she couldn't remember Mama going anywhere needing a party dress.

Then came a horrible thought: *Will I ever get to go to a social?*

~ 5 ~

One day after school, Veeza was doing homework with Irene at the Holihan house. A big ham simmered on the stove and the house was fragrant with the aroma of onions and cloves and doughnuts just popped out of the kettle. Veeza and Irene alternated between doing their arithmetic and nibbling the little rounds that had been cut out of the dough.

"If Veeza is going to stay for supper," Mrs. Holihan interrupted, "I want her to be able to tell her mother we fed her more than sugar doughnuts. Besides, we want enough left over for your sisters' gentlemen friends who are coming tonight."

Veeza crawled inside herself. She wished one boy in particular wasn't coming. He was the one who said that Jews have bony noses. When he thought Veeza couldn't hear, he had boasted that he could tell a Jew nose anytime. *But still,* Veeza thought, *it's so much fun eating here. The thick juicy slices of ham with the cloves and brown sugar topping baked into it after its skin has been pulled off, and the long slashes cut into the fat to hold the cloves and brown sugar. There must not be anything better to eat in the whole world,* she silently decided. Not even freshmouth Pete, the rude gentleman friend of Irene's sister, was going to deprive her of such a supper.

"Do you want to go with us when I get Mary Janes for the church social?" Irene asked. "We're going after supper."

Did she want to go? Veeza wanted to go so badly it hurt. Even if the shoes weren't for her, it would be nice to see and feel the shiny patent leather while Irene tried them on. Veeza thought of the cardboard in her shoes which would have to do until Mama had the money to get them repaired—but no one needed to know that.

After supper, while the older girls washed the dishes, Irene and Veeza dried and stacked them in the cupboard. Mrs. Holihan went to put on her corset, laced up her shoes, changed her skirt and waist, and put on her coat and wool hat. The beaus helped their girls with their coats and hats, and they all started off for the shoe store. Irene would be shopping for Mary Janes, and Helen and Lucy, the older sisters, would look for fancy high-heeled dancing shoes. Their gentlemen friends had insisted they be allowed to pay for the older girls' shoes.

As Irene slipped into the right size of Mary Janes, Mrs. Holihan motioned to the salesman to come to Veeza. Veeza pulled her foot back in embarrassment. "Not me," she said, "it's for the other girl."

"Both of you are getting Mary Janes," Mrs. Holihan stated. "It will be a present from us."

"And I'm going to pay for them," Pete called out. "I got a raise today, so I can be a sport."

Veeza held her foot back under the seat. Her mama would be angry. "We don't take charity," she would say.

The older girls started saying how generous Pete was, and Irene was looking at more samples the salesman had in his hand, when suddenly Veeza knew she wanted those Mary Janes more than anything in the world, no matter who paid for them.

Mrs. Holihan smiled and told Veeza to put her foot out for the man to measure her size. Big as life, the hole in the old sole showed—and the salesman saw the cardboard! But she didn't care. If Pete wanted to pay for her new shoes, good for him and good for her. She was getting Mary Janes! When the man slipped them on her feet, she wiggled her toes and tried a few steps. They were perfect!

Lucy and Helen pirouetted around in their high-heeled dancing shoes. Helen's beau insisted she get the ones with the bronze beads in the front; the beads glittered as the light shown on them. Twinkly toes! *Someday,* Veeza vowed to herself, *I'll wear twinkly-toed shoes!*

The walk home was like walking on air. "Wear them well," Mrs. Holihan called after her as Veeza said good night in a state of euphoria.

When Veeza got home, Manya was sitting at the kitchen table, material draped carefully in her lap. The only light she had to work by came from a kerosene lamp. Veeza knew that the gas, once more, had been turned off because the bill had not been paid. The room was gloomy, and Manya's head bent so low over the sewing that Veeza's first reaction was to turn and run back to the Holihans where they seemed never to have their gas turned off. There she would find laughter that came from kissing the blarney stone.

Looking up, Manya smiled a slow sweet smile of greeting. "You came up the stairs so fast, you must have been happy to get home."

"Oh, I was—I am!"

"You did your homework?"

Veeza nodded as she held the shoe package behind her back—the surprise that was to have been.

"Why are you standing there with your hands behind your back?" Manya asked. "Sit down so we can talk. You should ask Irene to come eat with us sometime and to do her homework here. It isn't nice to always go to someone's house and not invite them back."

"Is Baba here?"

Manya explained that Goldie was upstairs. She had taken a piece of honey cake up to the Murphys. Manya sighed a small, contented smile. "The Murphys are such nice people, and they like your baba so much. We're very fortunate."

"Especially me," Veeza answered, savoring how she would lead in to her surprise.

"I hope you're not imposing on Mrs. Holihan, eating there."

"Oh, Mama, there's always food there. They have ham left over from Sunday, and then on Wednesday they have corned beef and cabbage, so that's left over for Thursday, and fish on Friday—not gefilte fish like Baba makes, just fish."

"Ham," Manya shook her head. "It's bad enough not to live with kosher people or to have to be not–so–kosher like we are. But I wouldn't eat ham. A Jew has to be a Jew somehow; people respect you more."

"But Baba ate ham at the Youngs' Christmas party."

"She didn't know what it was. Baba would never eat anything so trayf."

Veeza wanted to say, "Oh Mama, let's not go into that again.

There's something more important to go into—the shoe package which is getting heavy behind my back." But instead she said, "Mama, shut your eyes and don't open them until I tell you. I have a surprise to show you."

Manya smiled, closed her eyes, and Veeza quickly put the shoe box down. She unbuttoned the uppers of her old shoes, slipped out of them, and stepped into her new patent leather Mary Jane slippers.

"Open your eyes."

At first, Manya looked at Veeza's hair, then her face. It seemed to take ages for Manya's gaze to reach Veeza's feet.

"Where did you get those slippers?" Manya asked, surprised and puzzled.

"Mama, don't be angry; please don't be angry." Suddenly, she felt like she was slipping into a bottomless lake and struggling for air.

"I can't be angry until I know what I have to be angry about."

"Mama, the Holihans bought them for me—as a present. What I mean is, Lucy's gentleman friend bought them. He bought them for Irene, too—for the church social Saturday night. They had an extra ticket, so they invited me, and I have that beautiful dress you made for me, but my shoes had holes in them. I couldn't go to the social with holes in my shoes." It came out in one long, agonizing breath.

"And so you told them you couldn't go because your shoes have holes in them?"

"Mama, you know better than that. I would never let anybody know that. I kept it hidden, but somehow they knew."

Manya put aside the material on her lap and went to the cupboard. She took out the tea glasses, set them on the table, and quietly poured steeping tea from the little pot into the glasses. Slowly and deliberately, she added hot water from the kettle. Veeza watched every movement without uttering a word, knowing that Manya was thinking.

"Mama, please . . . " Veeza finally said. "Please let me go to the social."

"How can you *not* go? You obligated us. You let them buy you shoes like a poor charity child. You ought to know that in our house, Veeza, we don't take charity. We do with what we have, and what we don't have, we do without. Have you ever been hungry?"

"No, Mama."

"And are your clothes something to be ashamed of?"

"No, Mama."

"Sit down and drink the tea and tell me where the social is going to be."

Veeza sat down and started in breathlessly. "It's in the church where Irene's family goes. You know that nice priest who was here? It's where he lives so you know it's a nice church—and everybody's going."

"Everybody?"

Veeza realized full well Manya's meaning.

"Well, not everybody. I mean, everybody who has a ticket. But I guess it's the Catholics who buy the tickets." She knew that her mama couldn't go even if she wanted to—there wasn't even enough money to pay the gas bill. And if there was ever a penny left over from anything, it would go into the pushke, to help someone who was poorer than themselves.

They heard Joey come whistling down the stairs, accompanied by Goldie. "Pour some tea for your grandmother and brother," Manya directed.

Veeza knew that Mama just wanted to get her up so that Baba and Joey would notice her Mary Janes.

Joey saw them first. "Take a look at those shoes!" he cried out.

Manya sucked on a lump of sugar while Goldie admired the slippers.

"Where'd you get them, Cinderella?" he teased.

"She got them in a shoe store, where else?" Manya shot back before Veeza could reply. "If you ask a silly question, you get a silly answer."

"But I need shoes, too," Joey protested.

"They were a present," Veeza stated defensively.

"I betcha Santy Claus came right down the chimney which we don't have, to leave her a present even if it isn't Christmas anymore on account of he wants to make sure she remembers Christmas next year. Oh boy, we got kicked out of Little Jewtown because we had Christmas. Now maybe we'll get kicked out of here because we *don't* have Christmas!"

"It has nothing to do with Christmas, silly!"

"Don't sass your brother, Veeza. And Joey, stop teasing!"

Goldie looked at Manya questioningly, and Manya told her

that Lucy Holihan's gentleman friend bought the shoes for Veeza because he got a raise.

"And," Veeza emphasized to Goldie, "they invited me to the social at the church Saturday night." Veeza danced, her arms out whirling.

"At the church? Oy, vay!" Joey threw his hand against his forehead, pretending doom. Then he grabbed Veeza and waltzed her around the room as he whistled a tune.

Manya left the room and soon returned with the butter-yellow dress she had hung carefully away last Christmas. It needed only minor adjusting—some lengthening since Veeza had grown nearly an inch. It was a perfect dress for the social. The Holihans would not be embarrassed by Veeza.

Goldie and Manya sat smiling. Goldie noticed that Manya's eyes had a faraway look to them and the lines in her tired face had softened. *In such brief moments, other heartaches can seem less painful,* she thought.

"It's a pleasure to see children happy," Goldie said. Manya nodded agreement as the lamplight sputtered feebly to announce it was running out of oil.

"Aaaarrreee!" Goldie's lively mind in her lifeless body recalled the pleasure of those moments. *The happiness of children is a gift to a home. Pleasure from your child is like medicine to your heart.*

A heart. She could hear a clock ticking. *My heart is still ticking, but what purpose does it serve? When it is time for it to stop—poof, like a light—you turn the jet and the light is gone. Meantime, is it better to have a mind with no speech, or speech with no mind?*

Gott in Himmel—it's no good either way.

"Aaarrrhee!"

~ 6 ~

By the time Veeza, the Holihans, and the beaus arrived, the social hall at St. Mary's was full of dancing, laughing, and chattering people. The group piled their coats and hats on top of others already on the chairs and racks while Helen and Lucy twittered over how their hair looked. Their beaus made jokes about how long it takes girls to get ready: "Even after they get to where they're going, they still fuss with their hair. They want to be sure their skirts are long enough, too, so that not too much of their ankles show—yet they hope that we fellows will see what pretty ankles they have anyway!"

Mrs. Holihan found herself a chair along the wall and joined all the other women and men who preferred to sit and watch the young folks enjoy themselves. The piano player thumped out "When Irish Eyes Are Smiling," and everyone sang, even those who were dancing.

Irene and Veeza stood with the other young girls, hoping some boy would ask them to dance. Shortly, a boy asked Irene.

"Do you mind?" Irene asked Veeza.

"Of course not," Veeza answered, worrying because she didn't know how to dance. After all, she'd never been to a social before. She edged herself to a place behind a post where she was sure no one could see her and where she could watch the dancing but wouldn't feel left out.

After awhile, she felt like she just wanted to get her coat and run. She looked down at the pretty Mary Janes and wished she hadn't gotten them—if she hadn't, she wouldn't be hiding behind a post because she wouldn't be at the social. How she wished she had the nerve to come out and be seen by a boy—any boy at all.

Suddenly, she noticed a figure standing quietly beside her—it was Fr. Malachi. He had a half-questioning look on his face.

"Does your grandmother know you're here?"

Veeza nodded miserably.

"Good. And how is she?"

Suddenly Veeza found herself saying, "She likes you so much. She feels you are a friend."

Fr. Malachi replied quietly, "I am her friend. I'll be stopping by to see her when I visit the Murphys. Please tell her that."

He glanced out at the dance floor, then questioned, "What are you doing behind this post? The boys will never find you here—in that pretty dress."

Sensing Veeza's shyness, he took her by the hand and led her through the milling dancers to the other side of the room where a group of boys was horsing around, mimicking the grown-ups, all too shy to step out on their own. They stopped the moment Fr. Malachi appeared.

Veeza looked up and into the eyes of Johnny Burke who

grinned a big Irish grin which spread all over his freckled face.

"Hey, I didn't know . . ." he began and stopped abruptly.

Veeza could feel that what he caught himself from saying was, " . . . that Jews were coming to the social." But she didn't care! Instead, he swung Veeza off into the crowd. The fact that she was all feet seemed to make no difference to him. He was tall and gangly and had three feet of his own. If they stepped all over each other, they weren't aware of it because there was so much happy jostling anyway. When the song ended, there was another boy already waiting to dance with her. Suddenly the social was wonderful and Veeza felt like she was floating on air.

As Goldie served tea that night, Veeza told them all about the social. She described the clothes the ladies had worn and her mother nodded her head encouragingly. Some, she observed, had dresses that had been "let out" because the ladies had gotten fat. Manya asked if Veeza noticed the blue silk Mrs. McGrority wore. The ladies' sodality had sponsored the dance and Mrs. McGrority, who was head of the committee, would surely have been there in the blue silk dress that she, Manya, had worked on.

But Veeza had to tell her mother with a glowing expression that she had been so busy dancing, she didn't notice.

~ 7 ~

Later that night in their little hall bedroom, Veeza confessed to Goldie that she had been going to the Catholic church every morning with her school friends, letting them believe that she was a Catholic. She hadn't told them she was Jewish until the day they went to the dairy farm and met Mrs. Holihan. Then she had to tell them the truth. Mrs. Holihan, who had taken them for Polish Catholics, was surprised because she'd always heard that Jews had horns. The best part of it was that it didn't matter because now they were all her best friends.

"Will you give me a penance, Baba?" Veeza asked, as she went on to explain what a penance was. Irene had told her a penance was for something someone did wrong, like a punishment, only you don't get spanked. You have to be deprived of something you like. Like if she had roller skates, which she didn't, then she might not be allowed to skate for whatever time Mama said, or even Baba said, because Baba is the boss of her while

Mama works. So if Baba would give her a penance, she would be forgiven for having deceived her friends.

Baba explained, "It isn't my place in the household to give out punishment; that is up to your parents. Because your papa is away, your mama is two parents instead of one. But it would be putting a heavy burden on her to punish you for deception, so perhaps you just better learn a lesson from it, and spare your mama the aggragavation—I will say nothing."

Goldie lay silently, so still that Veeza thought maybe Goldie had died! Finally, Veeza put her hand to Goldie's breast to feel if her heart was beating. Goldie thought it was because Veeza needed cuddling, so she turned over and held Veeza in her arms.

"Are you angry with me, Baba?"

"No child," Goldie answered, "but I am disappointed in you. Running frivolously into a church without contemplation, without a true feeling of dedication to God, is an insult to the holiness of a church, no matter whose church it is. And to cross yourself is a sin on yourself. You should consider it an honor to be a Jew and to tell your friend about the Jewish religion. Don't forget, Jesus was a Jew."

"Tell me about Jesus, Baba."

Goldie sighed. *Tell her about Jesus, the child asks. It would be easier to tell about the air, the light, and the dark than to tell about a subject that has brought so much pain to Jews. Yet, the child is growing up; she should know about some things.*

So Goldie started. "I remember your grandfather, he should rest peacefully, arguing for hours—the tempers that used to blow up at him—and how he would look in the books for hours and days to find some piece of information, some something to make his point. He used to argue that the Jews accepted Jesus as a Hebrew prophet . . . a fearless fighter for righteousness. But like all thinkers, Jesus became involved with something new. He believed it, and in the end it cost him his life." Goldie sighed, "I wish I knew more, but I know only what I heard. So you see, your baba is not too smart either."

"Did Jews kick him out like they kicked us out, Baba—because they thought he converted?"

"I suppose you could put it that way."

"And that's why they killed him?"

Goldie put her hand over Veeza's mouth. "Never, never say that, even to yourself. It is not true!"

"Then who killed him?"

"Who kills a man when he is hanged for a crime? The hangman? No, the law. The cross was the way of putting anyone to death in those days."

"Like a bad king who has people's heads chopped off?"

Goldie nodded. "Now, is all this conversation proper for a little girl to go to sleep on? The only thing you have to remember is that you are a Jewish child and should behave like one."

"But, Baba," Veeza persisted, "Irene says it's written in the catechism—it's their Sunday school book—that the Jews did it."

Goldie answered, "Someday, take my word for it, they will change it in that book. That's how it is with history: new ideas, new facts, and changes are made. That's how it is when men study to find out the littlest detail that could change ideas. Ah, how your blessed grandfather, he should rest in peace, used to delight in those times when rabbis from all over used to come to our house to sit and discuss and sip a little of my homemade wine."

They cuddled together awhile, each concerned with her own thoughts.

Goldie thought, *A Jewish child who goes to a Catholic church is susceptible, particularly when there is no other place to go. There should be a Jewish house of God.* Then she snorted to herself. *Why should there be? Here in this Catholic neighborhood where there is no Jewish face to be seen? What am I to do, go with a torch and proclaim? About what? Are we not happier here? And are there not other problems closer to me than only this?*

Veeza lay equally still with her own thoughts. *I will not think about Jesus, poor man. It is too sad. I will think about the dance until my thoughts are gay and my dreams filled with beautiful music.* Veeza shut her eyes and thought of the swirling couples, "When Irish Eyes Are Smiling," and of Fr. Malachi, his hand in hers. What was it that Helen Holihan had said? "That Fr. Malachi is too handsome to be wasting his life being a priest. He ought to be married and be home making babies." Mrs. Holihan had all but slapped her daughter's face, grown up as she was, with the sacrilege of it.

But really, can a priest make babies? Veeza planned to ask Irene; she would know—that is, if Irene even knew how babies were made.

Then she thought about Johnny Burke; how the freckles danced all over his face. He wouldn't know how to make babies; he was just a kid—well, not quite—but not much older than she was, so how would he know? Veeza didn't like Johnny's mother or father. Somehow, she had the feeling that they didn't like Jews.

Finally, Veeza decided that the best one to think about was Fr. Malachi. He was kind. She was sure he knew that Jesus had been a Jew that the Jews had liked. Fr. Malachi would not hold it against her that Jesus had made a mistake and gotten himself mixed up in some deal that was like converting which means you have to sign all kinds of papers and swear that you'll never be a Jew anymore. Of course, it did get Jesus into trouble which got other people into trouble. But she knew Jesus had been a good person—she just knew it. Otherwise, Irene wouldn't be saying that she would like to marry someone like Jesus.

The more she thought, Veeza had to admit, too, that she would like to marry someone like Jesus. She would wear a white dress and a long trailing veil. She would go across the tracks to Holy Cross and get the jelly doughnuts from Mrs. Streusel who worked at the German Catholic bakery there. Oh yes, she would tell Mrs. Streusel that she's marrying Fr. Malachi and that she's Jewish and very proud of it. "My grandmother is especially proud of it, because Jesus was a Jew and everyone knew that he was smart. Even though he was only a carpenter, he was a brilliant student of religions, and it wasn't the Jews' fault that he got mixed up with the wrong ones. But anyway, my grandmother says that the world is good because God made it, and there's only one God for everyone. I told that to Fr. Malachi and he agreed, but it's not true that all people are good. Some Jews, for example, kicked us out, just like they did Jesus, because my grandmother bought a Christmas tree on account of it being such a pretty holiday. And I'm going to marry Fr. Malachi so he can make babies, but can you tell me how babies are made? Well, now I have to go and see Fr. O'Neil and get his blessing. What? Oh yes, I'm sure I'll get his blessing because Mrs. Holihan is always laughing and saying that I'm going to marry a Catholic some day—and here I am, marrying Fr. Malachi. Everything Mrs. Holihan says comes true. She reads the cards, you know, and they said that Papa was going to have to leave because he has poor health.

"Well, I have to go and order lots of milk so we'll have plenty of milk for the doughnuts at the wedding. See, I'm wearing my new Mary Janes, and I have to be careful not to get them dirty. Ha, ha, ha! Laugh! Sing 'When Irish Eyes Are Smiling.' But you're German, Mrs. Streusel, and you go to the church where the Polacks and the 'Eyetalians' go. We live in St. Mary's where the wedding will be, and the Germans don't sing 'When Irish Eyes Are Smiling.' I'm going to marry an Irishman so I can smile all the time, and then maybe Mama will smile and laugh like the Irish do—and Baba will giggle and dance holding her skirt up like she did at the Youngs' party."

The bedroom door banged open, and Joey stuck his head into the room.

"Hurry and get up, sleepyhead."

Veeza forced her eyes open. It had all been a dream.

BOOK SIX

God's Messenger

~ 1 ~

"Uuuurrrrooo." Goldie let her brain stretch a little. *How far can a brain stretch when it's locked up in the pocket of a head; and when does it sleep? Certainly not when my body is sleeping, so it seems, the way the memories keep flooding in. They are like streams flowing into a river from every direction—the river flows into a bigger river, and the biggest river flows into the ocean.*

Yy, yy, yy—the ocean, like the one we crossed to get to America. What dreamers we were! But to be truthful, aren't we all dreamers . . . just like Columbus who discovered America? Veeza read to me about how he wasn't even looking for America—his ship got lost along the way and before long he landed here and named this land himself. Thank you, Mr. Columbus, I'll try to remember that for later. But in the meantime, I must remember how my discussion with Manya came out.

"What does the priest want?" Manya had asked.

Goldie recalled resenting the question. "Who said he wants anything?"

"That's what I don't understand," Manya complained. "A priest has more to do than keep coming to visit an old Jewish woman who can't speak his language, nor he hers. So why does he come?"

Goldie shrugged her shoulders, the pixie grin on her face. "Maybe he comes for my honey cake."

This irritated Manya. "Mama, you're acting like a young girl with a gentleman friend. Besides, what do you do when Veeza isn't here to interpret?"

Goldie smiled her reply. "Oh, I prattle and he listens."

"How can he listen to something he can't understand?"

Goldie remembered saying that sometimes a person doesn't need to listen or even to talk. "So if the Gallich doesn't do either, he has himself a little rest."

With that, Goldie ended the discussion.

~ 2 ~

Lying in her bed, however, Goldie continued to recall tidbits from the recesses of her dying brain. If the ladies' sodality had sponsored the social to raise money for Easter baskets, then there must be poor in Woods End just like everywhere else, she had concluded at the time. She thought about her Jewish tradition of almsgiving. For example, there was a pushke tacked onto the wall of the cupboard in their kitchen for the Milk Fund in Palestine and some Hebrew Home Society which, to be truthful, she didn't know what or where it was. Once a year or so, a Jew with a beard, a black hat, and a pushke would come collecting at the door. You were expected to drop a penny or more in, and he would leave a little receipt. He never said a word and refused even a drink of water for fear that it might come from a non-kosher glass. Where he came from or when he would show up, nobody knew. So, thought Goldie, if you live in a neighborhood where people need help and the church has to raise money for Easter baskets, a few pennies in a pushke, homemade from a matchbook, would be as much a mitzva for Catholics as for the Jews elsewhere. An empty stomach is an empty stomach, no matter whose.

So that night after the discussion with Manya, Goldie tacked a tin match box next to the pushke, and quietly dropped a penny into it.

She waited for Manya to say something, but all her daughter asked was "And who is going to collect the money? the priest? You're going to insult a priest by handing him a few pennies like he is a beggar?"

Coming into the kitchen, Veeza overheard and answered, "There's a poor box right by the door in the church. I saw it— uh, . . . when I went to the social."

"True charity has to be an unknown giver," Goldie remembered saying. "So, we don't need to be known."

Goldie knew Manya believed in sharing. It's just that she wouldn't want anyone to know it. She had seen her put a penny or two in the pushke if a child got over a cold or on some occasion of pleasure, like good marks in school. A few pennies in the pushke was proper. Life is empty without sharing.

Goldie smiled smugly. Was Manya not her daughter? She recalled now how Manya had taken a couple of pennies from her pocketbook and dropped them into the new pushke, for mazel.

It had been, in a way, an expression of her acceptance of Fr. Malachi.

~ *3* ~

April was approaching and, with April, Passover. But there were no Jews to discuss it with. Was it sooner this year, or later?

Regardless, Goldie cleaned every nook and cranny, readying the house for the festive occasion. The thought had crossed her mind that in their goyish neighborhood, it may already have come and gone! She had shut her eyes and mind to Laban's non-kosher home, but matzos he did bring all the way from the city one Passover. Leon also had found kosher treats for the children—little jellied candies carefully marked with the kosher stamp of approval for their Passover eating. "If goyisha children can have Easter egg hunts," Leon had said, "our children will have their own kosher candy hunt."

How Joey and Veeza and even tiny Shimon—may his soul be blessed—had hunted and laughed when they found the candies. Leon had stretched across the Morris chair and let the children maul him until they were all exhausted with laughter. Manya had glowed like a bride at the sight of their happy faces.

"Yiyiyiyi." *Life sometimes rubs like salt in a wound,* Goldie reflected. *Sorrows can follow one upon another.*

"Yiyiyiyi!"

Joey and Veeza came running in, terrified.

"Joey," Veeza trembled, "I'm scared to death Baba might die while Mama isn't home. What would we do?"

Hearing them, Goldie wanted to say, "Kinder, kinder, I'm not dead yet. I have a lot of living yet to do in my head. Go back to your books or your games, and I'll try to sleep."

She heard the children tiptoe out—and she shut her eyes.

~ *4* ~

"In the old neighborhood there is everything," Manya said, "and we didn't steal anything. So what if the merchants don't like us—where money is involved they don't have to like us.

You don't see them turning down a dollar of the goyish trade, do you?"

So Goldie and Veeza had set out. It was a long walk, longer than they figured by the distance. Goldie suggested they stop and have a glass of seltzer with chocolate syrup in it, and they both had a piece of peppermint candy. "Peppermint," Goldie said, "is good for the stomach."

Once they reached the old neighborhood, they went first to the fishmonger. Herbie, whom Goldie liked, wasn't in the store. Instead, they met his brother-in-law, a crude man—a grauber yung—whom Goldie disliked.

Seeing Goldie and Veeza, he turned his face away and shouted, "Avek, avek!" Waving his arms, he reviled them saying, "Goyisha Yids we don't need here." A couple of women raised their shawls to cover their faces, muttering, "The evil eye . . . "

Goldie looked as if she had been struck. "Who has an evil eye? I came for some matzos."

"Go buy matzos from your goyim, not from me." He turned to another waiting customer.

Goldie took Veeza's hand. "Come, we'll find a place."

"It's like the story of Joseph and Mary that Irene told me about. Everywhere they went, they were turned away, so they had no place for Jesus to be born."

Goldie put her hand over Veeza's mouth. "Don't mention that name here or we will be stoned."

They stood outside the store for a few seconds, then slowly and unhappily, Goldie said, "We will go home."

Manya was upset when they told her what had happened. "So," she said, "it will be a Pesach without matzos."

"And without matzo meal and chicken and gefilte fish," Goldie added.

"So chicken we'll buy like we always have to, and the same with everything else, like we always do," Manya stated, trying to be philosophical.

But Goldie was horrified. "You'll put trayfa—unkosher—food on pesachicha dishes? Never!"

"So where are you going to manufacture matzos?"

"Gott in Himmel," moaned Goldie, "somewhere there must be a place around here where there are Jews, and where they are, there will be matzos."

"So play like the children do. Put out your fists and say, 'pick a name,' then go ask from door to door, 'Are you Jews?' You'll wear out your shoes and we can't afford new ones."

Goldie snorted, but she had no ready answer.

That night, Veeza awoke and found Goldie sitting by the window, wrapped in her shawl and looking out into the darkness.

"Why are you up? It's not morning yet," Veeza noted.

"I'm trying to talk to God. He listens best when it is quiet."

"Is talking to God like praying?"

"I think so," Goldie answered.

"But how do you know he hears you?"

Goldie thought a moment. "Prayer is like a ladder. It goes up and up until it joins all the other prayers going up."

"Then how do you know God hears your prayers, if they are mixed up with all the others?"

"God answers the ones he feels are important."

"Is your prayer important?"

"I don't know, child. I'm leaving it up to God to judge."

They sat at the window until the dawn began to wipe out the dark. Finally, with a deep sigh, Goldie turned to Veeza and said, "We'll go to bed awhile. A child should not stay up all night."

They cuddled under the covers. "How long do you think we'll have to wait for God to answer?" Veeza wondered aloud.

Goldie's eyes were already shutting but she replied, "In his time, we'll know."

~ 5 ~

"Aaarrruuueee."

The sun and the moon and the stars have a job to do. Automatically, they know their places. A person—a mensh—is like one of those men on a board like Yussel, of sainted memory, used to play. He used to say it wasn't so much the game or who wins or loses. The important thing is to learn the various ways the other person can think—that is the challenge.

Goldie smirked. *How the pieces fall into place. Not because of anyone's wisdom, but because one piece falls at the right time.*

Fr. Malachi had sat, as usual, watching Goldie serve the tea and cookies. She remembered something, tapped her head self-deprecatingly, and mumbled, "Ach, mein kopf . . . zuker," as she bustled out to get the sugar bowl.

She had a mental conflict—how could she tell the good priest her problem, of their need for matzos and all the other things for the Pesach table? He knew a few Jewish words, so maybe he would understand. Besides, what harm would there be in trying? She returned to the dining room and furrowed her brow as she tried to concentrate.

"Headache?" Fr. Malachi asked with concern, pointing to his head.

Goldie caught the idea and nodded. "Kopfwetig." Then, pointing to her heart, she said, "Weltschmerz."

They sat quietly, yearning to communicate.

"Seder," she finally said.

"Ah," he nodded. "Passover."

"Matzos."

The priest repeated, "Matzos for the seder." He wanted to remark that the Last Supper was also a seder—but what would be the purpose even if he could? It would be a delicate subject at best.

Goldie's spirits picked up. "Keine matzos." She tried to show it with her hands, but her distress was more evident.

"There are no matzos?"

With that, Goldie went off into a stream of chatter, none of which Fr. Malachi could understand, except that the old lady was trying to tell him that there were no matzos. He patted her consolingly, but could offer nothing more.

That evening as Manya sat sewing and Goldie ironed a few pieces, Manya noticed Goldie's lack of worry. Finally, her curiosity got the better of her.

"So what did you do today?" she asked as though there was something other than house chores to do.

Goldie replied, "Nothing different than any other day." Then she thought she should relieve a little of the worry that Manya carried, so she dropped a casual hint.

"For every need, there will be a solution."

Manya listened, sewing carefully. "I haven't written down how many needs we have, so tell me which need you are talking about."

Goldie looked at her in surprise. "You don't mean you've forgotten that we have no matzos or anything else we need for the Pesach?"

"Mama, I thought we settled that. This year, if we have to, we'll do without."

"Maybe you settled it, but not I," Goldie retorted. She went on with her ironing, letting the silence sink in before she continued. "I told the priest about it."

"You went to the church?" Manya asked in a shocked voice.

Goldie snickered. "No, no. Here. The way I figure, God sent him here. Veeza wasn't home—he came and I told him about the matzos."

Manya could almost hear Joey ask, "In what language?" but she resisted the impulse to ask the question herself.

"And," Goldie added happily, "he understood." She sighed with relief. "It was like God sent him."

"Oh, Mama," Manya protested, "you're going too far with this. You think God has nothing else to do but send a priest so you can tell him about matzos? Don't you think there are Irish with problems that the priest's time is needed for?"

Goldie shrugged, "I didn't send for him—he *came*."

Manya argued, "The first time was by mistake; he didn't know new tenants had moved in so he was polite. But now he *knows* we're Jews. Why does he continue to come?"

"With God, you don't ask questions," Goldie responded, upset.

The tranquility of the evening had been shattered, and still Manya wouldn't let go. "Mama, you're getting yourself involved again. First it was with the Jews—and now it's with the Catholics. And we don't even know why."

Goldie suddenly felt inspired. "In the Bible, Malachi is one of the prophets. He was called God's messenger—Malachi, the messenger. So, who knows? Maybe God sent the priest to me as a messenger."

In a perverse sort of way, Manya still would not let it rest. "So couldn't God send you a telegram or a businessman—a Jewish businessman—instead of a Catholic priest?"

"Very funny," Goldie retorted. "But God doesn't have to answer to you or to me!" And with that, Goldie stalked out of the room.

The days passed. Manya went about her affairs and asked

nothing about what happened to God's messenger. Goldie knew by the avoidance of the subject that the children had been warned not to mention it either.

~ 6 ~

Nightly, Veeza would snuggle up to Goldie and say that she believed—at least a little bit. But Goldie would correct her, "You cannot believe a little bit in God's workings. You must fully believe." And with that, Goldie sighed to herself. *Why is it taking so long? Soon it will be Pesach and time is running out.*

"Jajajaja arruuu." Those were days which tested her faith, just as God tested her now as she lay in bed helpless. But there was a difference. She was a mensh then, a person living to fulfill some need in the family. *Ah, but I don't give myself enough credit. I was truly fulfilling not just some need, but an essential need. After all, what would Manya have done without me during the years she had to work? By the same exchange, of course, what would I have done without Manya—and yes, Leon. How many sons, no less a son-in-law, want a mother hanging around? So it is like that old expression, "One hand washes the other"—each has a need for the other's services. Like the good priest—he serves God and through God the people . . . or is it the other way around, he serves the people to serve God? Anyway, where do I, an alte baba, fit into the circle? Only God knows, and he isn't telling yet.*

Her resolution remained the same: to place her faith in God, to send her prayer along with all the others straight up the ladder to him. Simple. Life is built on faith. Without it, a person is like a doll stuffed with sawdust.

When God sets the time, I will know.

~ 7 ~

"Jajajajayyy." Goldie, in her bed, sensed again the same surge of relief in her body that she had had that afternoon when Veeza came running up the steps.

"Baba, Baba," she had called loudly. Goldie wondered if something awful had happened—had the child fallen and hurt herself? No, it wasn't that kind of calling; it was a different kind of excitement. Yes, excitement, that was it.

Quickly, she started down the steps and met Veeza. Together, they went on down and out to the street. There—there was a miracle! A wagon loaded with carrots, turnips, onions—jewels of the earth.

The produce man said his name was Morris—a Jew, yet. Evidently, the priest had explained Goldie's problem and asked Morris if he would go out of his way to see what it was the family needed. Goldie treated Morris like a long-lost relative. Imagine, a real Jew being friends with the priest, so Morris must be a special person also and, therefore, already a friend to Goldie. "Who is your family? How many Jews live where you live, Morris?"

The man looked at Goldie's eager face—a baba so like his own with a little babushka tied around her chin. Except his baba was long since gone.

He answered Goldie's questions. "Where I live, there are only a handful of Jewish families spread here and there, a few stores, some owned by Jews, some not. I own the grocery and vegetable store."

"And is there a place of worship? A barn, perhaps, like in Europe—or even a house like . . . " She started to say like the old reb's, but changed her mind.

Morris shook his head. "Each family lives its own life. No one questions who does what—so we all get along."

Goldie wanted Morris to stay a little longer and satisfy her longing for mama-loshen, but Morris was busy with a pad and pencil writing the order. He wanted to be sure to deliver it all before the holidays—yontif. He hopped back onto his wagon and snapped the reins; the horse started.

With the problem of matzos and all the other needs off her mind, Goldie relaxed. Thanks be to God for the Catholic priest.

BOOK SEVEN

An Extraordinary Seder

~ 1 ~

"Aaarrrooo." *Oh, the adjustments one makes on the path of life. Sometimes it's a straight road, and one comments as one walks along, "How dull; nothing to see but a road." How many times my blessed Yussel said "There is something to see everywhere—a bird chirping in a tree, a cloud shaped like a flower, a frog hop-hopping." Lucky frog! Ah, that Yussel, he had an eye for everything and a mind to match. From the Good Book he would take a jot, a word, a phrase, a mere mention of something, and expound on it like a learned doctor. "Outside," he used to say, "there is a world of mystery waiting to be discovered, but one doesn't have to go outside. Right here in our little village there is a whole world."*

Yes, Yussel, and one of the richest mysteries of life is people— like Morris the vegetable man. Whoever said that learning is all-important—and what kind of learning? Morris is learned in the way of human relations. He is, indeed, a true version of what a man should be—a feeling person. Yayaya, Morris came with the order, wished me happy yontif, and said he would be happy to deliver for me anytime. Little did Morris know what the devil had in store for me—well, perhaps not the devil. In any case, we are not the masters of our destiny, as the Good Book says. There is still a mystery in life.

With the delivery of the matzos and the rest of the order, the first thing Goldie did was to have Veeza wrap packages—one package of matzos for the Murphys upstairs, one for the Holihans and, of course, one for Fr. Malachi. With each package there was an invitation to the seder.

"But none of these people are Jews," Veeza reminded Goldie.

"Veeza, your baba has a kopf once in awhile. I know they aren't Jews. They don't speak Yiddish. But now is the time to return all the courtesies and exchanges of friendship. And who more than the good priest, without whom there would be no matzos? Besides, where else would he taste such food?"

Manya thought it would be an imposition on the priest's time. She had heard Mrs. Reilly say that this was a busy time for the church. The bishop—the important man—was coming. Everyone was preparing for communion, although Manya wasn't quite sure what that meant.

Veeza said that Irene had told her that on that day the girls wear white dresses and a veil like a bride, and the boys get new suits and things.

"That," emphasized Manya, "is a good reason why Fr. Malachi might not want to be invited. The bishop might not approve of mixing religions."

But Goldie didn't agree. "If the priest is too busy, he's friend enough to say so. But he should be invited." And so it was left.

In accord with propriety, Manya dictated invitations to Joey, the eldest son. The notes said it would be an honor and a pleasure to have the recipient's company at the seder. Then, in a precise script, Manya signed each invitation.

"Your mama," Goldie later told the children, "writes very nice English. But she is shy about writing an invitation. In Europe, it was not considered necessary that a woman know how to read and write. Your mama learned by practicing as soon as she came to America." To make her point, Goldie said that she hoped Joey and Veeza would appreciate how fortunate they were to live in a country where everyone can have an education—just a few blocks they had to walk and a whole world of learning was open to them.

Joey scoffed. "A few blocks! A couple of miles to get there!"

Goldie scoffed in return. "It's hard on the shoes, maybe, but not on the brain!"

With that, Veeza added her two cents worth. "Mama always says education is the key to knowledge, and knowledge opens the path to success."

Goldie nodded, " . . . with a little mazel."

~ 2 ~

Veeza dutifully delivered her package of matzos to the Murphys. "It's our holy bread," she explained, "and we're going to have a seder, which is a holy dinner. This is your invitation."

"Well," said Mrs. Murphy, "I'll be tellin' it to the mister. Jewish holy bread, is it?" Turning the wrapped package in her hand with curiosity, she added, "And be thankin' your folks for us."

Leaving the Murphys, Veeza proceeded to the Holihans. There, Mrs. Holihan opened the package, broke off a piece of the matzo, and mouthed it about. Veeza could tell that Mrs. Holihan wasn't sure she liked it. Irene said, "Maybe it would taste better if it had butter on it."

"Not butter," Veeza corrected her. "Chicken fat with salt." But they couldn't picture that either. Irene said that sounded like lard.

Veeza explained that she had to return home to pick up Fr. Malachi's package and deliver it. Mrs. Holihan slapped Veeza gently across the bottom, laughing. "We'll make a Catholic out of you, yet." Veeza suspected Mrs. Holihan was only joking, though, because the package came from her grandmother who, Veeza was sure, would not become Catholic.

At the flat, Goldie had emptied the Catholic pushke and wrapped the coins carefully in a piece of newspaper torn from one of the vegetable wrappings. "Remember," Goldie reminded Veeza, "first put the money in the poor box, but be sure no one sees you. A true Jew wants no thanks for a good deed. Then, deliver the matzos to the priest himself, not to anyone else."

Veeza promised to do just as Goldie told her, and took off.

Skipping along, she held the matzo package and invitation securely under her arm, and the coins in a paper wrapping clutched in her fist.

Johnny Burke, lounging by his doorstep, quickly caught up with her. She turned pleadingly toward him. "You can't go with me, Johnny. I'm going on an errand, and it's private."

Johnny's eyes lit up. "You mean you got a secret?"

Veeza felt her heart turn over. Since the social, Johnny had become special to her, and walking with him made him look like her fella. Although she was thrilled by his presence, she tried to tell him she was busy on a very private errand and that it wasn't a real secret she was keeping from him.

That didn't faze Johnny. "I'll go along with you anyway."

"But you can't, Johnny. I promised I'd go alone."

"Okay. If you don't let me go along with you, then I won't let you go along with me to the baseball game next week. St. Mary's is gonna play Holy Cross, an' they're gonna have popcorn an' all kinds of stuff."

Veeza stopped dead still. At this moment, she hated Johnny because she knew she was going to break her promise to her grandmother and let Johnny go along with her.

"All right, but first you have to cross your heart and hope to die if you tell anyone."

Johnny crossed his heart and swore he hoped to die before a word would come out of him.

They walked along, Johnny's long legs taking giant steps which made Veeza walk two steps to his one. His freckles seemed to glow in the sunshine, highlighting his carroty head. Veeza felt that she had reached the pinnacle of happiness. He was her fella.

As they approached St. Mary's, Veeza slowed down. "I've got to do something, but please don't watch. You stay here. Promise?"

Johnny promised and held back while Veeza went quickly into the church and toward the poor box. The coins were more than usual, and she found that the little packet would not go through the slot.

As she struggled to push it in, Fr. O'Neil entered the church and saw her. When she noticed him, her first instinct was to run, but then the coins slipped from the packet and scattered all over the floor. She quickly and nervously stooped to pick them up, but Fr. O'Neil was already standing above her, a giant in his flowing black cassock. He peered down at her through his glasses, a severe and questioning look on his face.

"I'm not robbing the poor box, Father. Honest, I'm not."

Fr. O'Neil looked at the coins spread across the floor as Veeza scrambled to pick them up. Just then Johnny came in. Veeza saw his shadow and looked up at him. "You weren't supposed to see what I was doing—you promised. Now I'm going to be in trouble with my grandmother!"

Fr. O'Neil, his stern face sterner, suggested that they go to his study to have a little talk. Holding on to the coins and the matzo package, Veeza turned to follow the priest.

Johnny stood awkwardly, watching Veeza follow Fr. O'Neil. When the priest became aware of his tarrying, he turned around. "You, too, young man," he commanded.

As they approached the rectory, Fr. Malachi came out and looked at the three of them in surprise.

"Hello, Louisa," he greeted her.

"Oh, Fr. Malachi! . . . He . . . " she pointed to Fr. O'Neil, " . . . I mean Fr. O'Neil . . . thinks I was trying to rob the poor box." She put out her hand and showed the coins and the torn paper. "My grandmother wrapped them but they were too many to put in at one time. So I was going to put them in a couple at a time, and they fell out of my hand."

Fr. O'Neil turned toward Johnny. "Is this true?"

Johnny shook his head. "I don't know, Father; she told me I was not to see what she was doin'—that it was a secret."

"But that's the whole point—it *was* a secret. My grandmother said a good deed is to be done without anyone knowing. That's what makes it a good deed—no one has to be embarrassed. My grandmother made a pushke—that's like a poor box—one for the Jews and one for the Catholics. This is the money for the Catholics so they can buy Easter baskets on account of that's why the ladies' sodality had the social, to raise money." Veeza was breathless from the effort to appease Fr. O'Neil.

Fr. Malachi interjected. "It's a Jewish family who moved into the parish, Father, and . . . we've become . . . friends."

Fr. O'Neil gave the younger priest a knowing look. "So I've heard."

It was time for Veeza to present the package. "It's a present from my grandmother. It's our holy bread."

As Fr. Malachi accepted the package, Veeza pleaded, "You won't tell my grandmother that you know about our putting money in the box?"

"It will be a secret," he assured her. Then turning to Fr. O'Neil, he said, "And we'll enjoy the matzos, won't we, Father?"

Fr. O'Neil's usual granite face had a slightly bewildered look as he nodded agreement to Fr. Malachi.

Then Veeza remembered the coins which she still held clutched in her fist. "I forgot to give you the money, but this time you put them in, please."

Fr. Malachi took the coins from Veeza's opened palm. "I wish I could tell your grandmother how much we appreciate this, but I will let it be a secret."

Mission accomplished, Veeza left, followed by a puzzled Johnny. He had never heard of Jewish Catholics, but he would ask his folks.

"Hey, what's a matzo?"

"It's our holy bread . . . "

"Like the bread of our Lord—that we take at communion?"

"Do you have a special bread, too?"

Johnny nodded. "Of course, it's not as big as that matzo package—we just get enough to put on our tongue. But it's special for communion."

"I bet it's the same thing, only broken up."

"We have wine, too!"

"So do we—special kosher wine."

"Kosher? What's that?"

"Special, like holy."

"Our wine is holy, too."

They walked along in silence, each meditating the wonder of having discovered this awesome coincidence.

"But Jews can't be the same as Catholics, even if they have holy bread and wine that are special."

"Why can't they? My grandmother said Jesus was a Jew."

"Yeah, but the Jews killed him anyway."

"They did not! My grandmother said they didn't."

"They did too! It's in our catechism."

"Then your catechism is a big liar!"

"Catechisms don't lie, stupid. It's printed like a book. All the kids learn that the Jews were Christ-killers."

Veeza stopped, her face white with fury. "Johnny Burke, don't you take one more step with me. And don't you ever talk to me again. I don't believe you!"

Breathlessly Veeza ran home, tears spilling down her face.

~ 3 ~

"Jajajaja." Goldie stared at the ceiling, remembering the child in near hysteria rushing into her arms and asking her baba to solve one of the greatest mysteries of all time: who was truly the guilty one who put Jesus on the cross? She looked at Veeza. Could this girl's baba, admittedly a good and sincere Jew, dare to answer the question of a child just beginning to cross the bridge from childhood to growing up? How could she help the young girl face issues that have persisted from century to century with no definitive reply except what we are told to believe by Jew and Gentile?

Goldie remembered a small example—not brilliant but maybe

realistic—that she used. Someone rides a streetcar to a certain destination. Someone else takes a different way to get to the same place. Which one can convince the other that one route is a better route?

Ach, what a poor example that was—a gurnicht—like which is better, tea or water, hot or cold, summer or winter. You believe what you want to believe—it's yours by right. Even Yussel of sainted memory would say, "Don't break your head on something beyond your capability. Leave it to the rabbis; they love to argue over the meaning of a word." So the child will learn with time that religion, for solving problems, is a man's world ... But who am I to have become such a philosopher lying in this bed?

Goldie remembered holding Veeza as they sat at the dining room table, the child's tear-stained face empty of any joy. Glasses of tea and a small plate of strudel were set out before them, but their minds were as far from the goodies as minds can be.

"You remember the story you told me about Columbus?" Goldie asked.

Veeza nodded, her face buried against Goldie's breast. Goldie gently pressed and caressed the child's hair. "Tell it to me again."

Veeza turned her head up to face Goldie's eyes, deep with the puzzlement of how to handle this situation.

"In our class they told us that Columbus discovered America in 1492."

"No, no. Go back to the beginning," Goldie said, "how he had an idea. Didn't you tell me that everyone said the world was flat?"

Veeza nodded. "They said the world was flat, and Columbus said it was round, and he wanted a ship to go out and prove it."

"And what happened?" Goldie asked.

"He proved it. The ship didn't fall off the edge like they said it would. It went around like he said."

"And so the world learned that the earth was round?"

Veeza nodded again.

"That's how it's going to be with the Jews. Someday the Jews will be cleared."

"But, Baba, even Irene says it is in the book."

"So," Goldie countered, "you think the children who lived in Columbus's time didn't have books? Someday—I told you before, kitten—when new children are born and go to school, they won't say it because it won't be in the books anymore."

"But what about Fr. Malachi? Does he believe it now?"

Ach, child, Goldie had thought, *I am not that smart.* But she answered, "When you meet someone, do you intrude into their private world? A priest has to believe what the church tells him. But maybe he can believe what his heart tells him, too."

Then Veeza asked the question that was tugging at her heart. "How about the Holihans, Baba?"

Goldie looked at the child, realizing the conflict which had arisen. "Do you love the Holihans? the mother who treats you like her own daughter? and Irene, your best friend?"

Veeza looked into Goldie's solemn face.

"I love them, Baba. I don't like Lucy's fella, but he doesn't really belong to them."

Goldie nodded. "If you love someone dearly, you believe in them. A person is judged by his deeds as well as his beliefs."

Veeza nodded. She knew she would love the Holihans all her life even if she didn't become a Catholic.

Thinking of Johnny Burke, she was sure she wouldn't want to marry him anymore, even if she did become a Catholic someday. Besides, she didn't like all those freckles on his face, and she'd rather he had brown hair instead of red.

It certainly is a complicated world.

~ 4 ~

"Eeeeyaaay." Goldie lay, her body unresponsive to her yearning to stretch. She was willing it to stretch, but the messages of her mind were not being received. Her body was uncooperative, but perhaps if she tried hard enough, she could recall the aromas of the Pesach baking that one year. The kitchen had teemed with the redolent freshness of cinnamon and nuts.

Manya was skilled with the needle, but Goldie took pride in her own handling of dough. And who could challenge her sense of taste? Or her judgment in measuring ingredients—a bit of salt, a drop more of vinegar for tsimmes, or a sprinkle of sugar. Where would any of the company eat such gefilte fish, or chicken soup with her matzo balls? That Pesach was, indeed, a special feast for very special company.

Goldie watched Manya steal a glance at herself in the looking glass. Why shouldn't she? Leon, after all, had been away for some time already—if he wasn't a ladies' man being so long away, he was surely handsome enough to have some fly-by-night woman try to ensnare him.

Goldie prided herself on the conviction that her family held their age well. Manya was still a handsome woman with a figure any man would be proud of in his wife. And Leon really loved her. There would be joy in the home with their reunion on this holy day.

Also, Sidney and his family would be at Manya's table for Passover. Goldie admitted to a certain smugness in this: she was sure Sidney and his family would be impressed with the neighbors and friends who would be there.

~ 5 ~

"Aaarrreeee." The screech was like a whistle piercing the air.

Joey came running in. "Baba, Baba, what's wrong? Where does it hurt?"

Veeza, too, came running from the parlor. *Oh God, don't let her die. I've never seen anyone die,* she prayed. Then, finding her voice, Veeza turned to Joey. "Joey, go get Mama. She's upstairs with Mrs. Murphy." Then, on second thought, she begged, "No, don't leave me. I don't want to stay here alone and watch her die!"

Goldie lay there, her eyes full of misery. Then, like a shade being lowered, her eyes closed.

Veeza and Joey stood there trembling, Veeza with her hands covering her eyes.

"Tell me if she's breathing, Joey; I can't look."

"You're a rotten coward," Joey accused.

"I know, I know," Veeza moaned, "but you don't love her as much as I do."

"If you say that again, I'm gonna wallop you one! I love her just as much as you do, but I'm a boy, and I'm not supposed to show it. I'd even change her diapers if Mama would let me, and that's something you wouldn't like to do even if Mama would let you!"

Veeza lowered her hands, and the two stood angrily facing each other, too terrified to look at Goldie. Then, happily, they heard Goldie moaning ever so little. The moan expressed the flame of memory which sears and creates its own fresh wound, but at least it was the sound of life.

Goldie remembered that Sidney had sat with his gloves on, leaning his folded hands on his fancy cane. He crossed his legs, showing the fancy cream-colored spats on his shoes. "So, how have you been?" he asked Goldie. "How are Manya and the children? How is Leon doing, wherever he is now?"

"Thank God," Goldie answered, "everyone is well, and Leon will be home for the seder. But why are you asking questions that you will know the answers to in a couple of days?"

Sidney quickly looked at his watch which hung from a beautiful gold chain across his vest, then changed the subject. "How are you fixed for money, Mama?"

Goldie shrugged, "Thank God, we make out." However, she didn't refuse the ten dollars Sidney handed to her—that ten dollars would pay for the seder dinner. She remembered thinking, *After all, he is a good son. Is it his fault he has an extravagant wife?* Then, in a flash, she corrected her thinking. *But when they come—which is almost never—it's Paula who says, "Give your mother something, Sidney." So thanks be to God for that. Manya works very hard at sewing before she earns ten dollars.*

Goldie watched Sidney stand, leaning first on one foot, then on the other. Finally, she said, "So tell me already, what is it?" She stood quietly, her hand gripping her apron. She felt the light go out of her eyes, knowing that what he would say would probably bring a sword to her heart.

"Mama, we aren't coming to the seder. Paula wants to go to the country for the holidays—at a Jewish farmhouse where they have kosher, and she won't have to wash the dishes or bother with . . ."

"And you, Sidney?"

"Naturally, I'm going with her. I take off from work anyway, so I might as well spend the couple of days with my family."

"And if your family don't see their grandmother, it's all right with you—even on Passover?"

Sidney had an answer as always. "It's not a case of not seeing their grandmother. It's just that by the time they get home from school and take their dancing lessons and do all the other things that children do, they're tired by the end of the week."

Goldie's mouth tightened as she waited for Sidney to continue, even if he had nothing more to say—but he did.

"Besides, I don't believe in that stuff anymore."

She couldn't believe her ears. "How can you not believe what is written in the Bible? There was always a seder—it's written!"

"So who knows who wrote the Bible?"

The first stab had been like a needle; the second was a sword.

"Gott in Himmel, what would your blessed father say, he should rest in peace. He taught you every word of Hebrew that you know. You brought him credit and pleasure at your bar mitzva—every word of your speech you wrote yourself. How can you say such things now? To be a nonbeliever is a sin and a disgrace to your family—to me!"

Sidney got impatient. "Don't carry on like this, Mama. You remember when we came to America, Papa said it's a free country. People are allowed to think what they please and say what they please, just so long as it doesn't hurt anyone. Well, I'm a grown man so I have to think what I think." He patted Goldie's shoulder. "You bought a Christmas tree, remember? I take after you; I'm a freethinker." He leaned down to kiss Goldie's cheek. "I'll see you after the holidays. After all that good cooking up in those farmhouses, I'll have to roll back here!"

Goldie had looked at the ten dollar bill in her hand, then threw it on the table in disgust. She started to take the tea things from the table—the tea which Sidney had not touched. *There's no need to punish Manya for Sidney's attitude. And who knows if Leon will bring even a dollar home with him?* she reasoned to herself as she tucked the money into her apron pocket.

~ *6* ~

The next day, a letter from Laban was waiting for Manya when she arrived home from work. Goldie sat down to listen with guarded anticipation. *Ach*, she'd thought, *such a big country here, one can't get to visit with each other. Knowing Laban, he probably can't spare the time from his business to come to the seder.*

As Goldie watched, Manya's expression changed from joy to despair. Goldie felt a rock settle in her chest as Manya read:

"Dear Manya . . . It would be easier to write a happy letter, but Leon is sick. The doctor says he has the early stages of consumption, which is contagious. I cannot make any arrangements

for him without you, so please come as soon as possible. Greta sends her love . . . Laban."

"Mama, Mama, did you hear? Consumption! It is a death warrant!"

They sat looking at each other in desperate distress. *Thank God for the ten dollars Sidney left,* was Goldie's first thought. *It will pay for Manya's fare.*

"Mama, the seder, the company."

Goldie reassured her. "Am I not a mensh? Have I not lived through emergencies, trouble that has come like a robber at night? I will manage. Meantime, you better eat something, and I'll make a nosh for you to have on the way. Thank God, you know the language and you will find how to go. The children will be home soon so you can get ready to leave."

Manya turned to Goldie and for one instant she pulled up the curtain of her emotions. "Mama, he isn't a good husband. I know he never provided for us. But he burns a fire in my heart, and I can't even show it to him. Oh, he mustn't die!"

Then Goldie watched the emotional curtain come back down. Manya's back straightened, and her head went up. She held herself with the bearing of a queen—that was Manya. She was a lady like the ladies in the gardens of Russia where she had sat with their children. She had learned early: the shoulders go back and the head goes up. Goldie could almost feel her own body move as she recalled Manya teaching Veeza how to hold a cup and how to stir it delicately.

"Grmmph! Grmmbrrr!" Even now, in her helplessness, Goldie sensed a pang of guilt as she recalled the comparisons she had made: Sidney—younger, ambitious, successful. Leon— good looks, charm, but a man who could not find his way in a world where a man has to be strong.

To be a mensh, even a young man has to learn to feel his way, to handle his power. Leon had the weakness that comes with charm. Laban, on the other hand, was a man with charm, but only on the surface; underneath the charm was a self-made man with power a competitor would sense.

And Sidney—who could fault him? He had been only a boy when they first came to this country, and he knew then that as a foreigner he would have to establish his position and his rights; even Laban recognized that in Sidney. But Leon, he was a charmer—a genuine charmer, not one who uses it like a mask. No, Leon would have been a success as husband to some rich lady—someone to whom it wouldn't matter whether he earned a little or a lot just so long as other ladies envied her for her handsome and charming husband.

As things turned out, Manya was the one who had the strength in the family, too much strength for her own good.

Gott in Himmel, Goldie had wondered, *what will Manya tell the children this time? How many times she's had to explain why this with Papa or why that. How they loved him—why couldn't their papa stay with them for his work like other papas?*

That night, even Joey wiped tears from his eyes. Goldie prayed this would be the last time Leon would be away. God willing, he should get well.

"Awwrrr. Ggrruu." *Who can foresee the path life will take? Like a turn in the road, you can't see it 'til you get there.* "Yeeeaarrr."

~ 7 ~

The house seemed empty without Manya.

Strange, Goldie thought, *she is only here mornings and evenings, yet her presence is so strong that a great feeling of emptiness is left.*

Moreover, there was no consoling the dog. The animal sat beside the door all night, waiting for Manya to return.

As the days passed, the children began to look peaked and pinched at the mouth, and the usual arguments between them faded into quiet. Joey's usual analytical monologue and Veeza's lively questions that her baba could not answer disappeared. It was like a house in mourning, and Goldie remembered spitting over her shoulder to ward off the evil eye.

"Ach, ach, ach." Goldie's mind raced. Well, not exactly raced. One races to get somewhere, to win a prize. But Goldie's mind was now moving to that time when Fr. Malachi had come to say he would not be able to attend their Passover seder. He explained that the bishop was making a visitation to the church and it would be a busy time. Goldie had been disappointed, but she wasn't offended. Indeed, she considered asking the priest if there was some miracle that might cure Leon and allow him to come home to make the family whole again. But she didn't ask.

Lying in her bed now, she recalled reaching the conclusion that miracles are a matter of God's judgment; they take place in his time and place. It would have been an embarrassment to the good priest to have to say he could not fulfill her wish.

Ja, ja, she had let it rest with the prayer that goes up the ladder straight to God, as Veeza said. She did not put the burden on this young Gallich. She had rested in the confidence that when it was time for the priest to be a messenger, it would be made known to her.

Goldie thought more about that seder night.

~ *8* ~

The Murphys sat, stiff and uncomfortable. Mrs. Murphy was corseted into a shiny satin dress, and Mr. Murphy wore his Sunday suit and high starched collar. Veeza liked Mrs. Murphy better in her everyday wrapper, with her hair up in rag curlers; that was the Mrs. Murphy she knew.

Mrs. Holihan, equally ill at ease, sat next to Mr. Murphy, and beside her sat Irene in her party dress. There was Tommy, Joey's friend, who didn't smell of horses because he was in his going-to-church suit, and Joey, hair slicked until it shone. He wiggled around and bumped into Veeza who sat next to the chair where Goldie would sit.

"Remember, Joey," Goldie had whispered, "you will explain to the company just what everything is for, and you will read it the way you wrote it, to explain about the Pesach."

"Jajajayyy" came from Goldie's throat as her mind poured forth its juices. *Who counts minutes, hours, even days, when the mind is so fresh with happenings?*

Joey had taken the paper from beside his plate just like he had practiced, and read slowly, but not so slowly that the guests would get hungry before he finished.

"The first Passover was celebrated in Egypt soon after our ancestors were freed from Egyptian slavery, and it became the custom to tell the story of how it happened.

When Pharoah refused to free the Jews, the angel of death

came and took the firstborn of every Egyptian family. But he passed over the homes of the Jews who had marked their houses with the blood of a lamb. So, the lamb's shankbone recalls the marks on the Israelites' homes . . . The bitter herbs are a reminder of the bitter hardships of being Egyptian slaves, and the matzo is a remembrance that they could use only flour and water, baked in the sun, for bread. And God saved the Jews by parting the Red Sea so they could cross, and the bad men got drowned, and we're supposed to have an empty chair for the coming of the Messiah—but we don't have enough room or chairs. But enjoy the dinner anyway. Written by Joseph Picker."

The company applauded, and the ice was broken. Everyone tasted the matzos and sipped the wine, and then Goldie served the dinner. First came the gefilte fish. With a chopping motion of her hands, Goldie tried to explain the preparation of the fish. The women understood, but then Goldie stopped and laughed, "Ach, kein Ainglish." So Veeza interpreted: "Baba had to chop, chop until the fish was like a pouf. She did not use a crumb of matzo meal or flour, just salt, a spot of pepper, and then carefully she shaped it into a ball. Meantime, bones and a carrot or two and a sliced onion are simmered very slowly because the chopping takes time. Then, the soft balls are placed gently over the carrots and onion to simmer until the fish balls are firm. After that, they can be eaten hot or cold—and, oh yes, with home-grated horseradish."

"Imagine," Mrs. Murphy said to Mrs. Holihan, "going to all that trouble for a bit of fish."

Then followed the chicken soup and the matzo balls. "A good matzo ball has to be light as a feather," Veeza continued to translate, "not like a bullet."

"My goodness," the ladies exclaimed to each other, "one could be cooking all day!"

Veeza nodded, "My grandmother does cook all day on Friday for the Sabbath or holy days."

They all expressed their regrets that the mister and missus were not able to be home. Mrs. Murphy said she would light a candle in the church for the mister's recovery, and Mrs. Holihan said she would, too.

Goldie's eyes lit up with appreciation as Veeza communicated the ladies' promise. "A schönendank—thank you—how fortunate we are to have such good neighbors and friends," Veeza translated.

As they finished their dinner, Irene whispered, "Your grandmother really is cute," and Veeza whispered, "So is your mother."

Tommy offered to walk Mrs. Holihan and Irene home, like a proper gentleman, even though he was only Joey's age. As the company left, Goldie thanked God for his goodness to her.

"It was a beautiful seder, Baba," Veeza said, and Goldie shrugged, "It was the best I could do." But Veeza could see Goldie was quite pleased.

"Tell me," asked Goldie, "did Joey write it good?"

"Oh yes, Baba. Every word was just like you said he should write."

"He's a smart boy—a good head on his shoulders. He would be a credit to your grandfather—a melamed.

"Joey wants to be an inventor," Veeza had said, but Goldie didn't hear. She was concerned with her own thoughts. *A melamed has to have a Hebrew education, and for a Hebrew education, you have to have a teacher, like Yussel, he should rest in peace.*

BOOK EIGHT

Bar Mitzva for Joey

~ 1 ~

Goldie lay in her bed. The house seemed so empty; she felt deserted. Surely it was only yesterday when there was a table full of people and Joey told the story of God saving his people. *The seder—how I enjoyed cooking and baking for it—without Manya, God forgive me.* There had been an air of "God-ness" present, even though all their guests had been goyim. No one threw a single stone—not real stones, of course, but word-stones like the ones thrown when they lived "over there." She was disappointed that the priest, a joy to her heart, was not able to come, but she understood—a priest has a boss, too, and when the boss comes, you have to do more than just tend to the store. *Yayaya.*

The day after the seder, the priest had stopped by to find out how Mr. Picker was doing, but Veeza was not there to translate. *Fr. Malachi looks warm,* Goldie thought. *Being a priest is like being a reb or a melamed—you deal with people of all kinds, good and bad.* Goldie didn't know any bad people, but then she had to admit that she knew only the Murphys and Morris, the little grocery man who listened to her chatter and then went eeny-meeny-miny-mo as he pointed to one item or another he knew she used. And then . . . what had she been thinking about? Oh yes, Fr. Malachi looked warm and she had thought about getting him a cool wet cloth. Fr. Malachi laughed and said something Goldie couldn't understand, but she knew he was pleased.

Goldie was relieved when, after a few minutes, Veeza came in. "Get the good priest a damp washcloth to cool his face," she told her. As Veeza came back into the room and handed Fr. Malachi the cloth, his head went back with laughter. "I knew you were my grandmother born again in this country. She used to do the same thing with the parish priest in old Ireland after he'd made the rounds."

Goldie smiled, seeing the priest was enjoying himself. "If my blessed grandmother were here, I'd sit just the way I am now

with you, pouring my soul out to her." He seemed to forget that
Goldie could not understand a word of what he was saying.

"'Bein' a good priest today is no easy job,' I'd be tellin'
m'grandmother. 'And didja think it would be?' she'd be askin'
me. 'Didja think you'd be learnin' it all in the seminary? A good
priest is one who gets out with the people. All that booklearnin'
is good, but it's no different than bein' a good doctor—'tain't 'til
he gets his first patient does he know if the booklearnin' crept
into his head—and his heart, for it's the souls of the people you
need to reach with your words and your preachin'. People can be
tirrible sinners . . .' And then I'd be sayin' to her, 'I'm only a
young priest—my first parish—and I'm still responsible to Fr.
O'Neil.' 'He's like the blessed old coot that we've had makin'
the rounds of this parish these forty years,' she'd say. And I'd be
tellin' her, 'Well, Fr. O'Neil's maybe not that old, but he's forgotten how to smile . . . and we're not goin' to draw any young
people into the church with a cranky priest.' 'Aye,' my old
grandmother would say, 'it's hard on the old ones. Agin' is a ter-
rifyin' specter. It's like a ghost's fingers. You'll be needin' the
patience of a saint to be dealin' with a cranky old man who's lost
his touch—but in the long run, you'll be a better priest and a better human bein' for it.' "

Goldie now recalled how she had sat listening. The young
priest talked his heart out, and it didn't matter to either one of
them that Goldie couldn't understand.

They sat for a while that day, each quiet. Then Fr. Malachi
got up to go.

"You're so understanding," he told Goldie, towering above
her. He touched his fingers to her forehead and murmured a
blessing.

Ah, my son, Goldie found herself thinking as she watched him
walk down the stairs. He had become as dear to her as a son—
maybe even dearer, God forgive.

~ 2 ~

Manya came home without Leon. It would be six months be-
fore he would be well enough to be released from the hospital,
God willing. She didn't know what she would have done without
Laban and Greta.

Goldie nodded with understanding. "A gutte neshoma, that

Greta. After all, what other woman would allow a family into a house as clean as hers that day that we came with bedbugs creeping around in the bedding. Even after we baked it out in the sun, who could tell where one might be hiding? That Greta—she has a Jewish soul in her."

Manya told her story. She had taken the trolley car first. Then, just as the conductor told her, she transferred to the train and rode and rode. It seemed forever. Finally, she arrived at the station, took another trolley and at last arrived within walking distance of Laban's.

"Ach, mein kind, you must have been exhausted."

"Oh, Mama, you should have seen him when I got there—so pale, lying in the bedroom where we all stayed before and where Papa . . . he should rest in peace."

Goldie nodded, "With God's blessings. But Leon—Leon is going to get better, yes?"

"If he stays there, keeps quiet, and drinks the milk and takes the eggs—raw eggs. And you should see how he does it. He sticks a pin into the top of the shell and into the bottom. Then he sucks at one end and draws the raw egg into his mouth. That way he doesn't mind it, he says." Manya paused to gain control. "Mama, we put him in a hospital."

"A hospital? Gott in Himmel, he truly must be on his deathbed!"

"Not that kind of hospital, Mama. This is a place where only people with consumption are. They take them out on the porch so they can have plenty of fresh air and rest. Mama, . . ." Manya's face showed the strain under which she was laboring. "Mama, it's a charity hospital."

Goldie sat quietly for a moment, then suggested that they have some tea. Tea was the answer to all problems. For a few moments, the warmth of the water is a balm to the innards as the warmth of the sun is to the body. The time it takes to pour the water into the glasses and set out the sugar can be a kindness extended to another—space for a proud soul in torment.

Goldie brought the tea glasses in and set out the sugar and the plate of cookies. "Which is more important to you, your pride or your husband's health? Can you afford a private hospital? People give money to build such a hospital so poor persons with consumption can have a chance to get better and live. A credit to the people, believe me, who think of others so much. You should be thankful there was a place for him to go and that they took him."

Manya sipped the tea through the piece of sugar in her mouth as she told Goldie what had happened. The workers didn't mean it, she was sure . . . and it was only the girls at the desks, but she had felt humiliated. She stood in line, waiting her turn to fill out the forms. Her fingertips had rested on the edge of the desk. The girl stopped writing and with an icy edge to her voice said, "Please don't lean on the desk." Manya remembered thinking, *How rude you are, how calloused your feelings. I have never leaned on anything; I stand straight on my heels with my head up. I wouldn't be leaning on your desk, but what if I were? Am I a leper that my fingertips are unclean if they touch your desk?*

Then, on top of this insult, an aide called to her with a beckoning finger. "Are you the woman admitting Mr. Picker?" "Woman?" Manya had wanted to retort. "What kind of expression is this? I am a lady and I am his wife." But instead she moved forward to give the needed information.

It wasn't only the charity, Manya thought now as she sipped tea. *For charity you should be grateful, and I am grateful. It's . . . it's what the taking of charity does to the taker—and to the clerks at that desk who dispense it.* Nevertheless, she was relieved. *What would I have done without it?* She was grateful to Laban, who knew who to ask and where to go.

"You see, Manya," Laban had reminded her, "what I meant when you first came here? Be a big fish in a small pond. I'm an important man here. People respect a businessman they can trust."

Ah yes, Manya had to agree. Laban had indeed become a person of importance.

"It isn't that Leon doesn't want to work," Laban had continued. "It's that he gets in with the wrong people. With his looks and his personality, he could have been a rich man by now—but he lets them make a shlemiel out of him. You can't run after every get-rich-quick scheme and make an honest living."

"Did he speak of us?" Manya asked.

"He spoke constantly of you and the family—even the shviger—how much he wanted for you, how smart the children were, and the girl—the apple of his eye. But he couldn't settle down and keep a job. Leon hasn't worked for me for a long time, but he asked me not to tell you, so I didn't. It was easier not to write than to lie to you."

And even if he had, Manya thought, *what difference would it have made? Leon is Leon and I will love him the whole of my life.*

"And the mishpocheh? You saw someone?" Goldie asked.

Manya nodded. "Laban and Greta took me one day. Not only did we see everyone, but we went to Hymie's boy's bar mitzva."

Goldie was amazed. "The smallest boy has already had his bar mitzva? How time flies!"

"Mama, what are we going to do about Joey?"

"Jajajaaaa!" Goldie's eyes sparkled even now, remembering that beautiful moment. She had not needed to remind Manya that it would soon be time for Joey to accept the mantle of manhood. She snickered to herself, but then found herself sobering. Who could have foretold how it would turn out?

"How strange that you should bring it up, daughter, because I was going to bring it up to you. All the children around here are having their bar mitzva."

"Around here? Where are there Jewish children here?"

"Not Jewish children—goyish."

"But Catholic children don't have bar mitzvas!"

"So it's not a bar mitzva; it's the same thing, though, only goyish. Veeza says the girls wear a white dress and a veil like a bride, and the boys wear white bands on their arms."

"It's communion, Mama. Mrs. Smith at work made a dress for some little girl—a beautiful dress, really like a bride."

Goldie nodded in appreciation. "A pleasure for a mother. But bar mitzva is only for a boy to become a man. Who knows, some day maybe it will be the same for the Jews as for the Catholics— to welcome the girls into the religion, too. But meantime, what are we going to do about Joey?"

Manya looked thoughtful. "Who's going to teach him? It's already so late."

"You're right. In the old country children of five years are already learning. A pleasure when a boy was born . . . as soon as they could take him out—you remember how they did with Moishe's boy—they brought him, so small, to your papa, he should rest in peace. They placed a drop of honey on a page in the book and put the baby's lips to it. In that way, he should know how sweet learning is."

"And also," Manya added, "they sprinkled a bag of coins over him, because with learning comes success. Yes, I remember that."

Goldie nodded. "It's right. It's the way it should be done. From earliest times, Jews have been associated with learning, and although God doesn't guarantee that you will be successful even if you have learning, it helps. And a Jewish boy is entitled to have a bar mitzva. In fact," Goldie added questioningly, "who ever heard of a Jewish boy not having a bar mitzva?"

Manya looked intensively at Goldie. "You know the reb won't take him."

Goldie understood the unspoken accusation, but ignored it. She merely answered, "You're the boy's mother. You have to try."

"You're right, Mama. No matter what they think about us, they shouldn't hold it against a boy who is ready to become a man . . . at least," Manya added as an afterthought, "in God's eyes."

~ *3* ~

"Ayayayayaaa." That was a pleasant gurgle. Veeza knew it meant that Goldie was comfortable.

Now, to get back to that day . . . The children were in school and Goldie hurriedly straightened the beds, put fresh water in the dog's dish, and carefully put on her sheitel. It was a proper day for her cape, also.

She took the walk in easy stages. *There's no use getting on the trolley car—it goes off in a different direction. Besides, a walk is good for a person. It strengthens the body.* Not that she needed to exercise. *Ach, the miles I walked in my youth, even in the dead of winter when the ice had frozen over the little river and not a leaf was left on the trees. Little jets of steam would come from my breath and my cheeks would be red from the kiss of the icy air. Sometimes, a wagon carrying logs cut from the trees in the forest of neighboring towns would offer me a lift and how I enjoyed watching the driver direct the horses pulling the heavy load. Where have the years gone? Now I am an old woman who has to stop for breath every so often.*

The woods beckoned. The trees were sprouting tiny leaves on the still, stark branches, and the little stream Veeza had talked about bubbled along the stones. She needed to rest a moment, but how would it look, she thought—an old lady with a fur cape and a bonnet sitting under a tree? *A passerby might think I'm shikker!* Still, she looked about. There wasn't a soul around. She pushed herself to walk on a little further. Finally, she compromised. She found a place hidden from view and sat down for a moment.

There was a boulder flush against the trunk of a tree, as if to form a seat. Next to the boulder was another smaller one, and nearby another. They formed a circle of rocks. Goldie stepped closer. Even the winter's snow and ice had not obliterated the signs of a charring. A fire had been made there, a fire to roast potatoes, properly protected from the wind and deep enough to keep the sparks and hot ashes within the circle. *Good children,* she thought, *and little did they know that it would form a perfect seat for an old lady.*

Goldie spread her skirts on the boulder, leaned her back against the trunk of the tree, and raised her feet to the smaller rocks. "Aaahh," she sighed, "mechaieh"—a pleasure. Here she could think about what she would say. But before she could have even a little thought, she found herself dozing as she watched the sunlight play among the branches of the trees and listened to the gurgle of the stream. It was like a melody—nature's tone poem put to music by God.

She forced herself to leave, thanking God for this little respite from the worry which was yet to be resolved.

As she reached the old neighborhood, she noticed three old Jews in their coats and hats sitting and lapping up the sunshine. As Goldie approached them somewhat hesitantly, they looked at her stonily.

"If you'll excuse me, I'm looking for Reb Herschel. Is he in his house?"

The old men mumbled in their beards and, as one leaned toward the other, their three hats and three beards touched, while their faces were turned away from Goldie.

Goldie waited a moment, then walked past them and approached the door of the reb's flat. She rang the bell.

The reb's wife, her head covered with a babushka and her body enveloped in a wide apron, came to the doorway.

"Good day, Mrs. Herschel. I came to see the reb . . . "

Beyond Mrs. Herschel, Goldie could see their familiar disordcred dining room and the reb sitting with his head buried in his papers. Mrs. Herschel stood for a moment, indecisive, then opened the door and spit three times over her shoulder as Goldie walked in.

"The goya is here—we shouldn't be cursed by her presence."

Reb Herschel looked up, his eyes fierce over his glasses which sat low on his nose.

Goldie spoke quickly. "I have a confession to make."

"What is your confession?"

"I came to confess that I have been possessed by the demon of another religion. You were right; it was stubborn and wrong of me not to have confessed earlier. But now I wish your blessing."

"And the demon? You're still possessed?"

"No, no, that is what I came to tell you. The demon has left me, thanks be to God. A Jew I am and a Jew I shall remain. I want your blessing."

Reb Herschel sat thinking and muttering to himself. *The woman came here of her own accord, admitting she did have the demon within her. Somehow by the grace of God, the demon has left her.* He turned to Goldie.

"Did you pray for deliverance?"

Goldie replied, "Every day, as soon as I knew that I was . . . possessed . . . every moment of every day until I felt the evil spirit within me had been exorcised by the grace of God, blessed be his name. That is when I decided to come to you to tell you and to ask your forgiveness and your blessing."

The reb looked piercingly at Goldie and thought to himself, *The woman seems sincere enough. I could, I suppose, demand proof. But how is one going to prove a demon that has already left? One can't exorcise what is no longer there.*

"And you've repented for your transgressions?"

"Every minute, Reb Herschel, every minute. I feel my soul is clean."

Reb Herschel put his eyeglasses down on the stack of books and papers, hefted himself from his seat, and shambled toward the front door.

The three rebs responded to Reb Herschel's waving arm and one by one they followed him into the house.

"You remember this woman?" Reb Herschel pointed at Goldie.

The three rebs nodded, their beards bobbing up and down.

"She has confessed that she was possessed of the demon, and she has repented and prayed to be cleansed. It appears the good Lord has cleansed her." At the same time the reb thought, *It would have been a great deal of trouble to find ten men of authority to authorize the exorcism of the demon. The good Lord has spared me that arduous task by cleansing her himself, thanks be to him for his consideration and goodness.*

"We will say the benediction over her and pray she may continue to go the good way of a child of Israel in God's light." Goldie bent her head while the reb placed his hand upon her, and the three rebs chanted the blessing over her.

Goldie prayed silently, *God forgive me for this which I have perpetrated upon these people and upon myself in thy name and in thy service.*

The benediction over, the reb's wife came forward to shake Goldie's hand. "A blessing, a blessing. Come, we will tell Herbie."

Goldie had nothing against Herbie. He'd always waited on her and had treated her no different than the other women. She followed the reb's wife to the store.

"See who is here?" the reb's wife announced to Herbie. "The alte baba is no longer possessed of the demon. The reb just blessed her. She is one of us again."

"Mazel tov, mazel tov! To be cleansed of the evil spirit is like being reborn!"

As the women bustled about, Herbie told Goldie that whenever she needed an order, she should let him know and he'd deliver it himself. Goldie, who always liked Herbie, gave him a small order right then—just some of her everyday needs. She thanked God that Pesach was over and they weren't asking questions. *If they do, I'll have to follow one lie with another. I'll say that at the time I had not yet been cleansed and had no memory of Pesach or whatever.* Goldie's mind was awhirl. *Meantime, dear God, who am I to chastise a child or to preach to one when I myself am even more guilty. I have broken the law, the law which says it is forbidden to steal the mind of any person, to fool him through words, even though he suffers no monetary loss thereby. But then, we must consider these godly ideals and their fulfillment. To cherish ideals is noble, but we are bidden to add utility to nobility. And utility is now my need—to gain the reb's acceptance of Joey as a student for his bar mitzva. So you see, God, my life is already well used up, but the boy still has a life to serve in thy name.*

She paid the little bill and told Herbie that she could carry the small package—another time it would be a bigger order to warrant his coming to deliver it.

~ 4 ~

"Rarararar." Goldie's body lay heavy as she recalled the guilt she carried on her shoulders during that walk home from the reb's house. How would she tell Manya about the ruse she had used to deceive the reb? Manya, who would not permit the children even a white lie, a small distortion of the truth for some convenience. What would Manya think of a lie as black as the one she had told to the reb? Should she tell her? Manya—who preached to the children to be truthful, who insisted that a lie could hang like a weight around one's neck for the whole of a person's lifetime. Surely there was some way to handle it truthfully.

Manya, Goldie knew, would be happy she had gone back and confessed everything. Most likely, she would even have insisted on accompanying Goldie to make sure she didn't weasel out of it. A fine example for the children—from their grandmother yet!

Goldie remembered unfolding a damp piece of something to be ironed and still thinking, *What if I don't tell Manya? Who would be hurt? In truth, no one. The old reb will make a few dollars, so he will be ahead, and what he and Manya don't know won't bring punishment to them.*

Somewhere in the Good Book does it not say that if you have transgressed and are too ashamed to confess, do a good deed and you will be forgiven? Ahhh! What better good deed than to add to the pushke? This time I'll add a little more than we would usually put in, including, of course, the good priest's box. It will mean an extra bottle of milk or an extra loaf of bread for some poor family. And is not a poor Catholic stomach also worthy of the benefit of a transgressor's penance? Goldie put the iron back on the stove, away from the hottest area, and went to look for her pocketbook. *What Manya doesn't know won't grieve her.*

Goldie had returned to her ironing, convinced that the whole thing was over.

"Jajajaja." Her mind turned like the windmill on the hill in their village when Yussel and some of the children he taught ran up the hill so he could explain how the wind has to be just a certain way. Yussel would go on to explain many other things that Goldie couldn't understand, but Yussel would comfort her. "As long as you understand what is necessary for you to understand, that is all that matters." Lying in her bed these many years later, her mind was like that windmill—turning, turning, using up what brain she had left in her body, which couldn't feel even the softness of a flower's petal. *Manya doesn't like cut flowers. She wonders why anyone would want to cut a flower from its stem, leaving the stem without the beauty of nature's handiwork. So here I am, no body at all, and how do I describe what is happening in my brain—turning, turning like a windmill on a staff.*

Shortly after Goldie's visit to Reb Herschel, Manya came home late one evening with good news. As Goldie had predicted, Reb Herschel said he'd accept Joey as a pupil to prepare him for his bar mitzva. The rate was twenty-five cents a week, which Manya said she would manage—a sacrifice she was more than willing to make.

The only one who protested was Joey: "Every day right after school?" Goldie had nodded and said, "That is how it should be, so the mind doesn't slow down. And don't you be late. Your grandfather, of sainted memory, tolerated no lateness from his pupils. Either you have in mind to learn or you don't."

Joey grumbled. "When do I get to have any fun? Probably never, and how about my riding the horse with my friend Tom?" But no one paid any attention to his griping.

Manya told the story of how she'd gone to the reb's house and of how cordial the old reb was. "You'd never have known that he was the same grouchy old man who came to the other place that time." She waited for Goldie to speak, but Goldie merely nodded. Without looking into Goldie's eyes, Manya prompted her. "Mama, Reb Herschel told me you were there."

Goldie lowered her head.

"Mama, you went and confessed that you had a demon in you, didn't you?"

"I went and confessed that I *didn't* have a demon in me—anymore."

"But it's the same thing. Your confession was a lie."

Goldie snickered. "You think I had a demon in me, that I was possessed, don't you?"

"But Mama, it's not the same. You didn't think so."

"What's the difference which way it was said? Nobody was hurt by it, and now Joey is going to get his Hebrew lessons for his bar mitzva. So you see, God isn't angry. Anyway you look at it, it comes out for the best."

Manya gave up. *Maybe Mama is right; it all came out the way we needed it to,* she thought.

And so it did. Every day Joey read his lesson to Goldie, and she would nod and smile in satisfaction, pleasantly remembering that it was done just that way in their old village. From miles around, relatives and friends would come to listen to a bar mitzva boy accept the covenant and become a man, gaining the right to sit in on a minyan for services and again on the Sabbath morning. Afterwards, they would have a Kiddush—a prayer—and then the gefilte fish and a little wine with challeh. Of course, the shul had been merely a converted barn, but it was used as a house of God, set aside every weekend for this purpose. It had its small bimah—the altar—and the ark holding the Torah which the whole village had pitched in to purchase. Yussel himself had designed and carved the ark—*Ach, what golden hands he had.* At last they would go to the house of the bar mitzva boy, where brandy and küchen would be served.

"And what are we going to do for Joey's bar mitzva?" Manya had asked. "What about everyone coming and eating?"

"We'll have honey cake and schnapps and—people."

"Which people? Who have we got?"

"Well, we have the Gallich."

"But Mama, he's a priest!"

"He's a friend."

"Did you ever hear of a priest going to a bar mitzva?"

Goldie's pixie face turned to Manya. "When Jesus was thirteen years old, he was still a Jew and he had a bar mitzva, of that you can be sure. So if priests learn about Jesus, they have to learn about his bar mitzva—and if the Gallich never saw one before, he'll see Joey and see something that other priests here haven't seen."

"And," Manya asked pointedly, "what do you think the old Jews and Reb Herschel will say when they see a priest here?"

Goldie remembered—ah, how she remembered slapping her

150

hands to her head. "That's all we need! Well, we could have the Holihans. Veeza said they were real pleased to be invited to the seder and to learn about the Jewish religion. They said Joey read it real good . . . And the Murphys upstairs . . . and Joey's friend, the one who was here, the one who has the horses."

Manya smiled ruefully. "It will be the first Catholic bar mitzva in the parish."

Goldie smiled and added happily, "For our boy, he should live and be well."

~ 5 ~

During the second week of Hebrew lessons, Joey came home with bruised knuckles and a tear-streaked face. Goldie bathed the bruises, shaking her head. *Ach,* she remembered now, *that was when I was still a mensh—a person who could walk and talk— not a log. But who am I to question God's judgment? . . . Never in our family was there a fighter—the Bible says to turn the other cheek.*

"Your mama will be very unhappy to see this hand." She had pushed at the knuckles just a bit, and when Joey winced she asked, "It hurts real bad?"

Joey shook his head. "It's not the first time he whacked me."

"What does it mean, he *whacked* you?"

"He hit me!"

"Who hit you?"

"The reb, that's who."

"Reb Herschel?"

"He's an old goat!"

"Yussela—Joey—you mustn't talk like that!"

"He called me a liar!"

"Reb Herschel called you a liar? Such a vulgar accusation from a reb. Why? For what reason?"

Joey's eyes burned angrily. "Are you saying I'm a liar, too?"

Ah, Goldie thought, *this is no time to pressure the boy. He's been hurt, whacked—what kind of a word is that? It sounds painful and the hand looks like for real it has been whacked.*

She prepared a basin of water, gently bathed the bruise, and carefully patted it dry with a towel. At the same time, she tried to soothe the irate child. "Tell me what happened to bring such a thing about," she said.

"I didn't mind it the first time. I was a little bit late, and then I didn't read as fast as he wanted me to because I was out of breath because I was running not to be late. So he took his pointer and whacked me across the shoulders. He said it was to get me to sway when I was reading, but it hurt. It was a whack, Baba, a good whack."

"And this time, Joey?"

"This time, I went to the reb's house like I was supposed to, and I put my hand in my pocket to give him the money—today is the day I was supposed to give him the quarter. I put my hand in my pocket and it wasn't there."

"But your mama gave you the money; I saw her."

"I know she did. I put it in my pocket, and when I put my hand in to get it out to pay him, it wasn't there."

"Are you sure you put it in the same pocket? Maybe your blouse?"

But Joey swore he had put the money in the same pocket. Goldie examined the pockets in his knickers and in his blouse, but there was no money.

"Baba, he called me a liar. He wouldn't give me the lesson, and when I went to pick up the book, he whacked my knuckles—and they swolled up right away."

Goldie sat back in her chair thinking, *It's not right to call a child a liar, especially a reb should not use such an expression. Even Manya does not allow that kind of talk.*

Joey continued. "The reb said he won't give me any lessons until I bring him another quarter."

The memories of this episode clung to Goldie's mind as she lay in bed. *Somehow my impression of that reb had never been the best. No matter how much learning he had as a reb, calling a child a liar was not the proper example for a man devoted to teaching God's ways. A reb learns from a book—the fact that it is the Good Book doesn't guarantee he will know how to deal with people.* As far as Goldie was concerned, this reb had not known how to deal with people.

Manya saw the bruised knuckles even before she saw Joey's face. She was enraged. Goldie offered to go and talk to the reb, but Manya retorted angrily, "Are you more competent to speak for the boy than the child's own mother? A boy loses a quarter due for his lesson; the rabbi is entitled to his money. But to call him a liar and hit him, that is something else."

Manya dressed in her best gray skirt and good shirtwaist. She combed her hair into a soft bun on top, as carefully as if she were going to something pleasant. Veeza wondered why Mama was dressing so fancy just to go and scold a cranky old reb, but then she remembered her mama saying that no matter what one must do, it is best to dress like a lady. Veeza was proud of her mother.

Joey's face was washed until it shone, his hair slicked back with water. He looked like a gentleman. Veeza wasn't quite sure what a gentleman looked like, but she was sure a gentleman was a nice person by the way people would speak of him.

Goldie sighed as she watched them go, and Veeza started clearing the table. Turning to Goldie, she said, "Baba, I'll put the dishes in the sink, and then we can go to the parlor and see if the moon is out yet. We can look to see how many little torches the angels are holding."

Suddenly Goldie felt old.

There was no smile on the face of the man on the moon that early evening. There were few angels holding their torches to make stars in the heavens. Goldie's heart was heavy with the burden that Manya was carrying on her shoulders. *What mother doesn't suffer at such a time,* Goldie asked herself.

~ 6 ~

Manya stood to the side as Joey rang the bell of Reb Herschel's house, and through the window she could see the old man shuffling to the door. Finally, the door opened wide and Reb Herschel peered at the two of them over the low-sitting glasses on his nose. Beyond him, Manya could see the dining room table and the floor around it piled high with books and papers in endless variety. *How can he ever find anything?* she wondered to herself. Her unspoken question was interrupted by the reb's query, "You want something?"

He obviously did not recognize Manya.

Joey tried to remain half hidden, the less to be seen by the old reb for whom his anger and fear still remained.

"Reb Herschel, I'm Mrs. Picker . . . you remember? You're giving my son, Joey, Hebrew lessons."

The reb let them in to the house. Recognizing Joey, he commented in Yiddish, "He's got a good kopf on his shoulders."

Manya thanked him appropriately for the compliment, but explained that she had come because of some misunderstanding about the quarter Joey was supposed to pay for the lessons.

Reb Herschel sat himself down in his usual place. "He didn't pay his quarter."

Manya nodded agreement. "Yes, I understand, but you should have believed him when he said he lost it—especially when he told you I had given it to him this morning."

The reb shrugged. "What a boy does between the time his mother gives him money and the time he is supposed to give it to the reb is not the reb's business."

Manya nodded, but insisted, "You should have believed him. If Joey said he lost it, then he lost it."

Joey interrupted. "We looked in my pockets, Mama, and my blouse and my knickers . . . "

"And then your son said, 'You didn't look in my shoes,' " the reb added, mimicking Joey.

Manya turned to Joey, "Did you say that?"

Joey nodded. "He made me mad."

"That was fresh, Joey. Whether he made you mad or not, you have no right to be fresh."

"He said I was lying. He called me a liar!"

Manya turned again to the reb. "You had no right to call him a liar, and you had no right to hit him. He did have the money when he left the house."

The reb shrugged. "Boys have uses for quarters—especially boys from poor families. A quarter is hard to come by; a crack on the knuckles makes them remember."

"Then you are saying he lied?"

The reb looked away and answered noncommittally, "He'll have to have another quarter."

"You mean for a quarter you are going to deny the boy his lessons?"

The reb gave Manya a shrewd look and answered, "You are the one depriving him if you don't pay for the lessons. I don't teach for nothing." With that, the reb turned his back on them and made no effort to stop Manya and Joey from leaving.

All the way home Manya walked so rapidly that Joey had difficulty keeping up with her. "Mama, why are you rushing so fast?" he asked.

Manya was busy with her thoughts and didn't have time to

voice them: *I'm rushing so fast hoping I can run away from my-self. "You're a poor woman" is what he implied, sneering at me; "You can hardly support yourself and your family, so a quarter a week is even more than you can pay as it is." I can still see the reb turn to his papers—and what was it he said? Oh, yes, "I'm not in the charity business. If you can't afford to pay for the boy's lessons, maybe you can get some charity organiza-tion to help you."*

She recalled a recent similar rebuff: *"Don't lean on the desk please . . . Are you the woman who is admitting this man? . . . This is a charity hospital, you know, the forms have to be filled out. Do you have any money in any bank? None at all? None at all?"*

Grovel, grovel. For Leon's life, yes, but for Hebrew lessons, no!

"Mama," Joey was asking, "what are we going to do?"

"We're not going to do anything, Joey. But you remember just one thing: your American education is given to you free of charge. Appreciate it and learn as much as you can."

With that, Joey knew that his mother would not send him back to Reb Herschel's.

~ 7 ~

After the Sabbath candles had been lit, Manya prepared the supper and Goldie sat with Joey and Veeza.

"I can't understand why there's a whole Jewish holiday about Ruth—she wasn't even Jewish!" Veeza remarked.

Goldie explained. "They tell the story of Ruth on Shevuoth because when she had a chance to go back to her own people, she chose to stay with her dead husband's mother. 'Thy people shall be my people and thy God my God,' is what she said. Be-cause of that, she later married a fine man and through her son's son, David was born and he became king of the Jews. You re-member, I told you that Shevuoth is the holiday to celebrate the giving of the Ten Commandments through Moses to the Hebrew people, and through the Hebrew people, they were given to the world for ever and ever. Remember that: it was through the He-brews that the world inherited the Ten Commandments!"

Veeza sat quietly thinking. She wondered if Mrs. Holihan knew about Ruth. If Ruth could marry a Jew, then Veeza could marry a Catholic. Of course, the story of Ruth took place long ago, and King David was already born—and dead—and so he couldn't be born again. And of course, it was all mixed up because she, Veeza, was Jewish, and she'd have to marry a Catholic and say "Your people will be my people and your God will be my God," and although it was great fun to be a Catholic like the Holihans, she had to remember that Jesus was once a Jew. He had turned away from the Jews, though, and even if he didn't really mean it, he certainly made a lot of trouble for everyone. She really felt sorry for Jesus, but she didn't want to get herself and all the other Jews in that much trouble. It would be easier, she concluded, to be Catholic and turn Jewish.

As she watched the children's attention wander, Goldie sighed. *What can one do? If nothing else, from holiday to holiday, even if we don't celebrate it, we can try to tell them the meaning of their religion.* She wished she could read to them from the Bible, but what would be the difference? Even if she knew how to read, the children wouldn't understand Hebrew. And there was no translating it into Yiddish; Yiddish was for conversation, Hebrew was for study. *Ah, Yussel, Yussel, if only you were here. What a joy it would have been for you to teach Joey.*

"What else do you remember?" she then asked Joey.

"Why do I have to go through it all again? You already told it to me once."

Goldie patiently pointed out, "The only way to learn anything that will stay in the head is to repeat it and to study the reasons—not just the words. You must understand why this or that happened. In Europe, the old rebs would spend years talking about the Great Word to make sure they hadn't overlooked some part of the interpretation. The law of God is very holy, you know, and you can't dismiss it with one reading. It's like when you get a letter from a friend—you read it over and over because you enjoy it, and you want to get the most out of it. Well, it's the same thing with the Torah. There is so much in God's law that you can't get the whole understanding of it just by skimming through it once or twice. A Jew, if he is a real Jew, is never finished with the Torah."

"Yeah, like the old rebs outside of Reb Herschel's," Joey said as he made a face.

"That's right, like the old rebs. That's the purpose of the law.

It is said that when God gave Moses the Torah on Mount Sinai and uttered the first commandment, 'I am the Lord,' the whole earth stood still. Not a bird sang, not a leaf stirred. They say, too, that the words were said in seventy different languages so that the whole world would know they were not meant for Jews alone but for all mankind. And then what happened? Do you remember?"

Veeza spoke up. "The angels protested. They said, 'Give the Torah to us because we're the best, we're holy, and we will always obey it.' "

"That's why God didn't give it to them," Joey added in singsong fashion. "God meant it for all people to learn by. People need a law to guide them, because people aren't perfect."

"You're right," Goldie confirmed. "Reb Herschel is a person and he's not perfect. If he makes a mistake, he answers to God. If we make a mistake, we answer to God. Remember, not a bird sang, not a leaf stirred, so that everyone could hear. Now, I'll say the Commandments so you can hear and repeat after me."

"Oh, Baba," Joey protested, "I learned them already at the old reb's."

Veeza felt a small chill of guilt run through her body as she knew she couldn't admit to her baba, mama, and brother that she, too, already knew them from the Catholics—but, of course, not in Hebrew.

They repeated the Hebrew words, stumbling with the strange pronunciations. Finally, Joey protested, "Baba, we really don't know what we're sayin'."

Feeling the frustration of someone trying to move a mountain, Goldie reminded Joey, "It was—and is—the language every Jewish boy must learn to prepare for bar mitzva."

Joey replied, "Baba, the world is not going to come to an end if I don't!" With that, Joey remembered that he'd promised Tommy to ride the horse with him. Grabbing his cap, he dashed out just as Manya came into the room.

Veeza related the whole story. With her usual, practical reasoning, Manya said, "Mama, don't be upset. So he'll grow up to be a man without a bar mitzva. Believe me, the world won't come to an end because of it."

Putting her arm around Goldie, Veeza added, "Baba, you can teach me, but I'm not as smart as Joey, so maybe I won't be able to learn."

Goldie placed her arms around Veeza and held her close. "In Russia, it was not considered important for a girl to learn, so don't break your head trying to learn Hebrew. Besides, to tell you the truth, I never learned either. But in America, everyone has a chance."

The subject of the bar mitzva was over, at least for now.

Goldie awoke, but her mind would not focus on her surroundings. *Yussel, Yussel, you are so close, so full of wisdom, so full of heart. You are as real to me as though yesterday had never left and life has yet many things in store for us.*

Then Goldie knew the searing pain of realization: Yussel was no more, only a memory to be drawn upon for the sweetness of life, locked away from all bitterness. As she let out a deep, heartrending cry, she felt a gentle and comforting hand upon hers, and she knew that wherever she was at that moment, something of life was still easing her sorrow.

Her eyes focused on Fr. Malachi, the good priest.

"Aaahhahaha." *My friend, you have come just in time. You, who represent God and are qualified to comfort the aching heart. Perhaps you will recall—or perhaps I never did tell you in sheer shame—about the one who should have had the wisdom and the gentleness of a teacher of children. Oh, I know, children have their moments when they try the patience of their elders. But to refuse a child his entry into manhood and the mantle of his religion was not the act of a true man of God—or so I believe in my ignorance. Women—wives—in Europe were not recognized as fountains of wisdom, so I plead guilty to that also. But how I wish now that I could have the comfort of your wisdom.*

Fr. Malachi sat next to Goldie's bed, holding her hand in his, smoothing, smoothing. Gently, he eased his hand from hers and let it slide lifelessly onto the coverlet. He could see she was in some distant moment of the past. How he wished he knew what her soul was unburdening.

BOOK NINE

An Irish Boarder

~ 1 ~

Goldie, motionless in her bed, remembered how spring arrived under the guise of summer with a sun that shed flesh-searing rays. The air was so humid that the perspiration rolled down in rivulets.

People, home from Sunday mass, would sit on the steps waving straw fans or folded newspapers to make a little hot breeze. The wavers deceived themselves into believing that they were a little cooler. With envy, adults watched the children, stripped of shoes and socks, as they ran about feeling no heat at all.

"Hello, Mrs. Picker," the bicycle man called over to Manya from the top of the steps leading to his cellar shop. "Hot as Hades, ain't it? But, then, I' been to mass this mornin' so I wouldn't be knowin' about how hot it is in Hades, ha ha . . ."

Manya didn't know what or where Hades was, so she just smiled.

Nearby could be seen Ryan's Beer Saloon with the swinging half-doors, and across the street was Dempsey's General Store which reminded Manya that she'd been too busy with her night sewing for Mrs. Smith's special ladies to pick up some needed items. She must get some material for Veeza's underwaists and drawers. After all, Veeza was getting old enough to enjoy those with pretty ribbons running through the edging, instead of the store-bought kind which are plain and would even cost more than ones Manya could make.

She watched Veeza and Joey contentedly sucking on a colored ball of shaved ice. They were only a penny apiece, but each penny was beginning to count, what with no money at all coming from Leon. She hadn't realized how the occasional dollars she had received from him had helped. *Oh God, not to have to move again to cheaper quarters. Even if I knew where to look, we're happy here.*

"You could put Joey to work," Sidney had commented.

"But he's only twelve years old. What kind of work could he do?" Manya half protested.

159

Sidney had a ready answer. "At the beach. I've seen boys of twelve and even younger selling peanuts and popcorn. All they do is hawk their wares. Joey could bring in a few dollars that way."

Manya had dressed as carefully as ever, and just as carefully saw that Joey washed his neck and ears, and that his blouse covered the top of his waistband.

It was a long ride to the beach—two transfers and a long wait for the right trolley to take them there.

The boardwalk was like a parade ground. Everywhere there were people in bathing outfits and summer streetwear sucking on popsicles, licking ice cream cones, or biting into hot dogs with sauerkraut oozing from the rolls. And hawkers abounded.

"Please," she asked one of the boys hawking popcorn, "where do you find the boss?" Wordlessly, the boy pointed out a cubbyhole on the boardwalk.

Manya and Joey walked over and entered a small door. Inside a tiny room sat a large man who gave them more than a cursory look. His straw hat was slid back on his head; his striped shirt and collar were pulled open at the neck, showing beads of perspiration streaming down toward the exposed hair on his chest. A cigar hung out of his mouth.

He was very polite. He leaned back on his chair and listened to Manya and looked at Joey as a buyer surveys cattle. Then, taking the cigar out of his mouth, he asked, "He a good boy?"

"Oh yes," Manya responded quickly. "He doesn't use bad words, and I raised him to be honest and respectful."

"Then take him home. This beach is a jungle. They'd eat him alive out there."

The man looked at Manya with an appreciative eye, but seeing her lack of understanding, turned back to his papers.

Manya stood, holding back her tears, her head high. *I will not tell him I need the money.* She heard the reb's words again, *"We're not in the charity business. Go to some organization for help."* And the words at the hospital, *"We're a charity hospital, we have to know. Do you have any money?" I will not tell him I need the money Joey would earn. I will not. I will not!*

Heading home, Manya counted the carfare they had wasted.

"Rraaayyyeeerra."

What time is it? Not that time matters, but soon maybe Veeza or Joey will be in to ask me if I would like a drink of something. Goldie would like to be able to say at such times, "Not for my mouth, children, just something for my brain. It's dry from squeezing the past out of it." *It's like a machine grinding juices out of something . . . or, rather, like a meat chopper—I've never seen a machine grinding juices. But, who knows, perhaps someone will invent it.* She played with the idea. *What a time-saver that would be, taking juices out of a mind and saving the heartache of remembering.*

Goldie remembered the time Paula brought a length of material for a dress for Veeza. Manya had found a ten dollar bill pinned to it. The worst of it was that it happened at a time when Leon was home.

Squeezing the juices of the brain, Goldie continued to remember. She couldn't fault Leon for being so angry. He had wondered why Sidney didn't come right out and say that Goldie is his mother, too, and that he wanted to give so much a month to her keep. But, no, it was always a few dollars slipped in like a secret favor. That day, the twins had sat as usual like two dolls, politely waiting for the visit to be over.

But the visit would take a while; Sidney had a proposition to make. Paula was going to the country for the summer with their neighbor and the neighbor's three children. "How would it be if Veeza were to go along to mind the children? That way, you could save on Veeza's food, she would have a summer in the country, and the mothers would not have to be tied down. After all, the whole purpose of a summer in the country is to enjoy and rest. How can they do this if they have to be watching that the children don't step into you-know-what from the cows?"

Manya was shocked. "Is that the best you can offer your niece—to be maid for five children? No, thank you!"

"But think of the benefit for Veeza—country air, lots of food—and the savings for you, Manya."

Goldie could perceive Manya's hidden rage. But with head held high, she answered, "Air is air! This is a clean, nice street. All I want is not to have to move from it."

Sidney and Paula shook their heads. Paula commented, "Sidney, I don't understand your sister."

Goldie didn't blame Paula. How could she understand Manya's feelings when she had a man who would jump through hoops for her, whose children, little balls of ice, knew a poor cousin when they saw one? Paula no doubt reasoned, "How else does a poor cousin get to the country except to be a maid for rich cousins?"

Later, Goldie watched Veeza's eyes follow a red-headed boy who lived down the street. *She's only ten, but soon she will be growing up. This is a nice, clean, airy neighborhood—but there are no Jews.*

~ 2 ~

It was baseball time. St. Mary's played Holy Cross in a lot behind the church. Over the years, little by little, bleachers had been erected. Veeza sat with Irene; Joey was selling peanuts for St. Mary's.

"How is it that Johnny's playing for Holy Cross?" Joey asked Irene.

" 'Cause they have a better team," Irene answered. "How is it you're selling peanuts for St. Mary's if you're a Jew?"

Joey laughed. "Because St. Mary's has Fr. Malachi. . . . Peanuts! . . . Peanuts! . . . "

"Are you folks takin' instructions from Fr. Malachi?" Irene asked. "Mrs. Murphy says he's at your place more than he comes to hers."

Veeza dug into her bag of peanuts and sank her teeth into the shell, spitting out the pieces of the casing. "Nah," she answered. "The priest and my grandmother are friends. Not like church friends—*real* friends."

"How can a Jew be real friends with a priest? Besides, she can't even talk to him . . . and he can't understand her."

It was true. As winter had faded into spring and spring blossomed into summer, Manya had become even more bewildered. "What do you do when he comes?"

"We sit. If it's cold, I give him hot tea. If it's hot, I give him cold water. Once, I gave him hot tea and he went to the ice box and chopped off little pieces of ice and put them into the tea. This I never heard of."

"But what do you do?"

"Why can't you understand, daughter? When you sit with a friend, you don't have to do anything! We understand each other. We don't need to understand what we say."

Veeza now answered Irene's question in the same way her grandmother had. "My grandmother says she doesn't have to talk to him. He understands her. . . . Hey, there's Fr. Malachi now."

They watched the priest walk along, smiling, waving, greeting familiar faces.

"That leaves Fr. O'Neil alone to hear confessions," Mrs. Holihan commented, waving her straw fan as she sat behind the children, her gaze set intently on the ball field. "They'll be losin' a lot of business today."

"You don't have to buy confession, do you?" Veeza whispered.

Irene shook her head. "Mama means that some people won't stay to confess if they find out it's Fr. O'Neil. He's too strict."

Irene munched her peanuts.

"Can't they go to Holy Cross instead?" Veeza asked.

"Uh-uh," Irene shook her head back and forth. "Holy Cross has mostly rich people in it."

"Play ball!" called the umpire.

"Peanuts! . . . Peanuts!" shouted Joey.

~ *3* ~

They stood around the piano as Sean banged out the strains of "Sweet Rosie O'Grady." Veeza held her singing down so she could listen—just for the sheer joy of it. She wished Irene wouldn't sing so loud in her off-key voice so she could better catch the beautiful tones of the voice which lifted itself above the clamor of the piano and the voices of the others. She thought, *If they sing in heaven, it will sound like Sean O'Flaherty's voice.*

All week long, the Holihan household had been in an uproar. Every room had been swept and polished since the arrival of the letter saying that Cousin O'Flaherty would be coming to stay a few days with them until he found a job.

Mrs. Holihan had tried to describe just how it came about that Sean was a cousin. "Well, it was on the mister's side of the family, and a handsome family it was. It was the mister's sister—or was it the sister-in-law?—who married into the O'Flahertys . . . But then, what difference does it make? Sean O'Flaherty is comin' and he'll be bringin' tales of the old country with him."

"And lookin' for a place to sleep and eat until he gets a job, no doubt," one of the girls' gentleman friends had commented.

"And what if it's so? Isn't it our Irish duty to provide the same? 'Tisn't money we had to be sendin' back to bring him here! An' if it's a place to sleep he needs, there's the couch."

"But Mama, he can't have the couch. It's the only place we have to sit when our beaus come—unless . . ." Helen's eyes sparkled, "it would be on their laps you'd be wantin' your girls to settle."

"Mind your tongue's waggin' like a hussy!"

But it was true. Every bed was doubled up, what with young Don, already half-grown, sleeping with his mother. So there would have to be a cot put up for Sean.

"Well, we'll cross that bridge when he gets here," Mrs. Holihan concluded. "He may be a big broth of a man who'll find himself a construction job right off and be put on a road somewhere layin' track or pipe or the like."

And in due time, Sean O'Flaherty arrived, his bundle on his back and in his hand a paper suitcase tied with rope. He was six-foot-two of Irish brawn, with black hair that competed with the night for its darkness, and blue-green eyes to charm the wits out of any lass, to be sure. *Now,* thought Mrs. Holihan, *it'll be no good havin' this broth of a man around here, cousin or not. The girls will be losin' their heads and their beaus. He's a real charmer, albeit they're blood cousins.*

But Sean O'Flaherty was no construction worker; he was a baker. A baker. Who in this world would have thought an Irishman would be a baker? And he had no qualms about finding himself a job. "I was born with the luck of the Irish," he told the Holihans who listened to him wide-eyed as the blarney rolled off his tongue. "To be sure, I have no intentions of takin' advantage of y'r hospitality. I could, if y'd let me, stay a bit until I find a job. Then I'd be findin' m'self a room close by it to be savin' the expense of carfare."

It was to everyone's surprise that Sean found himself a job right off—at the German bakery. Good Catholics they were, too. They didn't approve of the Irish priests in the churches, but there would be a German church soon with a priest who spoke their language. Meanwhile, the regular baker was sick with the "rheumatiz" and needed to stay off his feet awhile.

Sean mimicked the owner's wife: "Ach, du lieber Himmel, an Irish baker in a German bakery!"

Mrs. Holihan's eyes and ears rejoiced. She'd forgotten how sweetly beautiful was the sound of a good homegrown Irish brogue. They sat half the night talking about the old country until they realized that they'd not yet solved the problem of a room for Sean to rent.

It was not until Sean had gone off to work that night and had returned to sleep in the morning that Mrs. Holihan thought of a room. *Poor Mrs. Picker with her husband in the hospital an' sewin' day and night until the poor thing's eyes are bound to fall out—she could use the few dollars for the rent of the room. But,* Mrs. Holihan mused to herself, *she is a proud woman and it will have to be done tactfully.*

Mrs. Holihan figured that the best one to approach Mrs. Picker would be Mrs. Murphy, provided she did not have an asthma attack, what with all the rose fever going around. She would make it her business to see Mrs. Murphy after Sunday mass.

Stretch, stretch, Goldie thought to herself. *If I could only stretch one little stretch, or even feel the motion of stretching, like when I walked with the children. Gott in Himmel—how long ago was it?—like yesterday and like years.* "Take a long step, Baba. We learn in school that it stretches the muscles and strengthens the legs." Goldie would hold up her skirt with the yards of material in it—for sure it took a good grasp with each hand to hold the fullness up. The children thrilled to see her shoes and how long a step she was taking.

"Ayyayyayy."

How they had laughed when they outwalked her. Youth never considers age, of course. *In Europe, when they walk, they have a destination; who walks without a destination? But in America, we walk with pleasure, not to show how fast we can get there. You have to walk a distance? You allow time to talk a little, to enjoy the air, to stop to see a flower, a bird, or even a field mouse. To miss all that just to get somewhere or nowhere a few minutes sooner—narrish—foolish.*

"Ja, ja, ja." *Where was I in my memories? Ah yes, the Irishman. How could one stranger create such light where there had been so much shadow?*

At the suggestion that she take in a boarder, Manya had sighed with relief. They would not have to move to a cheaper place and the rearrangement would not be so difficult. Veeza and Goldie would move out of the little hall room and into the bedroom off the dining room which had been Joey's. Joey would sleep with Manya. After all, there was no Leon to occupy the other half of her bed, and Joey was only twelve, still a child.

And so Mr. O'Flaherty came to board. He had a private room which he could enter through the hallway; he could get to the bathroom from the hall door without even meeting the family. Usually, he was off to work before Manya got home in the evenings, and fast asleep by the time Manya left in the mornings. The family hardly knew he was there, except for the bread, the packages of sugar buns, or the jelly doughnuts he would leave on the kitchen table every so often.

Only on Sean's day off did the family become aware of the fact that there was a man in the house. Sean would fill the bathtub with hot water, steam himself until he was lobster-red, and sing old Irish melodies at the top of his lungs, filling the house with his music.

Veeza would listen happily; it felt like a good Catholic household. This man was alive, and his aliveness was infectious. His wild Irish eyes would dance with mischief as he strolled through the kitchen to heat some water in the kettle for his shaving. Oftentimes he'd stop to gently pinch Goldie's cheek. *A boldness, to be sure,* Goldie thought, *but the kind of boldness one cannot get angry at.* Sean would also tweak Veeza's braids and call her "Little Princess" when she brought him clean towels. Veeza would study her reflection in the mirror following Sean's sweet teasing. Her skinny braids had no resemblance to the golden curls or long blonde tresses of the princesses in the picture books, but all the same, she took to having Manya or Goldie roll up her hair in rag strips, hoping that by some miracle the curls would stay.

Goldie wished that Manya could be home more to hear the young man's singing, whistling, and laughter. He was so like a happy boy when he told the children tales of his childhood.

How good it is to have a man around the house again, Manya thought. *Not that Leon is like Sean, but when things are going well, Leon is cheerful and happy and handsome, too. Where,* she sighed to herself, *have our laughing days gone? the days of the summer sun, the walks in the fields, the moonlight, the air soft as a kiss, the laughing days of youth? But then, Sean is no youth; it's just the Irish in him. It seems the Irish are born with laughter. The Jew? His inheritance is sorrow. Well, let the children enjoy the laughter.* She was grateful Sean was there.

Manya wrote to Leon and told him that they had taken in a roomer. She explained to him that paying the rent was easier; she didn't want him to worry. She did not mention that the roomer was a man.

Manya insisted that the children write Leon regularly as well. But it was hard for them to write to a papa they had not seen in months and about whom there always seemed to be some tragic circumstance. "Write about school," Manya urged. Joey would feign enthusiasm to write about his latest invention which, he expected, would someday make them all rich. *We don't need to be rich,* Manya thought, *just to have enough.* But she never seemed to realize "enough."

Daydreaming one Sunday morning, Manya had been suddenly interrupted by the hall door opening and closing. It was Sean coming in to get washed up for Sunday mass. Manya quickly straightened her apron and brushed the loose hair from her face as the thought flashed through her mind, *Every Sunday he finds me at the same place—the washboiler on the stove.*

He stopped a moment at the doorway of the kitchen, the towel across his shoulders, suspenders hanging, and his undershirt open at the neck.

"Good mornin', ma'am."

Manya thought, *He's yet to call me anything but "ma'am."*

"Good morning," she answered, wanting to add his name, but unable to bring herself to be so forward even though Sean had come to seem like a friend in the household.

"It's too hot to be standin' over a washboiler."

Manya shrugged. What could she say? Should she go into a long story about Sunday being the only day in the week that she had, that hanging sheets had always been Leon's job, and that she was missing Leon's presence more and more? These are, after all, things you can't tell just anyone.

Sean hesitated in the doorway a moment longer. *I'm out of my head,* he admitted to himself, *but she's a fine figure of a woman, and a hard workin' one at that. She deserves a day off once in awhile, with a man to give her a squeeze or two.*

He watched Manya latch onto a sheet, square it off, and bring it to the window to hang out.

"Let me do that. I've got the arms for it, and it'll be takin' no time at all."

Manya hesitated, then stepped back. As Sean lifted the sheet out and let it settle loose, he quickly pinned the edges to the line. He gave them a brisk swing to shake out the wrinkles and then turned to take the next one from Manya.

"It's many a time I hung sheets for my sainted mother back in auld Ireland, and then after she went to her heavenly rest, I kept the house and did the wash—no different than you're doin' now—until I came to America."

"And you never married?"

"I had me a lassie, but there were reasons." *Two reasons,* Sean thought, *drinkin' and brawlin' . . . until the tears were dried out of my mother's eyes and there was no fire left in the lass's kiss. "I'll love you till I die,"* he recalled her saying, *"but it's away I've got to go to save me from makin' a mess of my life with you."* In the morning his lass was gone, and that afternoon he learned that her horse had run amuck; his lass would never see the light of day again.

Sean finished hanging the wash, emptied the steaming boiler, and hung it on its hook in the hallway. Then he came back into the kitchen. "I'd been thinkin' of goin' to the park after mass, and I'm wonderin' if you'd do me the honor of comin' along." As he saw Manya's look of alarm, he quickly added, "With the young ones, of course. Seems to me there's a whirligig or some such thing there that they'd enjoy, and a lake with rowin' boats."

No sooner were the words out of his mouth than Sean would have gladly taken them back. *I'm mad as a hatter,* he thought. *The woman's married, and hungry as I am for a wench, she's not the one. And if I want to take a decent woman for a stroll in the park, I'd better be takin' me cousin Kate Holihan before she finds out and blasts me all to Hades. But there's somethin' to this one, the saints forgive me, that stirs up the juices in me.*

Manya hesitated. She had no right to be out with another man, but with the children along and the day so beautiful, it seemed like an answer to a prayer. After all, she shouldn't deprive the children of a day of pleasure. A whirligig? Whatever that was, she was sure the children would enjoy it—all they'd ever had was the little pony ride on the merry-go-round pulled by a horse and turned by a hand crank. It was really a merry-go-round for tiny tots, but Veeza and Joey had enjoyed it anyway.

She looked at Sean who was waiting for her answer. In that long moment, a world of thoughts passed between them, and finally Manya's eyes dropped. "It's kind of you to ask us, but . . ." looking around as if to encompass the household, ". . . there is so much to catch up with. I'd better not."

Sean nodded, "I understand, ma'am," and he headed back toward the bathroom in the hall.

The heat of the kitchen had nothing to do with the perspiration which oozed from Manya's pores from desperate longing. Shortly, she heard Goldie returning from a visit with the Murphys upstairs—the Murphys were leaving for Sunday mass, too.

Book Ten
A Place for Worship

~ 1 ~

Bzzzzz. Bzzzz.

Goldie lay listening to the buzzing of the fly. *God forbid it should land on my nose or my mouth,* she thought as her eyes followed its hypnotizing flight. *It's like a hawk in the sky waiting to swoop down on some unsuspecting bird. A bird has a chance, at least. But a beetle sunning itself on a log is an easy prey for a predator. Ach, nature can be cruel*—as it was to her.

Silence.

Maybe the fly got tired of buzzing.

She closed her eyes.

Fr. Malachi sat on the chair beside Goldie's bed. She thought she would tell him she had just been dreaming about him, but on second thought considered that it wouldn't sound very nice. In her mind, she had been reviewing something. Maybe it had been only a little dream; whatever, she wanted to try to tell him.

"Aaahhhaaahhh."

How nice and soft her voice sounded. Surely the good priest could understand. "Aaahhhaaahhh." *What a mechaieh it would be to have some little sensation of the comfort he is offering me, his hand stroking my lifeless one. Dear God, just once, let me feel the motion of his stroking, the life that he is trying to impart from his hands into mine. I'll tell him just what I was thinking about. No, not in my sleep—a dream is a fantasy—but with the inside of my heart which still beats. I'll tell him how it was that day he came like a messenger from God. Let me see, God, let me remember, "Malachi is one of the few prophets who is deeply concerned for both moral behavior and ritual observance on the part of the people. 'Behold, I will send my messenger, and he shall prepare the way before me.' "*

I shall tell him about Manya, not in a mean way, but just to make the story more interesting.

It would soon be time to celebrate the next big holidays. Manya had scoffed, "The first time was a coincidence. You asked the priest how to get matzos for the Pesach, and it so happened that he asked an Irishman who happened to know a Jewish peddler."

"No, no," Goldie interrupted, "a Jewish businessman who happened to be in the vegetable business—and I did not petition God that his messenger should deliver the matzos. I merely petitioned God to solve the problem of the need for matzos. And with it, God threw in a little extra—we had all our Passover foods taken care of."

"Mama," Manya finally conceded, "if it makes you happy, then be happy."

Goldie recalled now that she had snickered to herself. "That Manya, she'll be a believer yet."

Fr. Malachi remained sitting with Goldie. *He doesn't know,* she thought, *or maybe he does know what a mitzva he performed by coming to talk to our roomer that day.*

Goldie had been concerned that something must be terribly wrong for the priest to wake up a man who had worked all night. Sean, in his undershirt and trousers, eyes heavy with unfinished sleep, came out of his room when Veeza rapped.

"You say Fr. Malachi is here to see me? Then there must be a need," Sean surmised confidently.

It turned out that the priest wanted to know if Sean would ask the German people at the bakery to donate donuts for the bazaar the ladies of St. Mary's were having.

"It's as good as done, Father," Sean told him. Then, feeling a twinge of guilt in the priest's presence, he added, "By the way, I apologize for not appearing for confession lately. It's on account of a temporary change in my working hours. But I'll be back on my regular shift soon."

"Good. We'll be glad to see you," Fr. Malachi responded.

Veeza explained this exchange to Goldie, who was readying the good priest's tea and cookies. Joining him, Goldie made her own blessing, "Gott ist gut," to which Fr. Malachi nodded agreement, "God is good."

He listened while Goldie struggled to explain something. Frustrated, she finally called Veeza, chattered to her, and Veeza translated.

"My grandmother wants to know if there are any Jews around here."

Fr. Malachi thought for a moment. "There are a few scattered Jewish families on the opposite side of the parish—over on Moore Street."

Goldie heaved a sigh of relief as Veeza translated. "How does one get to Moore Street?"

"The trolley car goes right by," Fr. Malachi explained. "The conductor will let you off."

That night, Goldie related the whole story to Manya. "A gutte neshoma, that priest."

"And how are you going to find the Jews?" Manya asked. "You're going knocking from door to door asking 'Are you Jews?'"

"If I have to," Goldie answered.

"Then you'd better take Veeza with you. By now she's so mixed up in your mishegoss, it can't get any worse."

The next day, Goldie put on her best taffeta waist, her petticoats, skirt, wig, bonnet, and capelet.

"Baba, it's too hot for all those clothes," Veeza protested.

But Goldie insisted. "If I am going to meet new people, I must look like a mensh." She stroked the fur, admiring its condition. "It's got many good years left—I should live so long."

As they started out, Goldie was excited. "Imagine. There are other Jews somewhere, and we didn't know it. That's what comes of living like a greenhorn—never going off your own street, never knowing what's going on in the world around you."

Veeza nodded. "It's like an adventure. Going someplace where we've never been before and seeing the different streets!"

~ 2 ~

Goldie lay like a log in her bed, but felt warm because of the adventure she was remembering. *Ja, ja,* it had been a short walk to the streetcar stop, and a pleasant one. The two of them also enjoyed the trolley ride: the new sights, the small houses, a bakery. They wondered if the bakery was where Sean worked. Gradually, there were fewer houses and more fields, and finally, the conductor called out, "Moore Street." They got off.

Goldie recalled how bewildered they felt looking at the wild growth of heat-scorched weeds. In the distance they saw structures, but no sidewalks—only a footpath made by others as a shortcut.

It was an uncomfortable walk, and Goldie began to weary. The little stones hurt her feet through her soled shoes. Eventually, the path ended at a sidewalk which led to small, newly built homes: a row of red brick homes with front steps which led to an entry door. Goldie stopped a moment to catch her breath; her fur cape felt too heavy on her shoulders and her bonnet strings seemed tied too tightly. She turned to Veeza and said, "I feel faint. I must rest a minute."

As she remembered now in her bed, Goldie had to admit that Manya had been right. *Who goes forth without knowing where they are going? . . . But didn't we go forth from Europe with God knows how many others, all uncertain of our final destination? We were looking for something to make our world right. So again, Veeza and I set out . . . looking for the right kind of Jews—But who am I to decide who's "right," as if I were God's judge.*

She remembered Veeza leading her to some steps and telling her to sit down; she remembered feeling faint and asking for a little water. *Ja, ja, taka, for sure, I thought that was my last day on earth. I felt so schwach, so weak.* Veeza had run up some steps to a house nearby and a young woman returned with Veeza to help get Goldie to their house. There had been a young child crying, and the woman had asked, "Where are you going—to walk across the fields when there is a regular streetcar stop close by?"

Goldie recalled looking at Veeza whose face was fire-red from the heat as the girl turned to her for an answer. Goldie had said, "Say the truth, child. We're looking for Jews."

The woman looked nonplussed when Veeza translated her grandmother's answer. "Why are you looking for Jews?"

Veeza looked at the woman and wondered. Would she understand? Suppose she didn't understand or didn't want to understand. What would they do then? *Mama was right,* Veeza thought, *you can't just go from house to house saying, "We're looking for Jews."*

"Please don't be angry," she explained, "but Fr. Malachi told us that there were Jews on Moore Street, and my grandmother, she doesn't know any English, so I came with her to find them—the Jews."

"Fr. Malachi? St. Mary's Fr. Malachi?"

Veeza nodded. "He's Catholic, but he's our best friend."

The woman smiled warmly. "He's my best friend, too. Did he tell you I lived here?"

"No, ma'am, but you see my grandmother didn't tell him we were coming. She only asked him if he knew where some Jews were."

"Well, he certainly knew. My name is Mrs. Bernstein."

As soon as Goldie heard the mention of Bernstein, she perked up.

"A Yiddisheh frau?" she asked almost unbelievingly. Then she started to rattle off her mission, but Mrs. Bernstein looked at her uncomprehendingly. "I don't speak the language," she told Veeza, and Veeza looked at her with the same lack of comprehension as did Goldie when she translated the information. Jewish people like Goldie understandably may not be able to speak the American language. But not to speak Yiddish?

"My husband speaks the Jewish language," Mrs. Bernstein quickly reassured them. "He's inside. Why don't you come in and get out of this heat?"

Veeza helped her grandmother up, and they followed the young woman into the house.

It was a pleasant little house, simply furnished. To Veeza's mind, however, it was beautiful. *They must be rich,* she thought.

"Excuse me a minute, and I'll go tell my husband you're here." Goldie nodded pleasantly, not understanding the words but feeling the friendliness of the tone.

She and Veeza sat down and looked at the walls with the framed pictures and the vase of flowers which sat on the table in the adjoining dining room. "How schön—a good little housewife. But whoever heard of a Yiddisheh maidel not speaking Yiddish?" Goldie commented.

In a few minutes, Mrs. Bernstein returned carrying her child and followed by a young man, studious in appearance, with a pleasant but questioning expression on his face.

"You want to speak to me?" he asked in Yiddish.

A broad smile and a look of relief lit up Goldie's face. In a stream of explaining, she told him that they were looking for Jews.

Mr. Bernstein nodded; his wife had told him that much. "But what kind of Jews? You just don't go looking for Jews from door to door."

Goldie shook her head in agreement. "That's what my daughter told me." Mr. Bernstein looked toward Veeza, obviously comparing ages. Goldie noticed and corrected him. "No, this child is my granddaughter. She interprets the language for me."

Mr. Bernstein indicated that he understood, then he said, "Why don't you tell me what you need the Jews for and perhaps I can help."

Goldie's eyes flashed excitedly. "I knew it," she glowed, "I knew I would be led to the right place."

Mr. and Mrs. Bernstein sat down, the baby on her lap, and they waited for Goldie to speak. Now that she had to outline her plan, she was suddenly unable to put the words together. Finally she started. "I'm looking for Jews to bring them together to find a place to have Rosh Hashanah and Yom Kippur services. The good priest—he's my best friend—told me there were Jews here in this area."

Mr. Bernstein looked at his wife. *Fr. Malachi is her best friend?* they thought. It puzzled them both.

"There's a Jewish colony on the other side," Mr. Bernstein explained. "They don't have a shul but they hold some kind of service there. That would be a place."

The light went out of Goldie's eyes. She shrugged. "Let's say we had a disagreement, and we moved away from there."

Mr. Bernstein was especially interested in Goldie's remark. "What kind of disagreement?"

Goldie hesitated, then replied. "Well, a misunderstanding. You know how people are. The old reb . . . well, no matter. Here it is a new development. Could we get together and have a service, and maybe later, more people would move in. Eventually we could make a shul, but for now all we need is a place to have a service."

Mr. Bernstein looked at his wife as if to say, "What have you gotten me into?" As he hesitated, Goldie questioned him. "Close by, there are other Jews? stores maybe? somebody?"

"There are some other Jews," Mr. Bernstein said, "but I don't know them well enough to know what they do on the holy days. The houses are new, and we haven't been here long ourselves."

"And where did you come from?" Goldie asked.

"From that neighborhood where all the old Jews are. The old reb is my zayde—my grandfather."

"Oy vay!" Goldie exclaimed. "You must excuse me. I didn't

know." She turned to Veeza. "You see how careful one must be when one talks?"

Mr. Bernstein smiled. "It's all right. I understand. You see, I had a misunderstanding with him, too." He looked affectionately at his wife, and she chimed in. "I am a shikseh—my name was McGrority."

Veeza listened openmouthed. "McGrority? My mother knows your mother! My mother works for Mrs. Smith, and your mother always tells Mrs. Smith that she wants my mother to sew her dresses because my mother makes such beautiful stitches—even smaller than a machine!" Then shyness overtook Veeza's outburst. "I didn't mean to butt in."

Kathryn Bernstein was delighted; suddenly, they seemed to be friends. But Veeza remembered her mama telling her never to overstay her visit at the Holihans—and she knew she mustn't overstay this visit with Baba at the Bernsteins. She stood up and moved to help Goldie up. "I think we should go now, Baba."

Goldie nodded with a sigh. "Yes, we'll go." She turned to the Bernsteins. "The other Jews, they're near here?"

Kathryn protested. "Oh, please, it's too hot to be walking." Then to Veeza she insisted, "Don't let your grandmother do it. She got so faint before, I'm afraid she will make herself sick." She turned to her husband, "Tell her you'll think about it, Dave."

Before he could speak, Goldie asked emphatically, "You'll let me know? Veeza, write down our name and the address."

Apologetically, Veeza asked Kathryn if she could have a pencil and a piece of paper so she could write down their name and address. Kathryn complied, and Veeza carefully wrote the information. Then, handing the paper to Kathryn, Veeza moved to the door with her grandmother, who bobbed her head and smiled gratefully.

As the door closed behind Goldie and Veeza, Kathryn and Dave Bernstein stood looking at each other.

"I didn't think she would take me seriously," Kathryn said. "I thought she would understand."

"Understand what?"

"Well, that you weren't interested, but that you didn't want to say so."

Dave Bernstein looked at his wife. "Now you don't expect me to believe that, do you?"

Kathryn looked at him with a smile in her eyes. "Not really, but I thought I would say it just to see what would happen. Are you interested?"

"The answer is no!" He sat thinking. *She has no idea of what it is to get a bunch of Jews together. And what happens when they do get together? It's one great big argument.* "We hardly know any of them." He shook his head. "I'm no organizer—I'm a teacher, and organizing a baseball game between classes is enough for me."

Goldie walked to the streetcar stop with more energy than Veeza had.

"What are you hurrying for, Baba? We're only going home."

That didn't diminish Goldie's enthusiasm. "Won't your mother be surprised?" And then with a second thought she added, "Imagine, the grandson of the old reb! Gott in Himmel, what a small world it is. But such a cranky old man to have such a fine grandson—a teacher. A credit to him, so the old man should have had more patience with Joey."

When the two arrived home, Manya's response was practical. "If the young man is the old reb's grandson, then he doesn't need to find a place to have Rosh Hashanah. Naturally, he will go there."

"But that's the whole point," Veeza interjected. "He said he had a misunderstanding with the old reb, too."

Manya passed it off. "By the time Rosh Hashanah comes, the misunderstanding will be over, and he'll go there, and it's no more than right that he should."

"But Mama," Veeza continued, "I don't think so, because Mrs. Bernstein said she is a shikseh—her mother is Mrs. McGrority, the lady whose dresses you sew on."

Manya was surprised. "If Reb Herschel's grandson is married to a shikseh, definitely the old man won't want him there. For him, it's enough of a shanda—a shame—without advertising it. And," Manya added, "it's understandable that the young husband would not want to get involved with a frummeh alte. He's got problems enough."

Goldie's enthusiasm waned like a balloon losing air. But she added hopefully, "He said he would think it over."

Manya scoffed at Goldie. "Of course he would say that. Did you think he was going to be disrespectful to an old woman?"

That night, Veeza snuggled up to Goldie. "Do you think he will think about it?"

"I think he will think about it, but I'm not sure he will do anything about it," Goldie answered.

~ *3* ~

"Yiyiyirra. Rrruhhh."

The moan echoed through the room. In the kitchen, Joey and Veeza fixed themselves peanut butter sandwiches and stopped to look at each other.

"How does it sound to you, Joey?" Veeza asked worriedly.

"It doesn't sound like she's playin' the piano, if we had one. An' she ain't singin' a song either. Anyway, how would I know—you're with her more than I am."

"Mama hadda go to deliver that dress to Mrs. McGrority, and I promised I wouldn't leave Baba for a minute. So will you stay with me until Mama gets back?"

"I'd stay with her even if you weren't here. I don't get scared like you do."

"Maybe it's because you don't love her as much as I do."

Joey slapped the peanut butter spreader down on the table and turned on Veeza. "One more crack like that out of you, and I'll smack you one!"

Hearing the raised voices, Goldie whimpered. *Kinder, kinder. Don't squabble. Life in sweet voices is so precious; don't waste them.* But all she heard was "Ayakdaih, yiiiii."

She recalled the days of tension as they waited to hear from the Bernsteins. How often she felt her disposition slipping out of control as she worried about Manya, too, who had greater worries than to think about the Bernsteins. As days passed, Manya noticed that Goldie seemed to droop.

"Are you sick, Mama?" Manya asked.

Goldie said she wasn't sick.

"Then something is wrong. You are keeping something from me. Is it Leon? Have you heard something?"

Goldie shrugged. "Why should I hear anything that you don't hear? You wrote to Laban, and he said he saw Leon, and Leon wrote you that he got the children's letters, and he was feeling better . . . "

"Then are you worrying about Sidney?"

"Why should I worry about Sidney?" Goldie remembered answering. She had wanted to say, "God forbid, Sidney can no longer spare the ten dollars for my care because the twins are taking ice-skating lessons. Our Veeza could learn to skate on the ice in the park like all the other children hereabouts, but the twins, God bless them, what do they know about counting pennies? No, it's not the twins' fault, but Sidney—with Sidney it's a little different." But she said none of this.

She thought again about Mr. Bernstein and felt a twinge of sympathy for the old reb. *It must have been like a stab in his back to have his grandson marry a shikseh—bless her, a lovely young woman. A pity on her to have a cranky old man for a mishpocheh. Ahhh, the twists and turns of life's path.*

Then Manya came to the point which she had been leading up to. "Mama, you are worrying about that business with Mr. Bernstein."

Goldie shrugged slightly in a manner that was almost an admission. "We gave him our address."

"But if he has nothing to tell you? . . . "

"Then he should write and say so."

"You are expecting too much, Mama. You walk into a stranger's home and expect right away that he should get involved with you and write letters to you. People write to friends, not strangers, and even friends don't always write because they're too busy. I owe a letter three . . . four weeks already to Greta, and if I don't have time to write to Greta, then I wouldn't have time to write about something that I'm not interested in. Mama, I can't get excited about the holidays. There are things weighing on my mind that are more important, and you know what they are."

Goldie couldn't disagree with Manya, but it didn't make her feel any happier. Were they trying to make something out of nothing—or were they trying to take nothing and make it into something?

Gott in Himmel! How mixed up can things get? From something it became a gurnicht. Or should I say, from nothing it developed into a something—a disagreement with Manya. Manya, who works so hard and has her own problems, shouldn't have to get involved with someone else's.

~ 4 ~

Veeza decided it was time to see if Mrs. Holihan would read the cards again. It would not be easy to admit that they had been kicked out of "Little Jewtown" and that because of this her grandmother had no place to go to worship—not a shul, a church, or just any old place. Of course, St. Mary's didn't have a regular church, either. It had only a basement, while Holy Cross already had a beautiful church. Mrs. Holihan could go to either place anytime she wanted, but Veeza's baba had no place to go. So that's what Veeza wanted Mrs. Holihan to tell her: would her grandmother hear from Mr. Bernstein? Veeza was full of questions but she didn't know which questions should come first. As she rang the doorbell and waited, Veeza practiced the questions which were the most important.

Irene was full of exciting news as she opened the door and let Veeza in. Helen's fella had given her an engagement ring and Lucy's fella was now talking about marriage, too. Veeza felt her questions evaporating into thin air.

Mrs. Holihan was slicing ham for lunch and chattering about wedding plans. "Now if Lucy could get her fella to get her a ring, then the two couples could get together and set the date." She bustled about the kitchen, getting the mustard from the cupboard and the bread from the bread box. "Oh, I can just see those girls now—beautiful brides they'll be."

Veeza felt that she simply could not break the happy mood even though it was important.

"Sit down and have a sandwich with us, Veeza," Mrs. Holihan invited, but Veeza didn't feel like she could swallow a morsel even though the thick slices of ham looked delicious.

The kettle on the stove whistled for attention.

"There's nothing like a spot of piping hot tea to cool one off," Mrs. Holihan commented, but Veeza thought of scoops of crushed ice with strawberry syrup running over it. Maybe older people just don't like crushed ice. Baba, too, had said hot tea is better than iced, even if it is sucked right into your mouth.

Veeza lingered at the kitchen door. Maybe if she sat with Mrs. Holihan, she might offer to read the cards. She eased herself into the chair while Mrs. Holihan poured the water into the little teapot, stirred the tea leaves, and poured the tea into the cups. Into that she spooned an overflowing measure of condensed milk, its thick, sugary substance holding to the spoon.

Aren't they all lucky? Veeza thought. *No worries.*

Mrs. Holihan continued to daydream about white bridal veils. *Once the dates are set, there'll be banns to post, sewing for the trousseaus, and flats to be found.*

Flats to be found! That will mean the girls will be movin' out, and with them will go their weekly contributions to the household . . . Ah, glory be to His name, I can't be worryin' about that now. I can try to rent their room and, if necessary, I could go back to takin' in washin' and ironin' like I did right after the mister passed when the girls were young an' Don was but a sprout. She shook her head as if to say, "Them were hard times, and I'm too old to be facin' them again."

Seeing Veeza sitting next to her brought Sean O'Flaherty to mind—and an idea! She could rent the girls' room to Sean. It was a hall room; he'd have privacy and quiet for his daytime sleeping. *And glory be, he'd be a cheerful soul to have around. The Sundays he comes over after mass, chuckin' me under the chin, he has me gigglin' like a hoyden.*

As Mrs. Holihan's face reflected the resolutions to her upcoming problems, something in Veeza's downcast face disquieted her.

"Is there something wrong at your house, Veeza?"

"Wrong?" Veeza asked, as if everything was always quite right at her house.

"You look like your papa went to jail—heaven forbid, he bein' a sick man an' all that."

"Papa is still in the hospital," Veeza told her. *Papa could never be in jail,* Veeza thought. *Jews don't go to jail! Once when Mama and I heard shots in the early dawn, and we got up to see what it was, we saw a man running and a policeman chasing him. Later, it was whispered that it had been a gangster. "It was Brockey," they'd said. "He's a Jew hold-up man." But Mama had pooh-poohed that. "Jews aren't hold-up men; they're students and scholars and teachers. But gangsters?—never!"*

Of course, Veeza knew she could not tell all of this to Mrs. Holihan. It might have turned out that Brockey was an Irishman, and it would not be nice to say that Irishmen are gangsters.

"Is your mama gonna have a baby, then?" Mrs. Holihan asked.

Veeza's head bounced up again, her eyes wide. "Is my mama gonna have a baby?" she asked in return.

"How would I know, child? I was wondering if that's what has dispirited you. After all, havin' a baby at your mama's age would be difficult. Lord forgive me for sayin' that, because it's a woman's duty to have children as long as the Lord sees fit. Is it your grandma, bless her heart? There'd be nothing wrong with her?"

Veeza hung her head. Now was her opportunity, and yet she could not bring herself to say a thing.

Mrs. Holihan asked more about Goldie, and Veeza knew that it was a good opening. Still, she could not ask Mrs. Holihan to read the cards. Then, in a rush of words, she found herself saying, "It's all started again like when we first got kicked out of Little Jewtown." Realizing what she had said, however, Veeza stopped abruptly.

Mrs. Holihan's eyes bulged, but just then Irene came into the kitchen asking about lunch, and Veeza realized that she was getting hungry, too. Besides, the whole thing seemed to be going wrong. "I think I'll be going home now." Veeza felt let down and wished that she'd never come.

"But we were going to do things," Irene protested.

"Maybe tomorrow?" Veeza suggested.

"But tomorrow I might not feel like it."

Glory be, Mrs. Holihan shuddered to herself, *getting kicked out of Little Jewtown would be like being excommunicated from the Church and switching over to become a Protestant, heaven forbid. No wonder Fr. Malachi is spendin' so much time with the old lady—and the child is migratin' into the faith of our Lord!*

"Arrrerrraarr."

Lying in her bed, Goldie remembered now that it was all over. *There is no pain now where there was once a body feeling like it was a pincushion with the jabbings of pins and needles and no way to turn from it. Ja, the kopfwetig and the weltschmerz . . . the body . . . no, the soul being tossed in its own pain.*

She recalled those gentle nights, sitting by the window with Veeza and talking about faith and prayers going up to the heavens like rungs on a ladder and wondering who up there would measure the importance of their prayer against those of others. She had told Veeza that God is our refuge and our strength, a well-proven help in trouble. *So am I to preach one thing to a child and believe less myself? It is the testing that the person must withstand.*

How could she feel a heartache when no feeling existed? Beating—beating—thump—thump. There was only the beat of the heart, and she wasn't even sure of that.

~ 5 ~

During Fr. Malachi's next visit, he asked Veeza if her grandmother was ill.

"What did he say?" Goldie asked, noticing his look of concern.

"The priest wants to know if you are sick, and I'm worried about you, too, Baba."

"I'm not sick in body," Goldie replied, and Veeza translated.

"Ah," said Fr. Malachi, "then she is sick in spirit?"

Veeza looked hesitantly at Fr. Malachi. "I don't know how to say 'spirit' in Yiddish."

Goldie remembered how she had made her right hand into a fist and gently pounded on her heart. The good priest indicated that he understood. When Veeza translated, Goldie's face lit up but quickly clouded again. "One mustn't impose on God's messenger. He has already done enough—with his friendship."

However Veeza expressed her grandmother's remark, it did not seem to faze Fr. Malachi. He asked Veeza to tell Goldie that we are all God's messengers and must spread his word.

As Goldie remembered this visit, she almost—just almost—felt as she had felt then, when she was a mensh, not like a log. *I wonder what a log feels when the ax cuts into it. It is a tree with its life juices until it is cut down by man for man's needs. Maybe inside it rebels, like I rebel. It is sad. But if the tree builds a house or serves some useful purpose, then who are we to complain? The tree certainly doesn't know.* She felt herself snorting. *Yussel, I'm a philosopher! I can't read; I can't write. But you, good husband, you talked to me and I learned. Who knows, maybe God will let me pass on something to this priest—not by language but by heart. God's beautiful invention: a feeling heart—and a young priest who shares his with me.*

Goldie recalled how she had gone on to tell the priest about the need for a shul, forgetting that she was speaking in Yiddish. "We need a place to worship on Rosh Hashanah and Yom Kippur, our holy days."

Fr. Malachi listened. Indeed, it seemed to Goldie, he understood the problem.

Veeza filled in. "Since Baba came to America, there has been no shul where she's lived. Even in their small village in Europe, Baba says they rebuilt a barn to make a house of God." Veeza felt good pleading Goldie's cause.

"But the old Jews . . . the Jewish neighborhood?"

Veeza shook her head. "We can't go back there on account of a misunderstanding." Her mama had always taught Veeza not to demean her own. "That's why my grandmother is so upset. That's why she asked about Jews living in other neighborhoods—she thought there might be a place there, but there isn't."

Fr. Malachi nodded, and Goldie spread her hands as if to say, "That's my problem."

"Let me give it some thought," Fr. Malachi assured the old woman, "but of course, I cannot promise anything." Veeza relayed to Goldie what the priest had said.

Goldie nodded happily and quickly said to Veeza, "I know the priest is heaven sent."

That night, Goldie dropped pennies into the pushke in gratitude for God's help. "You see, my children," she told Joey and Veeza, "you must have faith."

"So the Catholic priest is going to build us a private shul," Joey teased.

Manya shushed him, but asked herself, *Why can't Mama be satisfied with just saying her prayers? What did she do before we moved into that Jewish neighborhood?* Then Manya realized that moving into that neighborhood is what had brought all of her past life back again. Manya sighed to herself. *As a person gets older, the closer they get to*—she didn't want to even think of the black angel—*the more they want to feel close to God. I suppose that there is where the image of God is—in the heart, not in statues.* Manya decided not to argue with her mother. *If Mama believes the priest is God's messenger, then let her be happy—but what a priest can do with Jews, I wouldn't have any idea.*

~ 6 ~

The day had run smoothly. Dinner was unusually good and Fr. O'Neil, totally relaxed, sat in his study reading his breviary. When Fr. Malachi appeared in the doorway, Fr. O'Neil motioned to him to be seated.

The older priest sat back in his chair and thought, *I wonder if he is going to tell me that he is bringing a new family into the fold.*

There had been rumors, not much that he could pin down. After all, when a priest makes regular and frequent visits to a Jewish family in the parish, there must be more to it than passing the time of day.

"I've been meaning to tell you, Father, that you've been doing a fine job," opened Fr. O'Neil.

"Thank you, Father, I appreciate your telling me."

They sat quietly appraising each other.

Why is it, Fr. Malachi thought, *that I cannot converse easily with this man? No matter, there'll have to be a discussion, and I'll have to bring up the subject of Goldie—if there is to be any discussion at all.*

Fr. O'Neil, however, broached the subject first.

"Mrs. Murphy stopped by special to tell me how much she enjoyed your mass."

"That was thoughtful of her. She's a fine woman."

"A fine woman . . . and a good neighbor. She was telling me about those people who moved downstairs from them . . . the Jews. They invited her and Mr. Murphy to the Passover dinner—their seder—also the Holihans, good parishioners that family, too."

Fr. Malachi wondered where this was leading; he knew it was leading somewhere. Fr. O'Neil was not prone to make idle conversation. Since the opening gambit had been made, however, Fr. Malachi followed through.

"They are a nice Jewish family. The grandmother is the spittin' image of my own. Seems odd I've taken such a shine to an old lady not speakin' a word of English."

"Is it the child—the girl—who's takin' instruction then?"

Fr. Malachi tried to pass Fr. O'Neil's question off.

"No one's takin' instruction, Father. It's just a friendly visit I pay them—uh, for the goodwill of the parish, you know."

"You're courtin' the goodwill of the Jews for the benefit of our parish?" Fr. O'Neil's voice had a hint of incredulity in it.

Fr. Malachi stammered, "Well . . . that's not exactly what I mean."

"I've seen the child in and out of the church," Fr. O'Neil continued, "and then there's the money for the poor box that the grandmother sends. Seems to me there'd be a good possibility to bring a family of lost sheep into the faith—seein' as they're showin' that interest."

Fr. Malachi thought to himself, *If they are lost sheep, they certainly are not aware of it. Here the old lady is talkin' about a place of worship for her religion and Fr. O'Neil is talkin' about bringin' her into ours!* He took a deep breath. *I got myself into this and now I have to wiggle out of the whole thing or face the wrath of Fr. O'Neil for daring to overstep the bounds of my position.*

"As a matter of fact, Fr. O'Neil, it's that family, the Jewish old lady's, I want to talk to you about. It seems like the poor thing is concerned that there is no house of God to worship in—what with their high holy days coming up."

"That really isn't our concern, is it," Fr. O'Neil countered. "Just tell her that Little Jewtown is not so far out of the way from here. The place is crawlin' with Jews with beards down to their waists. Surely they must have a place of worship."

Fr. Malachi shrugged. "Seems like they hold it in someone's house. She calls him the old reb—and evidently, there's been some kind of misunderstanding."

After a moment's silence, Fr. O'Neil dismissed the subject casually. "That's too bad, but it's not our problem—nor yours either, Father."

This reaction had been expected. And Fr. Malachi had to admit that when he boiled it down to realities, Fr. O'Neil was right. Indeed, it was not his problem. The fact of the matter was, if he wanted to be realistic, he'd gotten himself emotionally involved with a Jewish old lady, and he should be aware by now that emotional involvement does not solve problems; it only complicates facts. The fact here was that he allowed his feelings toward his own grandmother to transfer to Goldie. Now how could he detach himself from her without hurting her feelings? Well, he would at least try another tack with Fr. O'Neil.

"You remember the McGrority girl, Father?"

Fr. O'Neil surely did. His eyes blazed. "The one who married a Jew, disgracing her family."

"Well, so they took it," Fr. Malachi countered.

"What other way was there to take it? A girl from a God-fearing, strong Catholic family! It was not only a disgrace to her family; it was a reflection on us!"

"Us?" Fr. Malachi questioned.

"One soul lost to the church can mean a succession of souls. It is our business—yours and mine, Father—to see that it doesn't occur. Did she come in to talk about it? Did she show faith in her church? Did she bring him into our church?"

Fr. Malachi tried to explain. "They eloped. Young couples eloping generally don't take the time to think things through. They jump into it on impulse." Fr. Malachi could see that he was making no headway but continued. "Besides, if she didn't bring him into the church, by the same token, she hasn't followed him into his . . . yet."

Fr. O'Neil raised his head sharply. "What do you mean, *yet*?"

"Well, she slips in and out of church. I've seen her two or three times. There's still a tie there, Father, in spite of the fact that Mike McGrority has disowned her—as well as the church. At heart, though, the girl is still a Catholic."

Fr. O'Neil roared angrily. "She's living in sin with a Jew!"

Fr. Malachi pressed his point further. "In the eyes of the law, she's a married woman, and in the eyes of God, she is a young girl torn between love for a man and love for her church. If we turn our backs on her now, Father, we may lose her completely, as well as the child she has and those to follow."

Fr. O'Neil was annoyed with the young priest, but his curiosity drove him to say, "What's on your mind?" in a voice that indicated no special tolerance.

In a brief span of silence, Fr. Malachi experienced an instant recollection of the hours he'd lain awake worrying about how to approach Fr. O'Neil. Now he felt as awkward as a novice.

"I've been thinking that we might allow the Jews use of the social hall for their high holy day services, providing you agree, Father. The social hall isn't booked, and there wouldn't be much needed that we don't have: the folding chairs, a table—not much different than we have when the sodality ladies have their meetings."

Fr. O'Neil listened without interruption, lost temporarily in his own thoughts. *When I turned Mike McGrority over to Fr. Malachi, I expected that the problems with Mike would be absorbed by this junior priest. Instead, here he is setting up another problem. Not that it has anything to do with Mike at this moment, but no doubt about it, it will. In the final analysis, it will end up in my lap!*

He envisioned the church overrun with Jews and a roar from Mike McGrority that would echo the length and breadth of the parish. It would stir up the old questions as to how it came about that a Catholic girl, Kathryn McGrority no less, had been so defiant of her parents and her church—which naturally included him, Fr. O'Neil—as to marry a Jew from Little Jewtown. And now, to complicate it all, here was Fr. Malachi putting another hot potato in the fire. *What,* he pondered anxiously, *has Fr. Malachi to do with the Jews?*

Fr. Malachi felt a twinge of guilt as he watched the older priest. He knew Fr. O'Neil had not been feeling his best of late, and now he was adding to his worries.

Actually, though, Fr. Malachi didn't feel it was such an ungodly thing to ask. Indeed, it was a godly gesture. He continued to wait for Fr. O'Neil's reaction. *If Fr. O'Neil refuses to entertain the suggestion, it could be just a thought forgotten, since I haven't mentioned it to Goldie. Besides, she might refuse to consider anything so radical as having Jews celebrate Rosh Hashanah and Yom Kippur under the roof of a Catholic church.*

He recalled his own grandmother saying, "Impulse will get you into trouble some day. A young priest should do nothing on impulse. Fools can step in where angels fear to tread, but a young priest can't afford to be a fool; he should leave the work of the angels to God." Yet here he was, involved up to his neck, seeming to be making Jews of Catholics or Catholics of Jews, but trying only to find a sanctuary for an old lady to worship God in her own way.

By the same token, Fr. O'Neil was lost in the thought that there might be some logic in Fr. Malachi's suggestion. If this tolerance on the part of the church could impress Kathryn McGrority's Jew husband, it might bring him into it. *Ah, yes, I can see a long line of new Catholics resulting from one generous gesture on my part: the children and the children's children.*

Fr. O'Neil broke the silence. "Do you suppose we'd be run out on a rail if we did let them have the social hall—what with

Little Jewtown being a sore subject as it is   for the sake of gaining one convert and, hopefully, the return of the stray Kathryn
McGrority . . . er . . . Bernstein?"

Fr. Malachi commented, "The Irish criticizing Little Jewtown
is a little ironic, Father. You've got to admit that they are clean
and orderly and there's no carousing. The old Jews sitting outside their homes isn't as bad as a bunch of drunken Irishmen hol-
lerin' their heads off singin' inside or outside the saloon in spittin' distance of their church—an' the policeman on the beat havin' to drag them home one by one!"

Fr. O'Neil nodded in agreement. "I remember the day when
no one wanted an Irishman around either: 'No dogs or Irish' the
signs would read big as life." He heaved a sigh. "Lord only
knows what will come of it, but . . . we'll take a chance."

"Thank you, Father." Fr. Malachi tried to hide his surprise.
The old curmudgeon had a soft spot under that crusty exterior after all.

"And by the way, Father, you haven't forgotten that I'll be
leaving for my retreat after mass on Sunday?" The comment
came with an almost visible sigh. "If Mike McGrority comes
running in bullheaded, remember— he's your responsibility!"

Fr. Malachi nodded. "I'll remember, Father . . . " *and I'll
cross that bridge when I come to it. It might, by some decree of
fate, never get noised around. The Catholics don't mingle with
the Jews of Little Jewtown, and the Jews can't care less.*

~ 7 ~

"Djeidjryfh."

The house was as quiet as a grave.

"Rrrrrh."

Who needed that thought!

Veeza came running in. "I'm fixing your supper, Baba;
Mama's not home yet so you just lie there a little longer, and I'll
feed you."

Goldie felt herself snickering. *No, I'll get up and dance a jig
like I danced at the Youngs' Christmas party when we bought the
little Christmas tree. What a time Manya and Leon and Joey
gave us. A poor, harmless little tree standing there like an orphan with people overlooking him to find a prettier child. Ridic-
ulous, maybe. But a live tree bleeds when it is cut. Does it feel*

pain? Do I feel pain? In my body, no. But, ah, the soul bleeds for sure. How long ago was that? And then came another Christmas, I believe, and another surprise.

"Aaahhhyayay."

What is it the children used to chant singsong?—"Sticks and stones will break my bones, but names will never hurt me."

Now sticks and stones will never hurt me either!

Ach, how long the hours are. I'll sleep a little.

But sleep would not come.

Instead, into Goldie's thoughts came memory of the day the postcard arrived from Kathryn Bernstein saying that her husband had called a meeting of the Jewish people in their area. It was to be held at the Bernstein home on the following Sunday, and the idea about the Jewish holidays could be presented to them by Goldie.

That same day, Fr. Malachi had come to tell her that the social hall would be available for the Jewish people to hold their Rosh Hashanah and Yom Kippur services in. How excited she had been. She could go to Mr. Bernstein's meeting with something definite to tell the people.

Fr. Malachi had been a little concerned that Goldie might not totally understand. He tried to clarify it for her by writing a note indicating the exact dates the hall would be available. Goldie could show this to anyone who might question her, particularly Kathryn McGrority Bernstein.

When Manya returned from work that evening, Goldie enthusiastically conveyed the information to her.

"Jews in a Catholic church? for such a holy holiday—or as a matter of fact, for anything?" Manya was sure Goldie had misunderstood.

"I understood, I understood. Gott in Himmel, where did I put it?" She scuttled around trying to find the note Fr. Malachi had written for her, then she remembered putting it in her apron pocket; she showed it to Manya.

"Where this involvement will lead us is beyond my comprehension, but it will have to run its course," Manya murmured, shaking her head. They could not now undo whatever it was the priest had to do to get the church's permission.

"It's a service in God's name," Goldie emphasized in her reasoning to Manya—and she had to confess, also, a service to herself. She couldn't leave a community of Jews to disperse to who-knows-what, but she couldn't define what she meant by "what."

But more important, she could not make a fool out of Fr. Malachi. She knew he could not have made that decision—such an important one—without his boss, the old priest. And the Bernsteins? What would become of them? No, that could not be her worry—or could it?

The worry began to feel like a stone—a boulder—rolling down a hill to stop suddenly, crashing against some obstacle. She recalled Manya saying, "You could tell them you changed your mind."

"But I haven't changed my mind. Are Catholics the only ones who should have a place to go during their holidays?"

"If those old Jews are willing to sit, year after year, in front of a store or in a house or outside a house and argue about the Talmud, and if Reb Herschel is willing to sit in his dining room and argue over a quarter for a boy's bar mitzva lessons, then why should you worry about them having a shul? Let each one make his own peace," Manya feverishly argued.

"And your peace?" Goldie questioned quietly.

Manya looked her mother straight in the eye. "Even my peace. I'll practice my religion in my heart, and then I won't have to answer to anyone."

"And your children's peace, daughter? Are you making their decisions for them?"

Manya replied, "They'll understand later. Religion doesn't need four walls. Do your praying in your heart and give to charity—that's my religion," and with that, Manya started toward the dining room.

But Goldie didn't give up. "It's not right to deprive a child of the knowledge of his heritage. A boy has a right to receive God's law."

Manya began to set the table. "Tell that to Reb Herschel. He refused Joey, and now everywhere I go I hear people—even the ladies where I work—say 'The young priest is a steady visitor at your house.' I hear it from this one or that one. Even from Mrs. Murphy upstairs . . . she's a good woman."

" . . . and Mrs. Holihan," Veeza added.

" . . . And from the Thomases because I told them," Joey chimed in. "I said my grandma has a fella—ha, ha! An' they said, 'Who? One of those old Jews from Little Jewtown?' And I said, 'Nah, it's Fr. Malachi,' and they thought I was jokin' and they all laughed. And there's everyone who saw Veeza at the church dance—they're all thinkin' we'll be Catholics—even if we aren't."

Veeza interjected, "Mrs. Holihan says I'm gonna marry a Catholic fella so I guess that will surely make me one."

Goldie remembered standing up and stating angrily, "No one is going to make us Catholics!"

She recalled stomping out of the room.

BOOK ELEVEN

A Rejected Proposal

~ 1 ~

The meeting started when Goldie, accompanied by Joey, arrived. Manya had said it was proper for a young man to escort his grandmother in the evening.

Dave Bernstein introduced Goldie, and she bobbed her head, not hearing names or even seeing faces in her excitement. He led her to a small table where she joined Kathryn Bernstein who was prepared to take notes with pencil and pad. Joey found a seat close by.

Dave explained to Goldie that there were a few other Jewish families who were interested but, for one reason or another, could not attend. In any event, there were enough present to discuss the issue. They all knew the purpose of the meeting. "Why don't you go right ahead and say what you need to say," he encouraged her, "and afterwards we can open the floor for discussion."

Goldie felt impressed and important. She was barely listening when Dave introduced her as "Mrs. Berron," and not until he nudged her did she realize that they were waiting for her to speak. This was an honor Goldie hadn't expected. She had never been to a meeting in her life, and now that she had created this situation, she wasn't sure what to say.

How strange, she'd thought, *with the good priest—who isn't Jewish—I can talk my heart out. Yet here with Jews, I am without words.* She didn't ever think that the priest might not understand her at times, but listened anyway; she hoped this would be the same.

"Don't be nervous, go right ahead," Dave whispered, and with that Goldie found her voice.

"My name is Mrs. Berron . . ." Goldie started, in her best Yiddish. "In Europe, my husband was a melamed." She didn't notice that some people were looking blankly at her, some with displeasure.

"We can't understand Yiddish," one man said in German-accented English.

For a moment, Dave was nonplussed. Then he said to the people, "I have forgotten that Yiddish is a language of its own—a jargon—with many variations. We'll go on and let Mrs. Berron explain as best she can, and then I'll try to explain it again."

"We lived in a village," Goldie continued, "a nice village near Kiev . . . but there was no shul. So wherever we could we made the best of it: in a house, a barn, a field—just to be near God."

Quiet fell on the group. Some nodded with interest, others sat with their heads down.

"But this isn't Russia," someone called out.

"There are no barns fit for a shul," another declared.

"A store?" Goldie questioned.

"A store," someone replied, "is for renting out to bring in some money for the owner. In a new neighborhood like this, the storekeepers barely make a living waiting for people."

"The neighborhood is more Irish than Jews, so they don't care one way or another whether the Jews have a place or not—some would say it's better that we don't!" someone else added.

As Goldie sensed the meeting getting out of hand, she spoke up, "I know a place!"

Dave Bernstein breathed a sigh of relief. *If the old lady knew of a place, why didn't she come right out and say so?* Then his second thought was, *Why did I get into this, anyway? I told Kathy that I'm no good at organizing this kind of thing. But she argued, "You're a Jew even though you married me and your grandfather declared you dead. You can't cut it out of your flesh and blood anymore than I can forget that I'm a Catholic."*

He remembered lying with her the night of their elopement, forgetting their families and thinking only of the soft way her body blended with his. His hands had cupped the full mounds with the strawberry tips rising firmly into his palms, until he felt his blood racing to a crescendo of shooting stars. Later, they lay as a single entity, gasping for air and marveling at the wonder of their oneness.

With difficulty, he brought his mind back to the meeting. The old lady was talking about a church. What church?

"The priest is most understanding. The Jews can have the social hall for their services with no charge, compliments of the older priest who is boss of the church."

As the group listened in stunned silence, Goldie waited for their pleased reactions.

The group's breathing was like the hissing of steam.

Kathryn looked at her husband as if he were interpreting the words wrong. How did a church come into this?

The watchmaker's wife raised her hands in horror. "I'm not a religious woman, but this I never heard! Jews should have their services right under the feet of Jesus? Ach!"

"Didn't you ever see those crosses, old woman," called out another, "with him hanging there for all the world to see that the Jews killed him?"

There was a babble of voices.

"Is this your idea of a joke . . . a rotten joke?" one asked Dave.

Dave started to rap on the table to reestablish some order. "Just a minute . . . just a minute."

Goldie tried to interrupt the clamor. "But you don't understand. All the world doesn't believe that the Jews killed Jesus—even the priest said so!"

"Tell it to the pogrom leaders in Europe and see if they believe it!"

One of the men stood up, shaking his fist toward Goldie. "Now I recognize her. I'm Sam Leibowitz, and they . . . " he pointed his finger toward Goldie, " . . . they lived on the same street as my cousin Jacobson. You're the bewitched one with the Christmas tree!" He turned to the group and continued, "She brought a Christmas tree into a religious Jewish home—her own household with Jewish children—and defied a whole Jewish neighborhood. Now she's trying to decoy us into the church by making us believe she wants to use it for a shul! She's trying to make fools of us. In her heart, she's a Christian, and that's why she's so familiar with the priest."

As the women stood up, their voices shrieking epithets, the men talked loudly and shouted at Goldie and at each other. Finally, they turned on Dave Bernstein. "You knew this!"

As Dave tried to protest, Sam Leibowitz looked at Kathryn. "Aren't you Kathryn McGrority?"

As Kathryn's face turned white, Sam Leibowitz gestured to the people. "Now we know the truth!" He pointed to Dave. "He's married to a Catholic—she's Mike McGrority's daughter, that Jew-hater! You see what a neat trick this is?"

As Dave went forward, fist clenched, Kathryn tried to protest. "But I married a Jew, didn't I?"

The women grabbed their husbands saying, "Let's leave this place," and Dave looked at his wife accusingly. "This is a rotten thing to get me into." The group began to disperse.

Finally, Joey took Goldie's arm. "Come, Baba, we better leave and go home." Joey couldn't understand why it was always Jews who got mad at Baba.

"Eeehhh. Eeeeee." No matter what her mind said, Goldie heard her own gibberish. She shifted herself but knew that nothing had actually shifted or moved even so much as an inch; it only felt that way. She had to be satisfied with letting her mind move for exercise.

That night on the way home from the meeting, Joey had said that he wouldn't tell a word to Mama or big-mouth Veeza about the big flop the meeting had been. Goldie tried to tell him that it was wrong to deceive his mama, but Joey said he wouldn't be deceiving her—he just wouldn't say anything.

Goldie looked exhausted when she walked into the flat that night, and Manya worried. *Does Mama think she is as young as she used to be, even taking a streetcar, going to a meeting? Since when is she a club woman, anyway?* She helped Goldie get into bed. "You can tell me tomorrow about everything," Manya said.

~ 2 ~

The following day there was a letter from Leon—and the proceedings of the previous evening were forgotten. Leon was feeling much better, and if he continued to improve, he would be able to come home. He might even be able to work at something light, something in the fresh air; fresh air is beneficial for anyone getting over consumption.

Manya spent the evening re-reading the letter and trying to figure out where Leon could get an outdoor job that would not overtax his strength. The meeting of the night before remained buried in her mind—which relieved Goldie's mind, at least for the time being.

Then another thought pushed the discussion of the meeting even further from Manya's mind: if and when Leon came home, Sean would have to go, and so would his room rent.

The following morning, Manya went off to work leaving behind a quiet Goldie. Veeza and Joey squabbled over who should get the jelly doughnut and who should get the cruller Sean had brought in that morning when he returned from work. Sean had also brought home rye bread.

"That German bakery makes the best rye bread," Joey exclaimed after gulping down the doughnut.

"Germans can't do anything that the Russians can't do better!" Goldie snapped. She put a piece of rye bread which had already been spread with butter back on the table. It would be adding insult to injury to eat it. Veeza, however, had no compunction about picking it up. She ate it with relish.

That night, Manya apologized for appearing uninterested in Goldie's meeting. "So what did they decide?" Manya asked.

Goldie shrugged off the subject. "The decision was put off, but whoever wants to go will go," and with that she gave Joey a significant, don't-you-open-your-mouth look.

~ 3 ~

As the high holidays neared, Fr. Malachi asked if Goldie had made the arrangements so that he could reserve the social hall for her. Veeza watched Goldie dig her one tooth into the edge of a lump of sugar and suck on it, but forgetting to follow it up with a sip of tea. Her baba's face was lined with deep thought. Finally, Goldie said to the priest, "I remember long ago when my husband—he should rest in peace—was a teacher, and all the talmudic students would sit around and discuss the history of the Jews. Sometimes a new interpretation would be presented and some of the hotheads got unruly. But those people at the meeting the other night wouldn't even listen. Why," Goldie commented proudly, "my Yussel even discussed Jesus . . . how Jesus said . . ." She frowned, trying to remember.

Veeza struggled to interpret, but finally Fr. Malachi dared suggest, "Jesus said, 'Forgive them, Father, for they know not what they do.' "

As Veeza translated, Goldie nodded appreciatively and went on. "I try to forgive those people for the hurt they caused that young couple more than for myself. Was it their fault that nature played a trick to make that boy and that girl fall in love?"

Veeza's mind jumped to the night Goldie had told her the story of Ruth, who wasn't Jewish either. *After her husband died, she could have gone back to her Christian family, but she said, "No, his people are my people."* If they can make all that fuss *over Ruth on account of that and write a big story about her in the Bible,* Veeza reasoned, *then those people in the meeting shouldn't have made such a fuss over the Catholic girl who married a Jewish boy because they were in love. Of course, I don't know if I'm in love with Johnny Burke, but I know I'd never say his people are my people!* So she concluded she really wasn't in love.

Fr. Malachi sipped his tea and then asked hesitantly, "You mean they didn't take to the idea of having your high holy days in a church?"

Veeza carefully translated for Goldie, and Goldie nodded sadly.

Fr. Malachi recalled his tense meeting with Fr. O'Neil when the subject was first introduced. Now, with a sense of relief, he questioned Goldie about concluding the matter. "Then no one will be at the social hall?"

But Goldie raised her head, almost defiantly, in protest of their lack of good judgment and to stress her own appreciation. "If I may have the honor, I will come—even if I am the only one there. I will not offend the courtesy your boss—the other priest—has extended to me."

As Veeza translated, Fr. Malachi thought, *She has courage, that old lady.* He replied, "It will be our honor to have you."

They sat quietly, sipping tea, each with his own thoughts.

Veeza was thinking, *I hope Baba is not getting herself involved with the Jews here—it's not even Little Jewtown.*

Fr. Malachi was thinking the same thing about Kathryn Bernstein—torn between the Jew she married and the Catholic blood in her veins.

~ 4 ~

It had been a typical holiday eve supper: the herring appetizer, the chicken soup, and the matzo balls made from cracker meal, all bought from the neighborhood stores and koshered by Goldie. After the meal, Manya put the finishing touches to a new dress for Veeza as Joey cleared the dishes.

"Why don't you sew a dress for yourself?" Goldie asked.

Manya shrugged. "What for? Where do I go except to work, and for that I look nice and neat. But the children, they need an appreciation for clothes. I want them to know by the feel that their clothes are well-made. They must understand that cheap wears like cheap. Joey will be out in the business world—a lawyer, please God—and Veeza too, whatever. And it makes a difference in their attitudes, their postures. There's more to clothes, Mama, than just putting them on, and I want the children to learn the difference by experiencing the difference not by the words of a salesman who has to sell or otherwise lose his job. So, thank God, I sew for them so they can appreciate God's blessings."

When the time came, Joey was slick and shining, and Veeza looked lovely in the new dress; they were ready. Manya handed Goldie the velvet case which Yussel had designed and which Manya had embroidered. She put the small altar cloth and prayer book into it, and with Joey holding the small menorah, candles, and matches in a paper sack, they started out.

"Mama, why aren't you coming with us?" Veeza asked. "It's for Jews, even if it is at the church."

Manya silently bent to straighten the hem on Veeza's dress; she had no answer.

"Yaaayaaa."

Goldie awoke to find Fr. Malachi sitting at her bedside. *How would he know that I was just thinking of him—or was it just now, or yesterday, or maybe tomorrow? Ha, ha, a joke!* But Goldie didn't feel like joking. *Does a prisoner sit in his solitary cell and make jokes while he is waiting for the executioner?*

"How are you?" the good priest is asking me even though I don't understand. But what else does one ask? A speaking person, a considerate person answers, "Fine." So here is my friend, and what else can he ask? How thoughtful he was that Rosh Hashanah Eve when we arrived at the church.

Fr. Malachi had come down the walk like he had been waiting for them. He greeted them with "Gut Yontif," like a proper Jew, and Goldie answered "Gut Yontif" in return. He shook hands with Joey man-to-man, and then gentlemanly with Veeza.

The priest then led them to the social hall which had already been lit. On the platform stood a bowl of flowers, and on each side a long taper was burning. Goldie thought, *How much those people are missing by not seeing this. They would have understood what I tried to tell them: we are all friends in God's sight.*

Veeza spoke up, "My grandmother was really worried that it would be bad for you to have only us here—that is, if nobody else comes."

Fr. Malachi reassured them. "It's our privilege," but at the same time he wondered what Fr. O'Neil's reaction would be if he knew.

Goldie smiled happily, bobbing her head, the little ribbons on the bow of her bonnet keeping time.

The priest then left them, and Goldie went about the small chore of setting up the menorah, inserting the candles, and setting out the prayer book on the altar cloth. She then lit the candles with a murmured blessing of the lights.

Finally, seating Veeza and Joey on either side of her, and with hands folded in her lap, Goldie sat in meditation.

"How are you going to say the prayers, Baba, if the prayer book is up there?" Joey asked in a half-whisper pointing to the makeshift altar.

Goldie put her finger to her lips and whispered in return, "I know them all by heart. The book is for those who don't."

Sometimes Goldie stood and other times she sat. When she stood up, Veeza and Joey followed suit until Veeza got tired of bobbing up and down and remained seated even when Goldie rose. It all seemed endless, especially with so many interesting distractions from the outside: someone's melodic whistling, the sharp cloppety-clop of a prancing horse pulling the fancy carts the rich ladies rode in. Veeza had wondered how anyone could stay in a place like that all evening.

Finally, Goldie asked them to repeat after her the Hebrew prayers.

They didn't hear the slim young woman slip into the hall and find a seat near the door. She thought, *This should be Dave here, not me. Why have I come?* She knew the answer—it was because she knew the old lady would be there, possibly with the boy or the girl. But the old lady would have to prove that what she was doing was right. She would have to show the priest that she appreciated the trouble he had gone to so that the Jews could have their service somewhere—especially in this church hall which had been offered to them in friendship.

Kathryn shuddered remembering that meeting in their home—and the aftermath. She remembered, too, an evening before they were married. Dave had puttered about outside until Kathryn finally put a wrapper on and went out to him. "I'm not sleepy," he told her.

But she had pleaded, "Tomorrow is a working day. You won't be able to keep your eyes open."

She had slipped close to him and had put her arms around his back until her palms reached his cheeks; her face rested between his shoulders. It was their favorite making-up position. That day, they had walked in the park, rowed on the lake, fed peanuts to the squirrels—and argued. Now, the argument started again—the same argument over the same thing.

"Dave, I can't marry a Jew!"

"You mean you won't!"

"I didn't say I won't—I said I can't."

"It's the same difference."

"My folks would never forgive me."

"And you think my folks will forgive me? My grandfather is a religious old man who can't say a good word about the goyim. You think he'll forgive me?"

"That's why we shouldn't get married."

"We're in love, Kathy! Or are we?"

Kathryn had turned pleadingly toward him. "Dave, why are you making it so difficult for me?"

He turned to face her, their bodies close, until their warmth intermingled. Dave reached for her lips, but Kathryn turned so that he only brushed her cheek. Dave then took her head in his grasp and forced her lips to his harshly, eating into her until it seemed he would tear her flesh. Kathryn felt herself fighting for air, and suddenly, there was no need for air. She was alive with fire, her body straining to his, and her kiss as vibrant to his lips as his were to hers.

"Oh, Dave, I love you so."

"I want you, Kathy."

They fell on the grass and clung to each other, their bodies entwined, their lips exploring each other's. Finally, breathlessly, Kathryn pushed Dave away. It took the full strength of her arms to break his grasp.

"My God, Kathy, don't do this to me!"

She felt her blood calm and her breathing return to normal. She looked at Dave still lying on the grass facing her, his glazed eyes beginning to focus, his breath coming slower and calmer.

"Don't ever do that to me again, Dave Bernstein!" Kathryn recalled saying angrily, knowing all the while that if he were to make one move to hold her close again, she would yield to him completely.

The air had been soft as a whisper, and the moon barely peeked through the clouds. Daylight had quickly faded.

Dave remained there, his body loaded with perspiration, angry at himself, angry at Kathryn, angry at the world for keeping them apart.

"God damn them all!" he had shouted as Kathryn watched him turn face down on the grass, his hands clenched. Slowly, she lowered herself to his side and rubbed her cheek against the hollow of his shoulders. She loved the feel of his firm muscles and his strong arms encircling her. He took her in his arms and they lay spoon-fashion until finally, Dave turned, and their lips met again—and again. That time, there had been no stopping their hunger for each other.

Later, as Dave wrenched himself away, all the agony and the beauty lay exposed between them. Dave had looked at Kathryn, the pins falling out of her softly braided hair, her disarrayed blouse pulling out of its skirt moorings. "It's no good, Kathy. If we can't get married, we've got to stop seeing each other. Please, let's marry."

Kathryn now recalled her father's blaspheming until every sentence was engraved into her memory. She remembered her mother's weeping and cajoling: "Yer father'll give you a trip to auld Ireland to be seein' his kin. If you can't find anyone here to yer suitin', there'll be plenty of young bucks over there who'll be after such a pretty lass as yerself—from America, no less!"

In the end, Kathryn had packed her valise while her father stormed, "You need never come back." Bridget wept and whispered, "There'll always be a door open for ya . . ."

Kathryn and Dave had married at city hall, with two strangers as witnesses, and moved into a furnished room until they could find a place near the school where Dave taught. Finally, they moved into a little house—a leftover from better days. It stood out like a sore thumb in an area which was building up with newly built flats and stores. But together, they had scrubbed and painted and haunted old furniture stores until they found just what they wanted to furnish their honeymoon cottage.

Indeed, it had been a period of adjustment. The two had agreed on a rest from religion until they adjusted to their marriage and their obligations to each other. Later, they would decide on how to combine or separate their religions from their personal lives.

But Kathryn missed her family, who had disowned her as Dave's family had done to him. After awhile, she also missed her church. But she had no intention of breaking her agreement with Dave.

Sitting there in the rear of the social hall, Kathryn sighed. She wanted to go and hold the old lady's hand and try to convey to her the admiration she felt for her courage. But she didn't want to embarrass the old lady or herself. It was Dave, the Jew, who should do that. *I wonder if Dave's anger was brought about by the same longing I have had and have been rejecting. The old lady is right. A person has to be in touch with God. True, one can worship anywhere, any place, with others or alone. To commune with God one doesn't need company. But churches are founded by communities—by people in communities, and if the Catholics can create their church right here, as they did, with my father laying the cement with his own hands, then the Jews should do the same.* She realized then that she had no business being there. It was their holy day, not hers.

Kathryn did not see Fr. Malachi on the walkway. When he recognized the slim figure, he paused and waited until she was out of sight. *What a kettle of fish this is!* he thought. *The Catholic one came, but the Jew didn't!*

Again he was grateful that Fr. O'Neil was away on retreat.

~ *5* ~

"Rrruuuooo." Goldie tried to scratch her nose; it itched. *Go away, itch. You know I can't scratch you.* Then she heard the dog: scratch, scratch. *You lucky dog. You probably scratched a flee who jumped right onto me.*

"Aaarrrugh." *Maybe that will bring Veeza. But then how will she know my nose itches? She'll probably say, "Baba, are you*

*hungry or thirsty or are you wet again and need changing? You
know what, Baba, Mama said to tell you she'll be back soon. She
went to pick up some work from Mrs. Smith."*

*How long have I lain here like this and how much longer will
it be?*

"Aarrhhee." The screech could be heard in every room.

When Veeza finally came in, Fr. Malachi was with her. When
she rubbed Goldie's forehead and face with a small, nice-
smelling cloth, the itch went away.

"The good priest hasn't been able to come much because the
older priest is away, and there is so much church business that
has to be taken care of," Veeza explained to Goldie.

Fr. Malachi looked at Goldie lying motionless in her bed. He
recalled that evening when Goldie and the boy and girl had come
to the parish house after the fiasco of the services. Joey and Veeza had explained that their grandmother wanted to apologize.
She felt it had been a mistake—in effect, a transgression—for
her to have forced her will against others, even in God's service.
She had decided to make her own peace with God—at home—
on Yom Kippur. She was sure of God's forgiveness for it was in
his name that she had tried.

The three of them had walked away somberly, and just as
somberly, Fr. Malachi had walked back into the parish house
thinking of what the old lady had said. Based on her wisdom, he
decided not to stop in to see Kathryn Bernstein, nor would he
pay a call on the McGroritys.

Manya dressed in her starched waist and herringbone skirt and
waited for the three to return. There was no sign of the sewing
she had done for Mrs. Smith; there was no point in stirring up
trouble by letting Goldie know that she'd finished the work and
had already delivered it.

"Gut Yontif," Manya greeted her family when they came in.

"Gut Yontif, daughter," Goldie acknowledged.

Joey and Veeza put the menorah in its velvet case, placed it
on the sideboard, and settled themselves at the table. Manya
went to set out slices of honey cake and the tea things.

"Can I have challeh and butter, too? I'm hungry!" Joey announced.

Manya smiled tolerantly. "After such a supper?"

"I'm a growing boy, remember?"

"Me too, Mama," Veeza added.

Manya smiled. "You're both growing so fast, I don't know how I'll keep you in clothes," she said, but there was no real worry in her voice.

As Goldie went to put her things away, Veeza whispered to her mama, "Don't be angry with Baba tonight, Mama, if she tells you anything."

Manya looked at her daughter in surprise. "One mustn't be angry on Rosh Hashanah. It's a happy holiday—the beginning of a new year. We should live and be well, a happy year . . ." *with your papa* she had wanted to add, but the thought of Sean's having to go was its own worry. She didn't want to think about any of it.

Veeza breathed a sigh of relief. She knew that Mama never meant to argue with Baba, but Mama had told her that everyone argues once in awhile.

"But it hurts Baba so," Veeza once tried to explain.

"And you don't think it hurts me?" Manya looked quizzically at Veeza.

Veeza put her arms around Manya. "Oh Mama, when I grow up, I'll never argue with you—even though you're old like Baba."

Manya patted Veeza's head, and as Goldie came to the doorway, Manya's voice was friendly. "How did it go, Mama? How many people were there?"

Joey quickly answered for Goldie, "There wasn't anyone there except us."

Holding the kettle for the tea, Manya stopped dead still.

Veeza turned on Joey. "You always call me a big mouth—well yours is bigger! Who asked you?"

"That's no way to talk to your brother, Veeza," Manya scolded.

"I don't care! He had no right! Baba was going to tell you!"

Manya poured their tea and motioned for them to be seated. She passed the sugarcone to Goldie, who snapped off a piece, placed it in her mouth, and then sipped carefully at the edge of her glass to test how hot the liquid was. No one spoke a word. Finally, Manya could restrain herself no longer.

"Is it true, Mama?"

"Is what true?" Goldie temporized.

"You know what I mean—is it true that no one came?"

Oh no, Veeza shuddered, *it's going to be an argument.*

Goldie shrugged, "If the children and I are no one, then it's true—no one came."

"Oh Mama, why do you have to make things difficult? Why can't you just answer yes or no? It would be so much easier for all of us."

"You didn't ask a yes or no question. Why couldn't you ask if it's true that the children and I were the only ones there. Then I would have said, 'yes it's true,' and you would have had the answer."

"Mama, you're just going around the bush."

"What kind of a bush?"

With his mouth full, Joey swallowed down his "Sunday" throat and began to choke.

"Slap his back! Slap his back!" Goldie cried to Manya as Manya jumped up to aid him. Veeza, too, ran around the chair and pounded on Joey's back until Joey finally drew a breath and yelled, "You don't have to crack my spine!"

While Manya asked Joey if he was all right, Goldie advised that he sip some tea, and Veeza smugly commented, "If I would eat as fast as you do, everyone would call me a . . ." She was about to say pig but caught herself.

The tension broke. Manya crumbled pieces of honey cake and put them into her mouth abstractedly. Goldie sipped tea, swishing it around the piece of sugar in her mouth, and Veeza sat, holding her breath and hoping that the argument would not start up again. Somehow, though, she knew it had to.

"It's a shame for the priest—he had to get permission and everything," Manya lamented.

"The priest wasn't mad at us, Mama. He said it was *their* shame and *their* privilege."

"Whose?" asked Manya.

"Theirs—the priest and the church."

"Anyway," Joey added, "he wasn't mad at us, and Baba told him we're not going back tomorrow because it's not fair to hold up the social hall, and the priest thanked us real nice."

"If they didn't come tonight, they surely won't come tomorrow. They'll probably all be taking care of their businesses," Manya pointed out matter-of-factly.

Goldie was shocked. "They can't! Nobody goes to work on Rosh Hashanah!"

Manya sat quietly for a minute. "I'm going to work, Mama. I was working tonight, in fact."

"You're saying that just to aggravate me," Goldie protested.

"No Mama, I mean it. It means bread and butter for the children. If I take a day off, I won't get paid for it. This week it's Rosh Hashanah two days and soon it will be Yom Kippur. I can't afford to lose that much money."

Goldie sat deep in thought. Then she conceded, "For the children, God will understand. You mustn't take food out of the mouths of children."

It seemed as though a multitude of problems had suddenly descended upon her. How simple it all seemed when she first started. But she knew better than to pursue the issue with Manya because she knew Manya had thought it all out: *Better not to be a hypocrite by going with them tonight and then going to work tomorrow.* But Yom Kippur, the holiest of holy days!

Goldie pushed away her tea glass and scooped up the crumbs into the palm of her hand. "Each one does as he thinks best, Manya. You have to do the same."

Manya sat quietly picking at one crumb or another at her place, trying to think of something to support her convictions. "Mama, we barely make out as it is." She sat a moment in silent distress. "There's nobody to put food on this table but me."

Goldie gently responded, "Nobody but you and God . . ."

"Aaarrrhhh."

The dog echoed, "Howlll."

Goldie thought, *Who says you can't teach an old dog new tricks? Lately, he sings a new song to me, like maybe he's trying to tell me the black angel is coming. But not yet, doggie. It's not time. I have much to think about, like the last chapters in my book of life.*

BOOK TWELVE

Leon's Homecoming

~ *1* ~

Mrs. Holihan shuffled the cards while Veeza sat with her heart exposed on her face.

"Well now," Mrs. Holihan said. "I see tears and I see gladness. Didn't you say your papa was well and is coming home?"

Veeza nodded. She was hoping she would recognize her papa, he'd been away so long—much longer than any of those other times. She felt a jab of guilt as she wondered if the tears Mrs. Holihan talked about would be hers if Papa didn't bring her a present. But that couldn't be. She'd never be that selfish. She really loved her papa.

Mrs. Holihan thought to herself, *Glory be to God, the timing will be just as it should be. The girls' room will be ready for Sean. Instead of a big weddin', they've decided to use their money for furniture, so they're plannin' to be married in the chapel without fuss or feathers. That way, there'll be enough in the till to hold us until Sean moves in.*

Mrs. Holihan smiled at Veeza. The cards looked very good. Veeza could hardly wait to tell her mother.

"That is a remarkable talent Mrs. Holihan has. Your papa is indeed really coming home," Manya confirmed.

"We're all going to be happy, aren't we, Mama?" Veeza questioned with a twinge of guilt as she thought again about a present.

"What kind of a question is that to ask?" Goldie chimed in. "Your papa has recovered from a serious sickness and that alone brings happiness."

A few days later, Manya brought herself to break the news to Sean. How the children would miss him and his morning offerings: large coffee rings studded with shaved almonds and raisins, the freshness of the cinnamon sugar still fragrant; huge loaves of German rye bread. Such little luxuries made life sweet.

Manya felt a pang of remorse. Sean was so vibrant. *Oh my God, don't let me remember again—so like Avrum. It's too many years for a memory to be so alive that it can still cause pain like the point of a dagger to a tender spot—and what is more tender than a heart?*

Sean's and Manya's eyes met. *If Leon's eyes are blue, then this man's eyes are the depths of an ocean.*

Sean felt the same fierce rush of desire for her as he had that Sunday morning he'd asked her to go to the park. They'd hardly spoken since, beyond a usual good morning or thank-you. He found himself barely containing a desire to bury his face in her neck, to suck the juices from her mouth, to carry her back into the little hallroom and smother her with his body. He was mad, he knew, but did not speak a word of his desire.

"I'll be packed and ready to leave by the end of the week, ma'am."

Manya felt weak. *Oh my God, spare me this. I have a husband coming home after a long illness, and who knows what condition he will be in.* Yet, her mind went to Sean's vibrant body.

~ 2 ~

"Yayayaya. Yayayay."

Goldie was bored. Her mind whirled like a mutchnik doing his whirling dance round, round, round. She was dizzy from it— or was it from thinking of that dizzy spell on Yom Kippur?

Nah, better I should think about the dancing back in our little town. How young we all were. Yussel, though, was no dancer; he was a learner, always studying books and writing down his thoughts. But others in the village could dance. None, however could dance like a Russian—not a Russian Jew, a real Russian— with muscles of iron, arms held out like, God forbid, a soldier holding a sword as he marches.

Thank God, our village was quiet. People left the village only to make a change for themselves—because of a marriage, a job, or to heal a broken heart. God Almighty, how many years it has been since I've thought of Avrum, who was the cause of our leaving our village. I wonder whatever became of him, sad soul. Poor Yussel, he should rest in peace, had no cause to leave. He had so much to offer the children of our village—he was so gentle. And he was respected for his talent and for his honesty, for his knowledge of religion . . . Ah yes, religion. What is it about Yom Kippur which brings the heat when it should be cool?

*It tests the fortitude of those who fast when not even a drop of
water is allowed to pass the lips.*

Manya had cautioned Joey and Veeza not to leave the house.
Even if they had no shul to go to, it was still a holy fast day to be
treated with respect, even by children who are not expected to
fast.

Goldie had sat silently, knowing that Manya felt she had to
work to survive—that was Manya. On a holy day, one doesn't
argue.

Veeza had pouted, though. "There won't be anybody to play
with. Everyone will be in school, so what am I going to do all
day in the house?"

"Learn about your own religion," Manya suggested.

No matter, neither were to leave in case Goldie got faint. After all, Manya impressed upon them, their grandmother was not
young.

Veeza put her arms around Manya. "Mama, nothing is going
to happen, and we won't leave Baba alone. You don't have to
worry while you're sewing."

The day remained special for Goldie. She sat in the parlor in
her yontif clothes and repeated her prayers. To all intents and
purposes, she was in a shul or some study house. Veeza was
glad they weren't in the church; a whole day of sitting and standing would surely be too much for someone as old as Baba. It
would even be too much for her and Joey. They'd had enough of
that on Rosh Hashanah.

"Baba," Joey asked, "what makes Yom Kippur different from
Rosh Hashanah?"

Goldie hesitated a moment then replied in formal fashion.
"Rosh Hashanah is a day of judgment. Abraham was asked by
the Lord to sacrifice his only son. But at the last minute, the
Lord let him substitute a ram."

"What's a ram, Baba?" Veeza asked.

"I know what a ram is," Joey interrupted. "It's a male sheep."

"Kinder, kinder, you can't learn if you interrupt. So, Rosh
Hashanah celebrates Abraham's act of devotion to God."

"You told us that already, Baba."

"So it won't hurt you to hear it again. Devotion to God is the
secret of a person's true belief in God. Anyway, God let Abraham sacrifice a ram, and from that time on, they used the horn of

the sheep which they call a shofar to welcome in the new year with a promise of goodness and joy.

"Now Yom Kippur is something different. It is the Day of Atonement—the holiest day of the year, when we ask God's forgiveness for our sins. For that, we have to wipe all our badness away. Come, kinder, it won't hurt you to learn a little. I'll say it in Yiddish, and you repeat it after me: 'Our Father, we have sinned before thee . . .' "

Veeza whispered to Joey, "That's the kind of prayer they say in the Catholic church."

Goldie shushed her. "Give us strength to make amends for our wrongdoings and grant us pardon for our sins."

"It's like confession," Veeza whispered again.

Joey pushed her. "Shut up!"

"For the sin which we have sinned against thee under stress or through choice . . ."

Veeza's eyes shut as if to blot out all those sins she had done.

"For the sin which we have sinned against thee openly or in secret . . ."

Veeza shut her eyes tighter. All her sins were coming out into the open. Then, with beautiful surprise, she realized that she was being really holy and truly praying the Jewish prayer for forgiveness. Her voice joined clearly into Goldie's Yiddish: "For the sin which we have sinned against thee in stubbornness or in error. For the sin which we have sinned against thee in the evil meditations of the heart. For the sin which we have sinned against thee by word of mouth. For the sin which we have sinned against thee by abuse of power. For the sin which we have sinned against thee by the profanation of thy name. For the sin which we have sinned against thee by disrespect for parents and teachers. For the sin which we have sinned against thee by exploiting and dealing treacherously with our neighbor. For all these sins, oh God of forgiveness, bear with us, pardon, and forgive us."

Veeza knew she hadn't done all those things—many she didn't even understand. But she was glad her special sins wouldn't stay on God's list anymore. *Wow,* she thought, *I sure am glad I stayed home from school.*

It was toward the end of the day when Goldie had her spell. From pale cream, her face went to beet-red. It was as if all the rays of the sun had suddenly focused on her. She panted for breath and could barely fan herself with her hand.

Veeza quickly ran to the sink, soaked a towel in cold water, and placed it against Goldie's forehead. As the towel would lose its coolness, she'd replace it with another until, finally, Goldie's skin tones faded back to their natural color.

"You're not to tell your mother about this," she warned Joey and Veeza.

"Are you sick, Baba?" Joey asked. "Maybe we ought to get Mrs. Murphy to call the doctor—or to send for Mama."

Goldie shook her head. "It is only the heat." She agreed to loosen her clothes and to lie down.

Subdued, the children watched their baba doze off.

"Do you think we should tell Mama?" Veeza had asked Joey.

"We promised that we wouldn't. We'll get a sin if we break our promise—especially on Yom Kippur."

Veeza had a quick vision of all the transgressions she'd just confessed and decided Joey was right. You don't start a whole bunch of new sins on Yom Kippur.

She looked at Goldie. Surely it was the heat and fasting. She was glad she and Joey had been there to take care of her. *But what now?* she wondered. *It's not much fun being so religious.*

In a short while Goldie awoke, refreshed and her usual self. "It is interesting," she told the children, "how God steps in. I had let myself get too tired, and he forced me to rest."

"Yayayaya."

As she lay in her bed, Goldie thought, *This much rest as he has bargained out to me is not what I had in mind that Yom Kippur morning.*

"Naaanaa."

But to whom am I protesting? To God, who has merely proclaimed his portion?

~ 3 ~

Veeza snuggled up to Goldie. "Oh Baba, I'm so glad we have our own room again—just you and me—like we did before Sean came. We miss the cakes and bread that he used to bring home, but it helped Mama out, so that is what matters first, isn't it?"

Goldie held Veeza close. "I missed you, too. Nature is funny; you can't snuggle boys when they're as big as you are, but girls are warm and snuggly."

"Baba?" Veeza hesitated.

"Yes, child?"

"Baba, you know when we asked God to forgive us all our sins? Does that mean I have to be Jewish Jewish?"

Goldie didn't understand. "What other kind of Jewish is there?"

"Well," Veeza tried to explain, "does it mean we can't be friends with the Catholics any more? Like they're Irish Catholics, so do I have to be *Jewish* Jewish?"

"That," Goldie admitted, "is a good question. And the answer is, a Jew is a Jew, unless," she hesitated, "like Jesus, he changes over. But Jesus did it for a cause—not like cousin Laban or Uncle Sidney. They decided not to be anything, which to my mind is even worse," Baba concluded.

"We don't have to give up seeing Fr. Malachi, even if he is a priest, even if it sounds in the book like we should?"

Goldie was surprised at Veeza. "Nowhere in the Good Book does it say to give up your friends. Besides, it is written in the Book, 'Malachi, the messenger of the Lord.' "

"But," Veeza reminded Goldie, "Fr. Malachi said that we are all God's messengers, to spread his word."

"Of course," Goldie answered, "don't you know that I know that? But the priest's name is Malachi, so he is the messenger God appointed. The others are his assistants. That makes our Malachi, our messenger, a very special person who has given us his friendship."

Veeza closed her eyes, a small smile on her lips. There was no one like her baba to explain things so she could understand.

In the room off the dining room, Joey lay in his bed, still keyed up from the day. He really didn't believe in all that prayer stuff. Besides, he hadn't done any of those things they'd confessed, unless it was riding a horse on Saturday at Tommy's place, which Tommy convinced him was no sin because "you don't go to church anyway on account of the Jews don't have a church. You can't sin if there's no place to sin against."

That was too much for Joey to think about, especially since the day was over. Whatever he'd confessed was already done, and he'd rather think about whether he wanted to be an inventor or not. *Maybe I'd rather be a lawyer, on account of a lawyer gets to outwit another lawyer, and everyone can see how smart you are. An inventor fiddles around with things and afterwards, what do you do with it if it works?—which nothing has so far.*

Well, I've cleared myself of whatever sins I've done, so I might as well try to sleep.

In the double bed, Manya lay alone feeling the emptiness of the side Veeza had slept on. She looked at the dark expanse of the parlor beyond the archway connecting it to the bedroom. Wide-eyed, she reviewed her error in judgment—letting Sean go before she knew exactly the day Leon would be home. Sean could have stayed until the day before Leon arrived; she still could have had the room swept and dusted and the bedding changed in plenty of time. Now there was no Sean, and the children were missing the crullers and the crumb cake that he'd leave them for breakfast. There was no money from his renting of the room, which made a sizable pinch.

Leon couldn't let his family know when he'd be returning because he himself didn't know until the day the doctor came in to say he could leave. Manya could understand that, but then shuddered. *No, I will not relive those moments again. "Haven't you any money at all?" Would they ask that of Leon? And does he have any money at all?* Then she felt guilty. *No, no. Wipe it out of your mind. Think of something nice.*

Leon's handsome face and blue eyes came to mind. Then, blending into and through the vision, she saw Sean's penetrating eyes. *Were they ocean blue or were they sea green? Why am I flushed? The man was hardly more than a stranger. "Good morning, ma'am. May I take you to the park, ma'am? Oh, naturally, with the children." The stalwartness of him. Will Leon be frail when he gets home?* She could not picture Sean as frail. Sean could take the world between his hands and shape it as if it were a loaf of bread.

Why am I concentrating on Sean so much? Oh, Leon, you were my love. Blended into her mind's eye came the power of Sean, untested but knowing. *Oh how my body needs to be loved.*

~ 4 ~

"Yayayaya."

Goldie recalled how sad it was during that period after Leon arrived home. They were all like strangers to each other.

Leon complimented the children on how much they had
grown, but the children hung back and didn't run to climb over
their papa or laugh until they were breathless as before. Manya,
never one to show her feelings, greeted Leon awkwardly, like he
was a guest she didn't know very well.

Ah yes, months—six or more—is a long time for a husband
and wife to be separated. Goldie felt for Leon as she had felt for
herself after that stay at Sidney and Paula's. She had returned to
find that the family had adjusted to being without her. Now she
felt sorry for all of them; the long awaited husband and father
was now more of a stranger in his own home than the roomer
had been.

Every day, Leon would leave the house to look for work—on
foot. Finally, Manya insisted he take carfare and "something in
the pocket" for a cup of coffee and whatever, even though it was
milk and eggs Leon needed. Every night, Leon would return, de-
spondent, falsely hopeful that tomorrow he'd find something.
The problem was that as soon as anyone heard he'd been in a
sanitarium for six months, they would turn away. Besides, most
of the jobs were heavy work.

Manya had been furious. "You've never done any heavy work
in your life, so why do you even think you can do it now?"

Leon would defend himself. "I have to feel I am trying even
though it seems a wasted effort."

"Aay! Aay! Yiyiyi." *How is it the bones can ache when there
is no ache in the body? Or is it only in my head that I imagine
the bones ache? So, what else is new?* Goldie's mind questioned.

"Ayayaya."

*I'll open my eyes and see what's going on in my world of four
walls and a ceiling and one dog who looks mournfully at me.
When he gets lonesome, he crawls up to my face, my neck, as if
to say he knows I'm going to leave him one of these days, but
meantime, he loves me.*

Goldie's eyes opened and she saw a figure sitting at her bedside. *Sidney? By what miracle did he find time?* Then she corrected herself. *He is my son—a product of Yussel's and my body.
Thank God for Sidney.* She resolved not to think of all those precious little bodies they'd left behind, little children in heavenly
rest. *Thinking so far back on God's judgment is a sin. You have*

rested in peace these many years, my little ones. Soon I will join you. A pleasure to think about.

Goldie remembered how Sidney, Paula, and the twins had surprised her after Yom Kippur. The twins—*God bless them*—were already inches taller, and they greeted their grandmother with proper respect, though Goldie could not envision either of them cuddling up to her like Veeza did, her little body full of warmth and budding life.

Paula had brought a length of material for a dress for Veeza. Goldie was moved. *Whatever Paula's life with Sidney is, she still has a tenderness hidden inside. Who knows?—if Paula hadn't started so early to make demands on Sidney, would he have given her so much? No matter, it is no affair of mine,* Goldie admitted. *Their life is theirs to live and resolve.*

The oil lamp sputtered as they visited. *Thank God no one is asking why we are using oil lamps when there are gas jets,* Goldie thought. But Sidney already knew; he didn't have to ask. In fact, he apologized for not adjusting the wick. Oil is difficult to wipe off, he said, and he didn't want the smell of oil on his gloves which, Goldie noted, he had not removed. Goldie remembered thinking how that small courtesy would have saved Manya's doing it when she got home from work. *She's facing enough problems,* she worried, *especially with Leon shlepping himself in after a day of looking for a job, more tired than a man who puts in a hard day's labor.*

"Ayyyaaa."

Goldie remembered yet another visit—and the stab to her heart—when Sidney broke the news that they'd bought a house upstate—as if Goldie had any idea where that was. They had come to say that they'd be busy with the moving, that as soon as they were settled they would write, that they wished the best for them all.

Paula reminded Sidney to leave something for his mother, ". . . maybe a little extra this time because you won't be seeing her so often." So the usual ten dollars became fifteen, and Goldie felt the tears come to her eyes. *A godsend.* Manya would be angry at the charity, but Goldie knew that part of it would go to pay the gas bill.

They wished the family good luck, and Goldie wished them mazel in their new home, knowing she would never see it—not that she would want to—because she would not be asked.

~ 5 ~

Veeza cuddled up to Goldie, who was deep in thought.

There was no man in the moon, Veeza had noticed that night, and would it have mattered? She might have asked him to look down on the world to see if there was one place that could have a job for her papa. *What about God's messenger? Maybe Fr. Malachi would know some place.* The last time he had stopped by after visiting Mrs. Murphy, he had said that he couldn't linger until Goldie woke from her nap, but assured her he would be by again.

On second thought, Veeza had reconsidered, *this kind of thing I should ask Baba about. Baba would know what is proper.*

And Baba did.

"No," Baba said, "this is not a proper thing to ask of the priest."

But Veeza couldn't understand. "We asked the good priest about where to get matzos and stuff for Pesach and about Rosh Hashanah, so why can't we ask him about a job for Papa?"

Goldie explained. "The first two—Pesach and Rosh Hashanah—have to do with religion. God's worship belongs to a priest's work. But a job for your papa is a personal thing and, if there are any jobs to be had, there must be Irishmen who also need them. No, you don't mix one thing with the other."

"Then can we ask God's watchman, the man in the moon? He oversees other places not far from Woods End, and maybe there aren't any Irishmen needing work in those other places."

Baba had considered that, but unfortunately there had been no man in the moon that night.

Veeza mulled it all over and finally said, "Baba, if we sit by the window and tell our thoughts to God without the man in the moon, won't they go up that ladder straight to him, just like they did the other time when you said God hears all prayers if there aren't too many and if they aren't unreasonable?"

Goldie admitted, "That's a possibility, especially the necessary part, and God knows how necessary a job is for your papa. Besides, what have we got to lose?"

Wrapped in a blanket, Goldie sat holding Veeza, and together they wished in their hearts that there would be a place for Papa. They wished until they were stiff in body and lighter in heart.

Then the two of them went sleepily to bed.

~ 6 ~

Mrs. Holihan read the cards while Veeza chomped on a sandwich of thick ham. The young girl eyed the crumb cake which she knew Sean had brought home to the Holihans like he used to bring home to her family when he lived there. She felt a little stab of jealousy.

Irene had asked her mother to read the cards to see if she was going to meet a fella who was as nice as Sean—since Sean was a hearty and kind Irishman, but so old, and kin at that.

"Away with you, child," Mrs. Holihan had said, giving Irene a healthy swat on the backside, but laughing as she did it.

Veeza vowed that she would marry an Irishman who could bake all the goodies Sean used to bring home and who could laugh and tease and sing and tweak her braids. She almost wished Sean was still rooming at her house, although it would mean not sleeping with Baba. It would also mean that her papa would not have come home—and the stab of jealousy became a stab of guilt. Her papa was once full of laughter, although she didn't remember him singing, which is understandable, because Sean sang like an angel—a boy angel who wears a robe like a priest and a halo on his head. Besides, Papa was Jewish.

Veeza's daydreaming was interrupted by Mrs. Holihan moving the chair close for Veeza to sit down. She started to shuffle the cards, and then one by one she laid them out.

Veeza shut her eyes and held her breath. It had been a long time since Mrs. Holihan had read the cards for her, and that was when the cards were not good. Now she hoped that there would not be bad news again. *Papa looks so sad most of the time and he and Mama never chatter like everyone does at the Holihans when the girls and their husbands are here. Talk, laugh, talk, laugh, play the piano and sing.* She envied them all.

"Mmm," murmured Mrs. Holihan, and Veeza watched with little pinpricks in her heart. Mrs. Holihan moved cards from one place to another, as if to find something good.

"Hmmm," she repeated, "I can't tell exactly what this means, but . . . there's definitely a letter."

"Is it a good letter?" Veeza asked, fearful of even mentioning the word.

Mrs. Holihan shrugged. "I can't exactly tell. I think it concerns your papa, though.

Veeza pleaded to Mrs. Holihan to try again. Maybe she could see more clearly if it was a good letter. With her heart in her throat Veeza waited as the whole procedure was repeated. Then Mrs. Holihan scooped up the cards, stacked them, and put them aside.

"Is it a . . . good letter?" Veeza asked worriedly.

Mrs. Holihan explained that it seemed to her it wasn't a bad letter, "so I guess I could say it is a good letter."

Mrs. Holihan then brought the crumb cake to the table, broke off a section of it, placed it on the table, and went to the stove to pour tea. "Will you be havin' a piece of Sean's crumb cake?" she asked Veeza, but Veeza said she'd have to be getting home. The truth was, she'd suddenly lost her taste for crumb cake.

"Baba," Veeza told Goldie that night, "I didn't tell Mama about the letter Mrs. Holihan said was coming. She read it in the cards, but I was afraid it might be a bad letter, and I didn't want Mama to worry about it ahead of time."

"That was very thoughtful," Goldie agreed. "Sometimes one has to know when to keep the mouth shut . . . You know," Goldie followed up, "that's one of my problems. Sometimes, I talk too much."

This thought caused Goldie to reflect, *I hope Manya never finds out how much I told Sidney and Paula that day they visited, to say nothing of the twins who don't know what tsuris is, thanks be to God.*

~ 7 ~

The letter Mrs. Holihan had seen in the cards arrived a few days later. Veeza had all she could do to keep from opening it in her anxiety. Joey snooped over her shoulder at the return address and asked, "Who is Mrs. Sidney Berron?" and Veeza had snapped, "Mrs. Sidney Berron is our Aunt Paula, stupid!"

Joey examined the postmark. "What're they writing from there for?"

"It is none of your business since the letter is for Mama."

"But if I'm going to be a lawyer, I have to get in the habit of checking out everything. Details could be clues," Joey argued.

"Are you going to be a detective, too?" Veeza snorted, but Joey wasn't fazed. "A good lawyer has to practically be a detective to sort out facts."

Veeza stuck the letter against the fruit bowl on the sideboard where Mama would see it. It can't be a bad letter if it came from Aunt Paula. She breathed a sigh of relief.

Leon noticed the letter when he came straggling in, haggard and weary from his job hunting. He picked it up saying, "They've hardly moved in, and they're writing already. That's certainly more than they did when they lived close by." He put the letter back to wait for Manya.

Goldie had supper ready by the time Manya arrived home from work carrying some of the dresses on hangers for her home sewing that night. "I'll read the letter shortly," she said, and in her mind she thought, *All I need is to read about the lovely new home they bought and how they are going to buy decorator furniture, and that we won't be seeing them for a while, it being some distance from here to there.* Manya knew what her reaction would be if they said their house wasn't far from the seashore or the mountains. Then she realized that she was just plain jealous. *Paula is entitled to as much as she can get from her husband.*

Veeza urged her mama to open the letter, but Manya decided it would be better if they could all have a quiet supper first.

With the dessert prunes, the argument exploded. Manya had finally taken the letter from the sideboard and read it, first quickly to herself and then, with pleasant surprise, to all of them, but directing her glances at Leon.

"Dear Manya . . . Sidney wants me to tell you that he has spoken to Mr. Jensen who is the owner of a business not too far from you by trolley and a transfer. Mr. Jensen is looking for a man who can write a good hand and is good with figures and who can speak well. Sidney did not discuss wages or anything, as those details would be up to Mr. Jensen and Leon. Leon can just go to the address, which I am writing at the end of this letter, and should tell Mr. Jensen that he is the person Mr. Berron spoke to him about. We wish you well . . . Paula."

Manya heaved a deep sigh of relief. "Imagine Sidney going to all that trouble!"

But Leon did not share Manya's enthusiasm. "Why wasn't the letter addressed to me? The job is for me—not you. And why didn't Sidney write the letter instead of Paula? It was a business letter, not a recipe that two women exchange. So, it means you all still consider me a gurnicht. It makes a big man out of Sidney, and everything else will be blamed on me."

Now Veeza could understand why Mrs. Holihan hadn't said it was a bad letter, but hadn't said it was a good letter, either.

Later that night, Leon and Manya lay side by side, as distant from each other as the bed would allow. They had not touched each other since Leon had arrived home—and Manya was relieved. She thought of the night she had tossed her hungry body about, torn with conflict and almost praying for forgiveness for her wanton thoughts. Would Leon be too frail? And there was the image of Sean penetrating her consciousness until she knew that if he had walked into the room, she would have welcomed what she had seen in his eyes that Sunday morning. Ah, to have let herself go!

As the days passed, Leon had made no approach to her. Had he lost his own capability? Manya felt her thoughts and doubts cut into her mind like a whip. *What kind of woman am I that I would measure that against the abiding love that has sustained years of privation and stress?*

In the dark, she gave a cautious glance at Leon, who lay unmoving, his eyes straight ahead, his face full of sadness. His eyes were still sky blue, and whatever weight he may have lost in those months, the nourishment and care given him had brought him home still able to withstand the pressure of looking for and being turned away from jobs. Manya knew—oh how she knew—what courage that took.

Not moving, still facing ahead, Leon quietly asked, "Why didn't you tell me it was a *man* roomer you had in the house?"

Manya caught her breath and parried the question. "What was there to tell? We needed the room rent. He was a cousin of the Holihans who just came to this country, and he got a job working nights as a baker. He came and went and I hardly ever saw him. In his free time he went to church and from church to the Holihans. And," Manya stated firmly, "that is all there was to it."

They lay in silence, the air seeming to have softened around them.

"But you are right about the letter from Paula," Manya went on to admit. "It should have been addressed to you. It was a man-to-man situation, not a wife-to-wife one like we were exchanging recipes."

Turning toward Manya, Leon asked, "Why didn't you agree with me when I first said that?"

Manya had no answer.

Leon shrugged. "Nothing has changed. Sidney is still . . . " he hesitated, searching for a word, " . . . a success, and by success he becomes the authority, and the authority has little regard for someone who is stamped a failure."

Manya listened to him and desperately wanted to remind him that her brother had made his own success just as he had made his own failure. They had each started on the same level. With a second thought, however, Manya thought, *Why rub salt in an open wound?*

"I'll go tomorrow to see Mr. Jensen, then we'll know."

Oh God, Manya prayed, *give Leon his one chance.*

As Leon turned toward her, Manya felt a surge of heat permeate her body—and she felt his strength.

~ *8* ~

"Arrraarrr."

Goldie yawned a wide, toothless gap. She was tired of sleeping—*day, night, who cares about time?* Where had she to go that it mattered, except she knew that time was running . . . for some too slow . . . for some too fast . . . but never stopping, a continuous circle of night to day, day to night.

Manya had put an extra blanket on the bed, and the winter's frost showed on the trees, bare of leaves. The cold brightness lit the room. *Oh, just to smell the air would be a mechaieh, and the luxury of a little exercise, even if it weren't bending to pick up coal.*

Then Goldie reasoned, *My brain is being exercised, but stretching the brain is not like stretching the arms and the legs. It's not like that good feeling of the shoulders making little cracking noises—a wonder how much the memory stores up.*

What a happy evening that had been when Leon came home to say that he'd gotten the job with Mr. Jensen. They all sat down to listen; nothing was more important. Even supper could wait.

"Mr. Jensen is in the trucking business," Leon explained, "not real big, but big enough, and being a Swede, Mr. Jensen wanted a family man. He says they're the most dependable. He wanted someone who could speak clear English and write a good hand for whatever has to be written, and to keep the books. Mr. Jensen's wife is expecting and has been doing the job with him, but now he wants to branch out both with his business and his family. She is going to stay away from the business from now on. He said that Sidney is a shrewd businessman that he respects, and when he recommended me he was sure I'd be the one for the job. It isn't too much money at first, but as the business grows, so will the wages."

As they all sat gasping with the excitement of the news, Leon added, "Sidney told Mr. Jensen about me being in the hospital, and Mr. Jensen said all the more reason why I would be a dependable person. Mr. Jensen said he was once laid up with a broken hip, and knew what it was to find a job after he'd been out of work for months. That's what brought him to start in the carting business, with an old horse and wagon which he bought on credit because the owner had faith in him."

It was as if Leon could not believe it all himself.

"Manya," Leon emphasized, "Sidney really recommended me!"

They all sat there, stunned with the wonder of the turn of events, and Veeza knew that Baba's and her prayers had gone right up the ladder, straight to God.

BOOK THIRTEEN
A Parting of Friends

~ *1* ~

"Jajajaj."

Goldie lay in her bed and thought, *Yes Sidney, my son, you did redeem yourself.*

"Guuuguuu." It was a pleasant gurgle.

Life had suddenly seemed free of worry, Goldie recalled. She had started going around spitting over her shoulder to ward off any evil eye lurking nearby, especially when she heard Leon and Manya discussing how much sewing she was doing. He wanted her to stop.

But Manya couldn't break the habit of worrying. She worried that one of the children would get sick or that the winter would be a hard one and more coal than ever would be needed. Manya wanted to continue working until Leon was well established in his job. Maybe, after he got a raise, she would slacken up a little. At least she would consider giving up her night sewing. Even if the gas bill could be paid on time, still, a little storing up for an emergency—*God forbid*—is good. One should be ready.

~ *2* ~

"Mama," Manya whispered to Goldie, "look who's here to see you."

Goldie's eyes focused on Fr. Malachi's sweet face. "Ugugugu," she stated with pleasure.

The priest sat next to Goldie's bed while Manya fixed tea, it being so cold out. Goldie smiled to herself knowing that Manya probably remembered the many times Goldie had told her, "The good priest comes to rest a little and to have a glass of hot tea." Goldie had showed him how to hold a steaming glass: "You don't wait for it to cool. You hold it with your thumb on the top edge and your middle fingers clamped to the bottom, not sideways like others do." She avoided use of the word goyim, but how better could one describe someone who isn't a Jew?

Goldie had also taught the good priest how to break off a piece of sugar from the cone, a solid piece of sugar shaped like an ice-cream cone. *Ja, ja. He's learned a few Jewish ways like he learned a few Jewish words,* Goldie thought to herself. She snickered aloud and blinked her eyes three times just to let Fr. Malachi know she knew he was there.

Goldie wanted to tell Fr. Malachi a few of her memories. "Aaarrruuu." It sounded strange to her ears. Perhaps it was a little loud, or maybe it wasn't loud enough. Lying still all the time, one forgets.

Goldie wanted to tell the priest about how Leon's boss had sent him a turkey just to show how pleased he was with Leon's work. She had planned to boil the turkey like she boiled chicken, but Veeza had said, "No, no, Baba, you stuff it like you stuff kishka. You put it in the oven until it browns, and when the drumstick—the pulka—moves easily, you know the turkey is done."

"You mean Mrs. Holihan doesn't make soup first from it?" Goldie questioned. "Such a waste."

"Oh, yes," Veeza continued to explain, "Mrs. Holihan makes soup, but after the turkey meat is eaten up. She saves the bones and puts in all kinds of vegetables and rice or whatever else is around and cooks it and it makes a thick soup to feed the family for a couple of days more."

Lying in her bed, Goldie cackled. *Who says the Irish can't teach a Jew something?* "Aarruu!"

Fr. Malachi sat listening, holding and patting Goldie's cold hand and nodding like he understood every noise. Shortly, Manya told him the tea was ready. She apologized for the store-bought cookies. "Mama has always been the cook and baker in our household."

"Indeed, I have had the pleasure of tasting many of her tidbits," the priest commented with a soft smile.

Manya thought, *How did Mama sit and prattle with this man? She would enjoy relating everything to him. When there was a problem, she'd spill out her heart to this priest. When Veeza was not there to interpret, he somehow still understood what she was saying. Yet, here I am with things I have to tell him, and I feel shy.*

Yet she had to know if for no other reason than she had to know. She felt awkward addressing him as Father; as a matter of fact, the few times they'd met, she didn't recall addressing him at all. She had usually responded with "Yes, Mama had a good night," or some such comment. Now she found herself sitting and making small talk. But still, she felt she must know.

"Excuse me . . . is your tea hot enough?" Then she felt angry with herself. She, the strong one, couldn't find the courage to ask a simple question of this priest who had been such a friend to her mama.

Suddenly, she found the words coming direct. "Did you know that my mother considers—no, believes with all her heart from the first time you started coming here—that you are, how shall I say it, the soul of . . . no, that is not the correct word . . . that you are Malachi, the prophet, God's messenger? She once asked me to read the section in Scripture where the prophets are listed, where it says, 'Behold, I send my messenger, and he shall clear the way before me.' From that time on, she has been convinced that you are that messenger sent by God on a special mission."

Manya went on to tell Fr. Malachi how she had poked fun at Goldie. "Why would God choose to send a Catholic priest to a Jewish old lady who can't speak or understand English when there are Catholics all around who might need him as much? But my mama never thought it proper to question God's motives."

Fr. Malachi placed his hand on Manya's arm and patted it lightly, as if to reassure her. "I feel honored. She is—forgive me for expressing it so—she was a remarkable old lady."

He sipped his hot tea as Goldie had taught him and lifted his glass in a small gesture of salute. "Guten Welt."

"I can hardly believe she's been . . . as she is . . . for so many months."

~ 3 ~

"Aaarruuu."

Goldie looked at Sidney sitting beside her bed, his face a mixture of emotions, as he turned from Manya standing by.

Ach, Goldie thought, *how tragic . . . we wait until it is too late . . . how many times he sat with one foot towards the door, without interest when I could talk. I'd think, Sidney, make a little joke, or laugh a little when I make one, or at least listen to my mama-loshening over some little something. Never mind that I am your mother, I am still a person. You go to a museum to look at a statue, but with a person you exchange a word here, a smile there ... not like I had to do—to shlep words out of you, like trying to pull a donkey who doesn't want to go. Now, the only difference is, I can't even do that ... and it is too late for you to start.*

Goldie could feel the tears welling up in her eyes. Sidney leaned over and asked, "Mama, are you hurting?"

"Aaarrrhhh," Goldie replied, but her mind was saying, *Not anymore, my son.*

Goldie remembered warmly how Leon had been the one to bring home the Christmas tree that year after coming home. Leon, who had steamed and fussed when Goldie and Veeza brought home a little tree the night of the Youngs' Christmas Eve party the year before.

He had tried to explain. "I was waiting for the streetcar on the way home from work and there were trees displayed. People waiting for the streetcar were friendly and said it was better to buy one early before the nice ones get picked over. There was this little tree, so symmetrical—not too large to sit on the parlor table." With a silly grin, Leon finished explaining. "There it sat, kind of looking like it was asking me to buy it, and I thought if I waited to come home and ask you . . . "

" . . . that I might say no?" Manya completed his thought.

Veeza was the first to come to Leon's support. "But Papa, I would have said yes, and Baba would have said yes, wouldn't you, Baba?" Veeza asked, turning to Goldie. "This tree even looks like the one we bought, doesn't it, Baba?"

"It's prettier, and that's the way it should be," Goldie said.

"Yeah, and there are no Jews around to make a big mishmash about it," Joey pointed out.

Manya looked at the tree appraisingly and admitted that it was a nice little tree, neither too large nor too small. And with that, the household relaxed. A mechaieh—a pleasure.

Goldie unearthed the box with the pompoms and the wool chain they'd strung across the branches the year before, only now the wool looked dull and shabby. No one seemed to notice, however; at least no one mentioned it. Manya even suggested that they buy some shiny things to fill in the spaces, but Goldie protested, "Don't even use mine. After all, they were a gurnicht put together just to make things for the tree last year."

"But Baba, Mama says that handmade things are better than storebought," Veeza pointed out, and Goldie's face glowed.

They all finally agreed that maybe a few shiny ones would be all right for such a nice tree, but not so many as to outdo the remembrances of their first Christmas tree.

"The rest of last Christmas," Goldie said, "can be forgotten, just like in life itself—remember only enough of the bad to double the appreciation for the good."

~ 4 ~

That Christmas Eve, the Murphys came down to bring a bottle of brandy, and Goldie gave the Murphys a loaf of honey cake she had baked. Irene and Mrs. Holihan came with a present for Veeza, and Tommy came with something for Joey.

Veeza was proud her papa was now working and didn't go out to play cards anymore. Manya had even given her and Joey a little something to buy a gift for each of their friends, so as not to be just taking all the time. Manya was fussy about "just taking."

Everyone admired the tree, and the party was almost like the party at the Youngs last year, but there was no harmonica.

Then Mrs. Murphy asked Mr. Murphy if he would whistle a tune. "He courted me whistlin' all those tunes that are old now, so maybe he's forgotten them." But Mr. Murphy whistled and everyone couldn't get over how good a whistle sound could be. Mr. Murphy didn't whistle like the boys do; it was more like music.

Mrs. Murphy started to hum "Silent Night," and then they sang "Jingle Bells." Manya served cherry wine—her very best—which everyone enjoyed, and Mr. Murphy joked that maybe Mrs. Picker could give him a few tips on making beer. Mrs. Murphy cuffed his ears for being so sassy, and Baba got up and danced a little jig like she'd done at the Youngs last year.

Later in the evening, the company returned home to rest for midnight mass.

Veeza thought, *This is the first party we've ever had, and it was a very good party with Mama and Papa and Baba—and Joey.*

"Aaarrruuughghgh." Goldie heard herself ask what time it was, what day it was, what month it was, and how long she had lain there. She remembered her first pain on Yom Kippur when Veeza and Joey had helped her to bed, and she had told them not to tell their mama. The pain had been like a hot poker burning into her head, which she'd thought was from the heat and the fasting.

If she had died on that holy day, she would have been cleansed of all her sins—such as they were, she thought modestly.

The next pain came that Christmas Eve, the night of their party. So it had been Yom Kippur and Christmas; at least God wasn't partial!

~ 5 ~

Goldie felt herself settling in to remember again—and more. If she was going to look back on yesterday, she might as well recognize that parting from this world quickly is not the worst way to go. It is the waiting—the slow torture of the waiting—which is so awful. She had lain motionless for many months now.

In the Scriptures it says that a person loses his hold on life when his time has come, like a leaf from a bough. When his time has come; not before, not after. A simple statement of fact. And it says that the body returns to the earth from whence it came, but the soul goes up to the heavens to shine in the firmament.

Beautiful. That will make Veeza very happy, because she believes every soul is an angel who looks down to watch over everything. She'll like thinking that her baba will be looking down on her, thinking of the many nights we've talked, and how we each learned something from the other.

How Goldie wished she could discuss this with the good priest. He'd be interested.

The next time she opened her eyes, Fr. Malachi was at her bedside, holding her hand. *How beautiful to wake up from sleep to find someone holding my dead hand. A hand is a pleasure to hold, to fondle, to squeeze. But a lifeless one? A man of God, truly, Malachi, God's messenger, to sweeten my soul.*

How clear her eyes are, the priest thought, *blue as little patches of sky. Amazing how smooth the skin and even yet, the faintest pink tones showing.*

As her eyes focused on him, Fr. Malachi felt a kinship with Goldie beyond comprehension. "God have mercy on her soul," he murmured.

At that moment there came an eerie wail from the dog and Fr. Malachi felt Goldie's hand quiver in his. He watched her eyes close like those of a drowsy child, the barest hint of a smile on her face.

Holding Goldie's hand tenderly in his own, Fr. Malachi whispered a loving farewell to his friend.

~ *6* ~

Mrs. Murphy and Fr. Malachi took control of the situation. The doctor was sent for and a certificate of death made out. Manya was put to bed with a sedative to keep her from fainting again; Joey and Veeza were kept occupied helping Mrs. Murphy.

Veeza showed Mrs. Murphy where Baba kept the white linen shroud. "Baba said Mama sewed every stitch while they were still in Europe. That means Mama sewed on it while she was a young girl. Once she told Baba that hopefully the shroud would not be used for a long, long time. And that's the way it worked out." Veeza added, "After Mama's other babies died, she didn't want Baba to die, too."

Veeza went to the closet where the box was, and Mrs. Murphy helped her lift the shroud from the tissue paper. Veeza showed her the tiny stitches and said proudly, "That's why my mama can sew for the rich ladies here."

Mrs. Murphy listened, knowing it was relieving the child's grief to speak so freely of her baba, now a corpse on the bed waiting to be washed. Mrs. Murphy had volunteered to do the washing, being so fond of the old lady.

Veeza helped Mrs. Murphy by making sure that the water was not too warm and not too cool. She made sure the washcloth was not ripped or shabby. Veeza tried not to look at Goldie, but when she did see her, Baba didn't appear any different to her. *The tiny smile on her face makes it look like she is thinking of something nice. If Baba can be dead and have that little smile on her face, she must already be in heaven.* That comforted Veeza.

When Leon arrived home, confusion set in. Where would he go for advice on how and where to bury Goldie? He knew he would have to get the advice of the old reb. Who else would know about burial for a Jewish soul?

Joey begged his father not to ask him to go along. "The old reb is a mean man. If he sees me, he certainly won't talk to you, Papa."

Then Veeza offered to go so her papa wouldn't have to go alone. Leon figured that the old reb might feel more kindly if a child was present. In any event, no old reb, no matter how arbitrary, would be so cruel as to abandon a Jewish soul to wander forever without a place to lay her head. There were tales of such punishment for the ungodly.

~ 7 ~

As usual, Reb Herschel sat in his cluttered dining room. He listened to Leon's tale and then shook his head dolefully as he commented, "A bad end—a bad end." Leon sat impatiently while the old reb continued. "What other end can a woman expect when she takes on Christian ways? I heard from Jacobson's cousin how that frummeh piroshka even tried to convert the few Jews in his neighborhood on the other side."

Leon tried to point out that time was short and that there was much to be done, but the reb would not be interrupted; he went on and on. Finally he paused, squinted his eyes, and pursed his lips. "Was there a . . . Christmas tree . . . again this year?" He spat to ward off a curse.

While Leon tried not to admit it, Veeza shook her head no, and the old reb invoked the devil on them both for conspiring in a lie.

Finally Leon admitted, "There was a tree, but *I* bought it, not my shviger."

"You are all accursed," the reb shouted. "She bewitched you all! Go to the goyim! She wanted to be one, so let her be buried like one! They have a party where they all get shikker, so enjoy yourselves. But get out of here before you bring the devil down on this house!"

Leon was immediately angry. "If that's the way a reb, the most respected of them all, behaves, then I don't blame my shviger for wanting to become a goy!"

After leaving the reb's house, Veeza tugged at Leon's sleeve. "Papa, she didn't want to become a goy! It was because she wanted the Jews to have a shul for the holidays that Fr. Malachi loaned her the church hall. He even covered up the cross, and Mama said that was the proof of a real friend."

"Then we'll go there to ask for his help," Leon concluded with hope.

In his study, Fr. Malachi listened to Leon as Veeza sat, her face frozen in misery. The priest took the certificate of death which Leon had intended to show to the old reb. Leon now realized that the old man wouldn't have been able to read it anyway. The priest suggested the two go home where they were surely needed. "I will take care of the necessities."

"Assure the undertaker that the costs will be taken care of; I trust your judgment, Father," Leon said, and Fr. Malachi thanked Leon for his confidence.

As they left the parish house, Veeza turned to Leon with a sense of comfort. "He really is God's messenger, like Baba always said, isn't he, Papa?"

Leon, his mind now on other problems, patted Veeza's head.

~ *8* ~

Hours later, the priest and the undertaker arrived with a plain pine coffin which they placed in the parlor. At the head of it, they placed the little Christmas tree, its ornaments shining like tributes in the soft winter moonlight.

The undertaker lifted the frail remains of Goldie as gently as a father would lift an infant. He placed them in the coffin as Mrs. Murphy slipped a soft pillow under Goldie's head and adjusted the pad. Goldie, in her shroud and matching ruffled cap, lay like a peaceful saint, the small smile testifying to her peace.

Veeza went to tell Manya that Baba looked beautiful, but Manya could not bear the thought of Goldie really being dead and lying in a coffin. Manya, the strong one, was powerless against this finality.

As Mrs. Murphy came in to comfort Manya, there was a knock on the door, and a tremor seemed to go through the flat.

Leon went to answer while Veeza cowered close to Joey, all of them fearful that it would be the old reb come to blaspheme them again.

Instead, in the doorway stood Herbie from the fish store.

Leon hesitated; he didn't know Herbie, but he knew it was someone from the old neighborhood. His first reaction was to shut the door and wipe out the memory of his encounter with the old reb, but Herbie quickly interjected.

"I heard about the alte baba, but I had to wait until the store was closed to come to offer help. No matter what the reb thinks, a person, a mensh, is still entitled to have a prayer man to cry over her. So, if you will accept me, I would like to sit and say the prayers over Goldie."

A myriad of thoughts ran through Leon's mind: the priest, the desiccated Christmas tree, and Irish Mrs. Murphy with a brogue as thick as clabbered milk comforting Manya and the children. This is hardly a Jewish household, yet this Jew wants to say prayers over Goldie. He opened the door and invited the man in.

Herbie seemed to take no note of the situation. He nodded to Fr. Malachi, sat down and opened his prayer book, and together the Catholic priest and the Jew prayed through the night.

As dawn broke, Herbie stood up and offered his hand to Fr. Malachi. "You're a good man, sir," Herbie said, "and a true friend to these people." The priest shook Herbie's hand in return and answered, "You are, too, and I appreciate it for them."

Wan but composed, Manya joined Leon in thanking Fr. Malachi and Herbie and offered them a cup of tea. But both men said they had to go about their own normal duties, and Leon showed them out, wordless in his appreciation.

Fr. Malachi privately told Leon that the undertaker would be there early. "It might be wise to feed the children a little breakfast to be sure that Manya has something to do. That will no doubt be a trying moment."

~ *9* ~

Joey, Veeza, Manya, Leon, Mrs. Murphy, and Fr. Malachi all rode together with the driver of the single carriage. Mrs. Murphy apologized that the mister was on the early shift—he knew the family would understand. Manya expressed appreciation and explained that her own brother and his family were away on vacation and could not be reached.

Joey and Veeza sat wide-eyed at this new experience, viewing the world from the seat of a carriage drawn by a horse with a lacy shawl on its back. Baba would have appreciated this touch of elegance. *And even if Baba is not here to appreciate for real,* Veeza thought, *I can hear her say, "Any first time is an experience in knowledge," so Baba and I are experiencing this together. Baba would like that.*

As she listened to Fr. Malachi's short eulogy, Veeza thought of how good God had been to give them Goldie as a baba and this priest as a friend. She didn't want to look at the hole they were going to put her baba in, though, so she closed her eyes, peeking just a little bit until it was done. Fr. Malachi bent down, picked up a clump of dirt, said something she couldn't hear, and tossed the dirt into the open grave.

With that, Veeza screamed, "Don't throw dirt on my baba!" Gently, Leon took Veeza into his arms and led her away, explaining that this was part of everyone's burial, Jew and Christian. "It only means that God made the world, and the earth is part of the world. So when a body is taken back by God, a handful of the earth goes back into the world from which it came."

But Veeza couldn't understand. *How can God, who is so good, have even thought of that? Baba would never let us throw anything at anybody, especially dirt!—and never on someone who couldn't throw it back!*

The funeral carriage delivered the family and friends home, but without Baba, home wasn't the same. It was just like that time when they had sent her to Uncle Sidney and Aunt Paula and the twins.

Veeza felt sorry for her twin cousins. Now, they'd never get to know what a wonderful baba they had had.

That night, Veeza curled up in a blanket and crossed her arms as she sat on the windowsill in the little hall bedroom; she peered up at the sky.

"You know, Baba," she said, "I saw the new star tonight, and I knew it was yours because it kept winking at me like you were saying, 'Here I am watching out for you just like I told you I would.' And when I see Fr. Malachi, I'm going to apologize to him about my screaming out at the funeral. I'll tell him about Papa explaining to me that even if it was only dirt, it was like giving back to God something that he loaned to us . . . because even dirt is important—plants get planted in it and vegetables, too, and all kinds of things. Papa said something like 'from the earth you came and to the earth you return,' but I didn't think it

really meant us. So I guess I have a lot to learn yet, and that's when I'll miss you the most—to ask you about lots of things we didn't get to talk about. But like you once told me, Baba, you learn something from everybody, even if they're not Jewish, and especially from a priest who has to go to a very special school for years and years—and Fr. Malachi even more because he is God's messenger. Of course, I don't know how the whole world can get along with only one of God's messengers, but like you said, the whole world gets along with only one God, and when he pronounced it, the whole world stood still and there wasn't a sound." Veeza sighed, "I guess the world was as quiet then as it is right here, now."

Perking up, Veeza continued. "Now, Baba, I have to tell you about the Christmas tree." She took a deep breath. "Mama helped Papa take the tree down, and Joey helped Papa put the branches in the stove. And like you said, it came to a good end, because it warmed the house, and it smelled good, and that's better than it bein' put out in the trash. And then we put the ornaments in their boxes and Mama said, "Put Baba's away very carefully because we'll use them—we should live and be well— as long as they hold together. So I guess we're gonna have a tree again next year, and I knew you'd be glad."

Veeza yawned. Looking up toward the sky, she smiled and said, "Star light, star bright, I'll look for you tomorrow night—if it doesn't rain, of course." She giggled. "I know you're smiling, too. Good-night, Baba. I love you."

Then Veeza tucked herself into bed and slept—and the man in the moon looked down and smiled.

BOOK FOURTEEN
The Covenant

~ 1 ~

Fr. Malachi sat in his study, his thumbs and forefingers rubbing at the ache pounding in his temples. He was not given to headaches, but knew he had been brooding over the death of the Jewish grandmother. Why? Death in itself is no novelty, even to a young priest, and months had passed since the family moved. They had come to say good-bye—and to leave a generous offering, and to thank him for his friendship. That should have been the end of it.

Then why wasn't it?

The answer, he conceded to himself, is that he had been blocking out a basic fact: the old lady had started the wheels turning in his mind, causing him to wonder why the Jews weren't doing anything about a place of worship of their own. *Of course,* he reasoned, *that's none of my concern. After all, St. Mary's is still without a real church, despite Mike McGrority's earlier bragging about the beautiful structure he would build the parish. . . But Mike is an embittered man, and it will take more than a pat on the back to win him back to the Lord's graces.*

The problem of the Jews having no place to worship is, in effect, their problem, not mine. To each his own.

But Fr. Malachi, in total honesty, knew he was avoiding deeper thoughts. He was blocking out the one fact which the child's mother, Manya, had revealed to him and which was now hanging like a noose around his neck. The grandmother, Lord have mercy on her soul, had accepted him with total conviction as Malachi, the prophet, God's messenger. He could see her blue eyes trusting as a child, and he felt a sense of impatience with himself. Goldie had gone to her heavenly rest, the family had moved, and that should have been the end of it.

But instead, it plagued him.

Malachi, chapter three: *"For he is the messenger of the Lord of hosts. Behold, I send my messenger, and he shall clear the way before me, and the Lord whom ye seek will suddenly come to his temple. And the messenger whom ye delight in, behold he cometh. And he shall purify the sons of Levi and purge them as gold and silver that they may offer unto the Lord an offering in righteousness. Then shall the offering of Judah and Jerusalem be pleasant unto the Lord as in the days of old and in former years."*

Fr. Malachi's weary head buzzed with quotes, in and out of context. Finally, he let go, whispering a prayer for guidance.

He felt a sense of relief that he would not have to face Fr. O'Neil who, unquestionably, would have no sympathy for his headaches. He allowed himself a wry smile; Fr. O'Neil was away on retreat again, in an effort to conquer his own recurrent headaches.

Realizing that his stomach was growling, Fr. Malachi looked at his watch only to discover that it wasn't ticking. He shook it, held it to his ear, and commented to himself, "I guess a watch is like a human being; it needs a little doctoring once in awhile. I'll stop by the watchmaker on my rounds." Flexing his weary shoulders, he went to have his breakfast.

"You look a little peaked this mornin', Father," the housekeeper commented. "What with Fr. O'Neil away, you're doin' the work for two people, and that takes extra nourishment—for body and soul."

Suddenly, Fr. Malachi felt especially weary. *"Malachi, the messenger . . . and he shall clear the way before me . . . and the Lord whom ye seek will suddenly come to his temple . . . and the messenger of the covenant whom ye delight in . . ."*

What was its portent?

~ 2 ~

The watchmaker was a little surprised to see the priest, and for a moment was uncertain as to why he was there. Still, he thought, even a priest can be a customer. He recalled the evening at the Bernsteins when the old lady had mentioned that she was friends with the priest. He hoped that the old lady was not the reason which brought the priest to the store. Then, when he went to attend the priest, he was relieved to notice that the priest had a watch in his hand. Obviously, the call was business.

Fr. Malachi explained that the watch had stopped running. As the watchmaker snapped open the case, he complimented the priest on the quality of the movement. "Ah, there's nothing like a Swiss watch." After examining it closely, the watchmaker told the priest that it merely needed cleaning. "If you'll be in the area, you can pick up the watch this afternoon."

As the priest left the store, the watchmaker felt annoyed with himself, a feeling he could not quite understand. Then, shrugging it off, he went back to his work.

It was Bridget McGrority, on her way to a meeting, who next crossed Fr. Malachi's path. She apologized for having only a moment to pass the time of day as she was late already. It was obvious she wished to avoid the subject of her errant husband and his absence from the church. Fr. Malachi made a mental note of that and wished her good day as they parted. He knew there were times when one pushes religion and times when one doesn't. This had not been the time.

Next, Mrs. Collins, groceries in arms, sighted Fr. Malachi coming toward her and made an apparent effort to hide the out-jutting feet of a goose. With a slight smile, the priest helped her to readjust the packages and commented that there was nothing tastier than fresh-killed poultry and fish snagged right out of the tank—and the Jews surely have a knack with their breads. He could almost see Mrs. Collins's body relax as he bid her good day.

Then to the Murphy flat.

As he reached the first landing, the priest realized how strong habit is; he almost expected Goldie's welcoming smile to greet him in the doorway before he started up the stairs to the Murphys.

It proved to be one of Mrs. Murphy's good days. She bustled about with no sign of the asthma which plagued her constantly. She served him a cup of tea and filled him in about the new tenants. "So far, there's been no minglin' with them. Ah, I miss that Jewish family, especially the old lady and those well-behaved children." Then she snickered. "I never let on to the family about a funny incident which, of course, would have upset them. My mister was on his way to work one day when he saw this one little girl cryin', and he bein' the softie he is, he stopped to ask her what was wrong. She told him that she'd lost the dime she'd been sent to get milk with and she was afraid to go home because she might get a beatin'. So he gave her a dime and went on his way. It occurred to him that he'd seen that child somewhere, an' as he turned around, out of nowhere came another little girl; both little girls laughed and laughed. Then the first child hid and the second one stood in her place waitin' for the next easy mark to come along." Mrs. Murphy chuckled. "Of course, we never let on we knew the little girl was Veeza, no matter how many times we saw the family—Mrs. Picker bein' so proper about raisin' the children."

Mrs. Murphy refilled the tea cups and went on. "No, we figured we'd let Veeza's conscience do its own work. Each time she saw us, we knew she'd be fearful the mister would recognize her, and that's a lot of punishment for a little girl to face."

Fr. Malachi's mind wandered back to the time he'd come to call on the new tenants in the lower flat and found Goldie and Veeza instead. He recognized Veeza as one of the little girls that always stopped at the holy water font to bless themselves before continuing on to school. He had been surprised to see her with the Jewish grandmother.

The priest brought his mind back in focus and gave Mrs. Murphy a blessing before he left. For a brief moment he considered asking Mrs. Murphy if Veeza had ever mentioned any of her grandmother's ideas about him. Then, with a pang of guilt—vanity—he knew he couldn't ask such a question.

As he slowly walked back toward St. Mary's, he was aware that some concept was beginning to lodge in his consciousness like a rock. With this realization came the question, "Why am I taking this nonsense seriously? Malachi, the messenger—indeed. But then was not Jesus a lowly carpenter who rose to godly heights?"

Then Fr. Malachi chastised himself. "How dare I make such a comparison?"

A little Jewish old lady had designated him as God's messenger—but only because of the coincidence in names. Anyone could have done the few good deeds he'd done to help her out. Nevertheless, the old lady believed it. But did that make it enough for him to give it a second thought? In fact, did not his giving it even a single thought make him guilty of vanity?

"Behold, I send my messenger, and he shall clear the way before me . . . behold he cometh . . ."

The rock in Fr. Malachi's consciousness settled heavier as he slowed his walk.

That night, dinner was like ashes in his mouth. He made a

pretense of eating so as not to alarm the housekeeper, who displayed a strong tendency to mother the priest. If she noticed the good priest losing his appetite, she would immediately prescribe any number of cures, none of which, he was sure, she'd ever tried herself.

~ 3 ~

In his study, he gave himself a scolding. *As a young priest, I have a moral obligation not to think above my station and duties. A priest is God's handyman.* He recalled his sainted grandmother saying that even a priest is not God. He also reflected on the joy with which his family had given him to the Lord.

A group of young men in spotless albs had advanced to the altar in solemn procession. On the left arm of each was folded the priestly chasuble which they had not yet the right to wear; the right hand held a lighted candle. They knelt with heads bowed, and the archbishop crossed the stole upon each candidate's breast as he said, "Receive the yoke of the Lord for his yoke is sweet and his burden light." The chasuble of charity was then placed on each young man's shoulders, and the archbishop spread the oil of catechumens upon the opened palms of each candidate in turn, from thumb to fingertip in the sign of the cross. He then closed the hands as one of the attendants wrapped them about with a linen cloth—a little white strip which remained the dearest treasure of any woman who had a son at the altar. It would be carefully put away at home, and when the mother died and her body laid out for veneration, her hands would be wrapped with the same little linen strip as her boy's had been at his ordination.

As the candidate went forward to touch his fingers to the chalice and paten of gold with the host upon it, the archbishop said, "Receive the power to offer sacrifice to God and to celebrate mass for the living and the dead." This was an awesome moment for every young man ordained to the Catholic priesthood.

In the middle of the night, Fr. Malachi awoke, his mind feeling like he'd had a stroke. Then he realized that he hadn't had a stroke; he'd had a brainstorm!

"Dear Lord," he prayed, "sustain me. If Fr. O'Neil were here, he'd throw a fit."

His dear old Irish grandmother, on the other hand, would giggle like a young girl tiptoeing back to the buggy to kiss the boy again, saying "nothin' ventured, nothin' gained!" And Goldie, the loving optimist, would say, "Alle Menschen gut, danken Gott."

Sleep escaped him and the daring of his thoughts stimulated his body. Hands locked behind his head, he planned his strategy.

Not until the bright sunlight streamed into his room did he realize that he had finally gotten up and paced the hours away. "Dear God," he prayed, "it will be more than one lion I'll be facin'. Give me the courage and faith I'll be needin' in your name. Amen."

~ 4 ~

As Fr. Malachi wolfed a man-sized breakfast, the housekeeper commented, "You're sure fit as a fiddle this mornin', and here last night you looked like a droopin' piece of wet wash."

"Yes, indeed," the priest agreed. "Seems like the sun came up real early and dried it till it snaps in the breeze." He could hardly wait to be off and about the church's business. Especially did he want to investigate the practicality of his middle-of-the-night inspiration.

First he checked out the rundown building. Indeed, it was not too far from here and not too far from there. All in all, it was in a fairly central location.

He chalked step one off the "no" list.

With that much established, Fr. Malachi started using his nights to plan, and it amazed him how refreshed he felt in the mornings. He knew he had a mountain to climb, but his heart and his flesh supported him. At the same time, however, he realized that this was not a one-man job; he would need the cooperation of Kathryn and Dave Bernstein.

One morning, after planning for hours the night before, Fr. Malachi set off for the Bernstein home. He knew that in all likelihood he'd tangle with Dave Bernstein; he'd find no ally there. Not that he had anything specific against Dave. He recognized that in the midst of this hot seat of mixed religions, Dave had his own cross to bear. Fr. Malachi snickered to himself. "Heavens alive. This is Dave's problem in many ways. Maybe there is a plus in it, too." A tremor of hope came to him; he would wait to see.

Kathryn McGrority Bernstein's first reaction to the sight of Fr. Malachi on her doorstep was a natural one. "Is anything wrong at home?" The priest assured her that all was well as far as he knew and, with a sigh of relief, Kathryn invited him to come inside.

Dave Bernstein looked up from the newspaper, a puzzled expression on his face when he saw the priest. Momentarily, all three seemed suspended in space until the priest finally asked if he could speak with them for a few minutes about a certain matter on his mind.

Kathryn broke the tension. "Sit down, Father, and have something to drink." But the priest considered this church business rather than social, much to Dave's obvious relief.

The moment of truth faced them.

Fr. Malachi wondered how they would react to his plan, his idea. Granted, it needed to be developed. He began to explain it, focusing on Kathryn.

"Of course, I'm familiar with the location of the store my father owns," Kathryn commented. "In fact, I've heard that unless it's put into repair, it most likely will be condemned."

The priest noticed the puzzled expressions exchanged between Kathryn and Dave. *How does Mike McGrority's property concern us?* the wordless glances seemed to say.

Gradually, Kathryn began to feel as though she was about to be propelled into something she knew nothing about. As a result of the couple's uncertain glances, Fr. Malachi found himself wondering what had happened to that brilliant idea he had had earlier. It seemed in danger of evaporating into thin air.

He took a deep breath. *Either they'll go for it or they won't, but no matter what, I'd better get on with it. Without them, after all, the whole project can crumble without even a push. The Jews would say, "If the Bernsteins don't want to be involved, then why should anyone else?"* Then he had a second fleeting thought. *Ye gods! What am I getting into—and why?* Then into his brain flashed the words, *"Behold, I send my messenger."*

He took another deep breath and continued. "Remember the old lady and the meeting in your house? Perhaps the whole thing was a fiasco; nevertheless, the intent was good. How it was received has nothing to do with the fact that where there are Catholics or Protestants or Jews, there should be a place of worship. After all, the freedom to worship is everyone's right and privilege in this country. I believe that Mike's dilapidated building would make a nice little synagogue."

As he studied their faces, Fr. Malachi could feel he was getting in deeper than he had anticipated when his brainstorm first occurred. But having stated his mind, he persevered. *Onward Christian soldier,* he thought. With Mike's cooperation and Kathryn's and Dave's support, hope remained.

"You mean Mike is actually going to get involved in fixing that store up as a shul?" Dave asked incredulously.

Before Fr. Malachi could reply, Kathryn declared with delight, "Dave! It's my father's way of giving in—to our marriage—to us!"

The young priest was stunned. This interpretation was as far from the truth as one could imagine, but before he was able to clarify it, Kathryn continued. "Dave, of course we've got to help. How would it look to everyone if we didn't? You know my father; he's a stubborn Irishman. This way, it gives him a chance to prove to everyone that he's forgiven us and that he doesn't hate the Jews!"

Fr. Malachi's mind was boggled by this turn of events. "Fate steps in where fools fear to tread" or some such quotation seemed to be all he could think of. In that crucial moment, he decided to let come what may. He looked at Kathryn facing Dave, who seemed stunned. She was already planning strategy. "We could have a meeting right here in our house, and it will be a good meeting this time."

Dave scoffed. "Fat chance that anyone will come."

But Kathryn disagreed with him. "This is different. We'll be talking about a store, not a church, and my father is offering it for the good of the Jews to use as their synagogue. You have to offer friendship before you can receive it, and that's what my father is doing!"

The priest sat there almost believing it was a fact. What a kettle of fish Kathryn's enthusiasm had stirred up, but in no way was he about to toss it out.

And so it was planned. Fr. Malachi would canvass one side of the parish where there were some Jewish families, and Kathryn and Dave would telephone others. The meeting date was set for two weeks hence to give people a chance to make the time clear to attend.

With that ticklish situation smoothed over, Fr. Malachi accepted a much-needed drink to stabilize his bewilderment over the unexpected development of his well-planned idea. All he had to do now was latch onto Mike, wherever he might be, and accomplish the impossible: to get him to consent to rent the store to Jews for practically nothing, as Dave had interpreted it—or should he say, *as he had let* Dave interpret it.

Fr. Malachi anticipated a whale of a headache that night. He almost admired Mike McGrority's ability and freedom to drown his worries even at the cost of a massive hangover.

He tossed and turned in his bed. *Drat it all,* he thought, *there are a zillion ways to approach Mike, particularly since Dave and Kathryn think I've already done it. I'd just better latch onto some idea quickly before Dave has a change of heart and backs out of the whole thing.*

The priest's tortured mind went round and round—but sleep finally came.

~ 5 ~

A brilliant sun streamed in through the bedroom window and awakened the priest. *Ah,* he thought, *a beautiful day. Weather like this is perfect for walking the parish and feeling the blessedness of being alive and stirring.* He experienced a little stab of pity for the housebound, and with it came the recollection of the old lady and the tragedy of her final days. *A pity but, ah, her appointment of me to that state of grace as God's messenger— perhaps "saddled with" is more like it. Heavenly Father, where do I go from here?*

Of course, he knew. Onward, Christian soldiers.

A small house. No one home.

Another small house. A young woman answered the door, surprised at the priest's appearance and at his purpose. With some suspicion, she agreed to discuss the idea with her husband.

Another small house. "Would it be within walking distance? There is no streetcar close by."

Another small house. "Would it be an Orthodox shul? If so, count us out. We're Reformed."

Another small house with two small children playing in the yard. "Who would go?" asked a tired-looking mother. "The wife, leaving the husband at home to mind the children after a hard day's work? Later, when the children are older, religion will be more important. Maybe then."

Fr. Malachi returned to St. Mary's a weary man.

Ah, he mused, *the life of a priest is not an easy one, and of course no one ever said being God's messenger would be a bed of roses. No wonder the old grandmother always had her tea and cookies or sponge cake or kugel set aside for me. She herself was battle-scarred and had her own crosses to bear.*

Then he said aloud, "Be careful how you speak, good Father," and his weariness lifted. He thought of the many times, unknowingly, the old lady had displayed a sense of humor and understanding in dealing with those who make up the human race—all created by one Father. *Gott in Himmel!*

~ 6 ~

The following day Bridget McGrority called and Fr. Malachi could hardly believe the miracle. But then, why should he disbelieve the very ideas he preached? Miracles can happen—or at least doors can be opened to allow them in.

According to Bridget, Mike swore he was dying and wanted the last rites. Having heard from Fr. O'Neil how many times he'd been called at any time of night and day to smooth Mike's way through the gates of heaven, Fr. Malachi felt free to doubt Mike's condition. But of course, the church would not fail him.

Fr. Malachi forgot his priestly dignity as he whispered a prayer of thanks to the good Lord—for Mike's health, of course.

When he arrived at the McGrority home, Mike was sprawled out on the parlor couch, a sad sight to behold. The priest knew that Mike was a tough bird with his fists, but the Irishman had apparently met his match this time by the sight of him.

"Help me, Father, I'm dyin'! Restore me to a state of grace so the gates of heaven will open for me."

The priest took a deep breath. "The gates of heaven are never open to sinners who have disowned the Church and have abused their families, Mike. You're a disgrace to the community, you've embarrassed your good wife, and you've killed your own love for your daughter!"

Mike screamed out, "Save me, Father. I'm askin' to be saved!"

"At what cost?" Fr. Malachi was shocked at his own daring. "We need a leader in this community, Mike, like you were when you first came to St. Mary's. The stories I've heard tell about your contributions to this parish make it hard for me to believe that you are the same man. Soon, the prosperity of St. Mary's will be movin' over to Holy Cross, and people will be sayin' that Mike McGrority, the leading builder in Woods End, lost his grip!"

Mike was so taken aback by Fr. Malachi's outburst that he stopped bemoaning his aching head and began to bemoan how bad business had been. "The empty store is one big headache, and I'm only tryin' to drink my troubles away."

"What good will that do," asked Fr. Malachi, "if tomorrow you go out and forget your repentance and start all over again? Repentance comes with sincerity."

Mike grabbed at the word. "Sincerity? Oh, I'm sincere!" His head was feeling better already, just knowin' the priest was there.

"Well," challenged the priest, "prove it!"

"Just tell me what to do," begged Mike, thinking, of course, that the priest would give him maybe a hundred Hail Marys to say, or make him promise to lay off drinkin'.

Instead, Fr. Malachi made a business proposition. He asked that Mrs. McGrority listen to it as well. "A family should be a team, working together."

Mike yelled for Bridget, who came in, a worried expression on her face as though the good priest was really performing the last rites for Mike. Fr. Malachi came to the point quickly. "I would like to rent the vacant store for a period of six months."

With a sly look, Mike's head popped up like a jack-in-the-box. "At how much?"

When Fr. Malachi replied "One dollar a month," Mike's head flopped down and his sly look was replaced by a grimace of pain. "Y're jokin', Father. 'Tis that store that's drivin' me to drink—the repair an' the taxes an' the lights. Who'd be payin' for that? Certainly not me at a dollar a month!"

The priest reminded Mike about their earlier discussion concerning sincerity. It was a promise made with no strings attached.

Mike looked at Bridget, his eyes pleading for her to come to his support. But she glared back at him, her heart in her eyes. "Mike, m' love, it was a promise given to the priest."

After several long minutes, Mike conceded.

"We'll be expecting you at mass, Mike. That, too, goes with the sincerity for the Lord's work."

Fr. Malachi then indicated for Mike to bow his head, and he gave the Irishman a blessing.

Bridget led Fr. Malachi to the door. "God bless you, Father," she whispered.

As he walked back to the parish house, Fr. Malachi wasn't quite sure how God would interpret the small deception he had just employed with Mike.

~ 7 ~

The following morning greeted Fr. Malachi again with brilliant sunshine. As he planned his day, he almost wished for a pat on the back for his coup with Mike McGrority the day before.

The pat on the back came sooner than he expected when the housekeeper came to tell him that Patrick Riley was there to see him.

Patrick explained that his good wife had been to the sodality meeting of which Mrs. McGrority was an active member. Evidently Bridget McGrority had proudly related that her husband was a changed man. Not only had he made a vow to the good priest to become temperate in his imbibing habits, but he also made a contribution of the use of the vacant store to the church. According to Pat's wife, Mrs. McGrority had proudly related that Mike had such faith in the good priest that he didn't even inquire as to what Father intended to do with the store. "The ladies," Patrick's wife had told him, "were much impressed with Mike's generosity."

"So, I've come to offer the use of my services, Father, as a painter and plasterer. No doubt you'll be needing help that way, too."

Fr. Malachi made a special point of saying that, indeed, Pat's services would be greatly appreciated when the time came—and he hoped that would be very soon. Pat thanked the good priest for the opportunity to be of service.

That night, Fr. Malachi slept like a child, at peace with the world. He knew now that there'd be a whole crew eager to get on the bandwagon.

The following morning there was a letter from Fr. O'Neil, and the serenity of Fr. Malachi's previous night's sleep was subconsciously jarred. He held off reading the letter, but his conscience jabbed at him. He half hoped that Fr. O'Neil was writing to say that he was not feeling well enough to return yet.

Instead, the letter revealed that Fr. O'Neil was much improved, free of headaches, and missed his parish. If all continued as well as he hoped, it would not be long before he could return to St. Mary's. As usual, he hoped that all was well with Fr. Malachi, and he sent his blessings.

As he finished reading the letter, Fr. Malachi felt sinful for hoping that it would not be such good news about the older priest's return. There was just so much to accomplish before facing him. Fr. Malachi shuddered as he considered the next item of business—the meeting at the Bernsteins.

~ 8 ~

The preliminaries were short. Kathryn reminded the group that since she had explained the reason for the meeting when she contacted them earlier, she would let Fr. Malachi tell them what he had in mind for the Jews in their community.

Fr. Malachi remembered that Goldie had stood in this very house, in this same way. He sensed the same animosity she had, but he went right to the challenge at hand. "Your Jewish community is growing, and you really should have a house of worship. There is a building available—not large, but large enough for a start."

The initial reaction was explosive—a jumble of questions—but Fr. Malachi raised his hands to quiet the group. Then he went on. "The building will not have to be bought; it can be rented at first. The owner has agreed to accept a token payment of a dollar a month for six months. At that time, you can negotiate further."

The group guffawed. "That's a joke! Who will rent a place for a dollar a month, no less a building? And when the six months are up, what then? Will the hammer come down—clop—right on our heads? Meantime, we'd have to spend money to make the place into a shul, and we'd be stuck with what we'd laid out, and no place to go from there!"

Finally, a voice in the group asked, "Who was so thoughtful as to go out of his way to be concerned about the Jews not having a shul?"

"I was . . . " Fr. Malachi stumbled with his response.

"Is it your building?" someone else fired.

The priest took a deep breath. "Mike McGrority owns it," he stated calmly.

The group's reaction was alarming. "What kind of trick is this?" was the demand. "Mike McGrority is a Jew-hater!"

Kathryn felt her face blanch as her mind flashed back to the aftermath of the other meeting when the Jewish old lady had been there. She recalled her arguments with Dave which had lasted for days. This time Dave wouldn't forgive her because, again, she had forced the issue against his wishes. She closed her eyes; if she couldn't close her ears, at least she did not have to see those irate faces. Hearing would be enough.

Then she heard her husband's voice. "In no uncertain terms, your attitude has been an insult to a member of the clergy who happens to have in his mind the memory of a religious old lady who told us all about the need for us to have a place in which to worship. Myself, I don't care one way or another. I'm married to a shikseh who happens to feel like the alte baba did, that everyone should have a place to worship in their own religion. Because she happens to be the daughter of Mike McGrority, who has disowned her, is no reason for you to be suspicious of this good priest who, by coincidence, also happens to believe that Jews should establish themselves as a people, respected, and able to join in and grow with the entire community to make it better for everyone!"

As Kathryn listened in amazement to Dave's outburst and noticed Fr. Malachi's look of total surprise, the group burst into applause—and began to attack the subject with enthusiasm. One recalled he had an altar cloth belonging to his family; another had a Bible he'd received as a bar mitzva gift; another had candelabra which had belonged to his grandparents.

Then one pointed out that a shul needed to look like a shul! "That means work to be done. But I'm a bookkeeper. I can't hit a nail in straight."

Another said, "For the time being, we can sit on folding

chairs or maybe even just plain benches like we do at the concerts in the park."

"A shul has to have some appearance of dignity, not like a barn."

"My grandfather used to tell how, as a young man, they would have services outside when the weather was good, and they would go to a barn when the weather was bad or too cold."

"A shul is where the heart and the mind concentrate on God."

Fr. Malachi reassured them, "We already have a volunteer Catholic crew to make whatever repairs are necessary."

A buzz went around the room. If a Catholic could volunteer to work for free on a synagogue for the Jews, could the Jews do less than accept in brotherly love?

Kathryn McGrority Bernstein poured wine, and the group raised their glasses to say "mazel tov" on the birth of their first synagogue.

Fr. Malachi thrilled. He knew he would not easily forget that evening.

~ *9* ~

Bridget McGrority got the brunt of it. The ladies of the sodality club accused her of keeping secret from them the purpose of the building. They were also upset because Fr. Malachi had not revealed to their husbands to what end they were offering their services. Others wanted to know what the Jews ever did to help build St. Mary's—which wasn't even built yet.

Bridget felt their attacks on Mike like a lash. It especially hurt when they started complaining that at the rate Mike McGrority was spending his time on other interests, the Jews might well have a house of worship before the Catholics in St. Mary's.

As the stories spread, they enlarged—and Mike began to roar, "I put my faith in the church and in the priest, and where did it get me? All I asked for was absolution, and I got suckered out of a building." Then Mike rationalized, "Fr. Malachi's deception wipes out my promise about only havin' a social drink or two now and again." With that, Mike went off on a toot without so much as a word to Bridget, who then felt that Mike had deserted her when she needed him most. After all, she had been frantically defending him for supposedly conscripting free labor to build a Jew church.

~ *10* ~

Officer Brody, walking his beat, passed the old store about which there was such a stew. *Glory be. Never did I think old Mike would ever do such a damn thing as help a Jew.* Then he spotted a figure lurking close to the store, but before he could do more than change his pace, the figure darted off. Brody gave chase, drawing his nightstick.

The figure skirted in and out and finally stumbled; Officer Brody was atop him in a flash. To Brody's amazement, it was young Mike McGrority! The boy struggled to get away, but Brody held on and they headed back to the store to stomp out the flickers of fire which young Mike had lit.

Brody shook the living lights out of the boy. "What on earth did y' think y' was doin' settin' fire to y'r pop's property?"

"I don't want any Jew church in my pop's store!" the lad answered.

Young Mike was hauled back to the McGrority house.

"Retribution," Bridget McGrority moaned. She had spent the whole day arguing with Mike because he was determined to call the whole deal off. She had insisted that he must keep his word. "Imagine that," he complained, "a priest pullin' a fast one on me." He argued that the good father had never said what use he was intending to put the store to.

"But a word given is a word given, I figure," Bridget flared at Officer Brody. "And now, the divil really has got hold of young Mike. I warned the mister this would happen, what with the young whippersnapper givin' me the lip, and if it wasn't for you doin' y'r duty walkin' the beat, the store would have burned to the ground, more'n likely, before the fire engine could have got out of the station. An' all the disgrace that would have brought us! Sure, and the mister wouldn't have needed to be worryin' over the Jews havin' their church in the store because more'n likely there'd be no store left. An' all of Woods End would be knowin' it was our son, young Mike, who'd set the fire to his own father's property!"

Officer Brody read the law to young Mike and Bridget promised that the seat of the young man's pants would be as hot as fire if he didn't toe the line. "Shenanigans by the young are understandable, but settin' a fire anywhere is somethin' else."

Officer Brody said he would overlook the whole matter this time and accepted a warm drink to seal the pact.

~ *11* ~

Fr. O'Neil returned from his retreat full of health and vigor as he went back to his desk. It didn't take Fr. Malachi more than a glance to learn that the older priest had already heard a great deal about the state of affairs at St. Mary's. No doubt, there were probably several versions to the story.

Fr. O'Neil lost no time attacking the subject. "If you had any free time, Fr. Malachi, which during my absence you shouldn't have had, you should have been making efforts to bring strays back to St. Mary's instead of conscripting free labor from the parish to help build a Jew church!"

The younger priest responded to the reprimand by saying that he had had no need to conscript. "They came running, offering their services without question!" He emphasized "offering." "It may very well be that those offering might be expecting to gain something from their generosity instead of giving wholehearted-ly without intent to gain! A technicality, and a conjecture, to be sure," Fr. Malachi admitted to Fr. O'Neil, "but one to consider under the circumstances before passing total judgment!" He concluded, "As a result, I must continue until the entire matter is re-solved. I cannot retract my word to the Jews no matter the conse-quences to myself."

Fr. O'Neil stared at his subordinate in astonishment. As the two priests surveyed each other, the younger priest had a mo-ment's pang of conscience. Fr. O'Neil's eyes were squinting again—the preliminary to the headaches he suffered before go-ing on retreat.

Fr. O'Neil felt he had given enough time to the discussion; his desk needed to be tended to. Fr. Malachi breathed a sigh of relief for whatever respite he could get.

Kathryn Bernstein was restless, cross with the baby, angry with Dave, and sorry for Fr. Malachi, who now seemed involved with—she made the sign of the cross—the ghost of the Jewish old lady. It seemed to Kathryn that Fr. Malachi was mesmerized to defy the precepts of the Church. After all, a priest's obligation is absolute; he should not be drawn to other values. As Kathryn thought about it, she scolded herself. "How dare I make a judgment—me of all people, who defied my Church by marrying a Jew!"

She needed to talk with someone . . . someone impartial . . . who could separate facts from emotions. The watchmaker came into her mind.

She put the baby in the buggy and started out, no telephoning in advance for fear the watchmaker would say there was nothing he could do.

It was a troubled and lonely walk.

The watchmaker listened while Kathryn conveyed her worries to him. He shook his head. "The good priest, indeed, is well-intentioned but very unwise. A priest's business is religion; he should stay out of the building business, especially to be the middleman for a faith not his own!"

He noticed Kathryn's tears forming in the corners of her eyes. The baby whimpered.

Finally, the watchmaker agreed to contact a few people. He conceded that the priest should not be left friendless by those he had tried to help.

Word of Fr. Malachi's predicament traveled like brushfire fanned by a brisk wind into the neighboring parish of Holy Cross. Parishioners there picked up whatever bits of gossip they could about the handsome priest at St. Mary's—and with the gossip came their varied attitudes.

Holy Cross storekeepers had welcomed the modern Jews. "Some of them you might think were Protestants, not having any singsong Jew-English. And they like the best in everything so their money is just as good as any Catholic's."

In "Little Jewtown," the old Jews murmured in their beards. This one heard from that one who heard it from someone that the frummeh piroshka—the religious dumpling—not only made trouble for them there with the hoax of being bewitched, but had left behind the demon in her to stir up a whole megillah among the goyim.

Herbie, the fish man who had offered prayers after Goldie died, lost his temper. "Did not all of us here move from the crowded tenements because our children and our parents deserved something better? We knew it was a goyisha neighborhood—the few farms and stores—but it was a good place to become Americans and to live with Americans! So, did we build even a little shul over the years, like Jews should do? We could have introduced the goyim to Jewishness American style. But no. We let our parents gather together in the old reb's house, no different than before, never progressing to learn how to be Jews in America, to be respected in a new community, to grow with it. Instead, we remained clannish, bickering, critical of any person who wasn't like us!" Herbie continued, "I'm going to do everything I can to help the shul get built over there and then I'm going to become a member. Furthermore," Herbie emphasized, "from here on, I had better not hear anyone say that the alte baba was bewitched!"

~ 12 ~

One by one, the "American" Jews canvassed the parishioners of St. Mary's and explained that it was they, the Jews, who were at fault for Fr. Malachi's predicament. From the very start, they'd walked out on an old lady who had tried to explain that life without a shul to worship in is an empty one, that there is a sense of oneness under a holy roof. They pointed out that it was because of her depth of devotion that Fr. Malachi was carrying God's message to the Jews. It was in the Bible somewhere—God spoke the words, "Behold, I shall send my messenger, and he shall clear the way for me."

Some admitted, sheepishly, that they hadn't read the Bible much, not like their folks did. Yet here was a Catholic priest carrying God's message to the Catholics as well as to the Jews, to help the Jews get a shul! The priest, they said, could not have told Mike McGrority what the store would be used for until all the Jews had agreed they would take it over. But as often happens, the news got out ahead of time.

In St. Mary's parish, the ladies of the sodality called a special meeting and Bridget McGrority was naturally invited. She worried about the reason, but no amount of hinting brought any light as to why the meeting had been called.

She telephoned Kathryn. *Merciful God in heaven,* she thought, *I haven't had this much contact with my daughter since she married that Jew, and here we are, telephonin' each other in emergencies like we'd been the best of friends all along—and all because an old Jew lady stirred up a whole to-do over the Jews not havin' a church of their own!* Goose pimples rose on Bridget's arms. *Haven't I been taught that the Lord has mysterious ways for workin' out problems?*

Then, with doubt, she wondered again about the special sodality meeting. *Could they be askin' me to resign because of Mike's involvement with the store, and him, God forbid, really lettin' the church down as Fr. Malachi plainly told him?* She whispered a Hail Mary to sustain her. *The truth is that Mike has let the church down. He built that crypt when we were scrapin' for a dollar, but then the more dollars he made, the less time he had for the Lord's work.*

Bridget dressed for the sodality meeting with a heavy heart.

The watchmaker and a few of the solid Jewish citizens made their appearance at St. Mary's parish house. The housekeeper, grim-lipped, said she would inform Fr. O'Neil that they were there. Uncomfortably, the Jews waited until they were admitted to the older priest's study.

With the watchmaker as a spokesman, Fr. O'Neil listened, thinking, *It's the same story I've heard from Fr. Malachi—at least now it's confirmed.*

When the watchmaker finished, the priest told the contingent that he would give it all some thought. "The matter of discipline," Fr. O'Neil emphasized, "is strictly between myself and Fr. Malachi. Thank you for your interest and time, all the same."

As the committee left the parish house, there was a shaking of heads. It had obviously been a waste of their time.

~ *13* ~

When the sodality meeting convened, Bridget listened to the constrained small talk until everyone was accounted for. As she played with the thin slice of lemon lodged at the side of the delicate teacup, she mused, *Stubborn little thing, and what do I care about a slice of lemon in a cup of tea anyway. I'm too nervous to drink.* She felt like a pariah, yet she didn't know what the meeting was about. *So why should I feel this way?* she questioned.

Finally, all members accounted for and the teacups put aside on the little serving table, the hostess called the meeting to order.

Bridget held her breath. Indeed, the meeting was about what they, the sisters of the sodality, should do about Fr. Malachi's predicament. Bridget felt like she wanted to put her hands to her ears and close out the whole discussion before they reached the subject of Mike.

She let her eyes and her mind wander to the outdoors, visible from the windows. There were the woods where she had taken the children when they were toddlers. Kathryn had already been in school and young Mike was just learning to throw a ball. Life had been hard, but it had been full of the peace of grace.

She was brought back to reality when her name was spoken.

"Bridget, do you agree this would be more effective?"

She felt like she'd been snapped in two: one half in yesterday and the other half suspended, standing like a victim with the hangman's loop in place, ready to have the life choked out of her.

She wanted to scream, "No! I don't agree if it is anything more about Mike than I've been hearin'. I don't want to hear anything more about how Fr. Malachi suckered your husbands into promises they don't want to keep about the old building, an' I don't want to hear any more about the old lady—Lord, forgive me—with her good intentions. The only thing I do want to hear about is my renewed relationship with my daughter, Kathryn. I beg that it not be only because of this emergency meeting . . ." But Bridget heard herself reply instead, "I agree; it would be more effective." She dared not ask what "it" was that the ladies had been discussing and voting on.

The meeting came to a close, and each went her separate way, none stopping for the usual chitchat.

~ *14* ~

In his study, Fr. O'Neil felt like he was holding a hot potato in his hands. He had listened to the sodality ladies; he had listened to parishioners who were far from being paragons of virtue; he had listened to every argument presented, some with information so distorted he wondered what other variations were floating around. Even the priest at Holy Cross, St. Mary's archrival in the diocese, had a version, and this, Fr. O'Neil had to admit to himself, was the blow which had reactivated his headaches.

He recalled the peace of his retreat, aware that, indeed, it had been a retreat from the pressures of being the leader of a parish that needed to expand and had not expanded—pressures compounded now by the philosophy Fr. Malachi was espousing.

Like a needle into his flesh, the question challenged the old priest. *Blessed Mary, how many doors were closed to you before the child was born in a stable?*

~ *15* ~

The air of St. Mary's parish seemed suspended. Fr. Malachi's name was mentioned only in whispered tones as if not to offend the Holy One by bantering this unique situation back and forth. Furthermore, Holy Cross parishioners developed an unusual interest in the Sunday masses at St. Mary's. After all, no priest in St. Mary's had ever become involved with the Jews in Little Jewtown. Of course, buying their fresh-killed chickens and the fish netted right out of the tank—"as good as goin' a distance to the bay to throw a line out and hope for a bite"—was different from having a synagogue, with old men walking around in their caftans and their skull caps and their beards, right in the middle of St. Mary's parish.

And it being Mike McGrority's property no less!

Who would have thought that Mike McGrority would give a damn about any Jew—especially after his daughter had left the Church to marry one and have a child, no less, and no baptism. Who would have ever thought that Mike would get himself entangled in such a mess by giving his property to a Jew church! Mike—who could squeeze a dollar until the eagle on it squealed.

~ *16* ~

Fr. Malachi walked the floor. Over and over the questions buzzed through his head: *Lord of mercy, have I sinned by overstepping the bounds allowed a junior priest? Lord of mercy, whose jurisdiction relates to all living under your bounty, are we not all your children? Lord of mercy, are they—the Jews—not direct descendants of thy creation—and in fact—the essence of that creativity? Lord of mercy, should we not be our brother's keeper to aid and abet in his worship of you? Lord of mercy, forgive this errant servant for attempting to juggle your whys and wherefores, but it is this thy servant's soul which is being tossed between heaven and hell in this conflict of judgments, and which is now released into your hands—and may your will be done.*

Having cleared the air between himself and God, the priest went to bed.

~ *17* ~

The following Sunday, Kathryn and Dave Bernstein, with the McGrority family of Mike, Bridget, and young Mike startled Fr. O'Neil, but he greeted them as he did the other parishioners entering the basement serving as their church. Later, Mike admitted it had been Bridget's nagging that had given him no peace of mind.

Bridget interjected to the good father, "For the benefit of Mike's soul and in gratitude to the good Lord for our family problems bein' resolved, Mike has agreed to tear down the old store and start afresh for a little Jew church. At the same time, Mike will be buildin' a real St. Mary's. That way," Bridget added with some pride in her accomplishment, "Dave and Kathryn and their children can attend both churches. Learnin' the Lord's will in either place can only make their understandin' better."

Standing nearby, Fr. Malachi could almost see Goldie's blue eyes glowing with pleasure as Veeza would translate: "Ja, ja, ja, how the paths of life twist and turn and then finally meet . . . with the Lord's blessing." And then, Goldie would bustle into the kitchen to ready the tea and cookies.

YIDDISH EXPRESSIONS

ach, du lieber Himmel! Good Heavens! O My!

Alle Menschen gut, danken Gott: All human beings are good, thank God.

avek! Out!

averah: a sinful action, an undesirable act

baba: "little grandmother"

babushka: head shawl

baleboss: owner, manager; master of the house

bar mitzva: ceremony which marks a Jewish boy's entrance into manhood and acceptance of religious responsibilities

bentsh licht: the blessing over Sabbath or holiday candles

bimah: an elevated platform in the synagogue from which the Torah is read

broche: a blessing, prayer of thanksgiving

challeh: a braided loaf of white bread glazed with egg white; a traditional Sabbath bread

Chanukah: holiday, usually falling in December, which commemorates rededication of Temple in Jerusalem after profanation by Syrians in 168 B.C.E.; also known as Feast of Lights

cheder: the room or school where Hebrew is taught

chozzer: pig

Danke schön! Thank you! (German)

dybbuk: demon, an evil spirit

frau: woman

frummeh alte baba: pious old grandmother

frummeh damas: pious ladies

frummeh piroshka: a religious dumpling, i.e., a hypocrite

frummeh weib: pious woman

Galitzianer: a Jew from Galicia, a province that overlaps Poland and Austria

Gallich: a Gaelic, i.e., an Irishman

gefilte fish: fish cakes traditionally served on Friday night

gontser macher: a real operator, a big shot

gontser mensh: a real man

Gott in Himmel! God in heaven!

goy, goyim (pl.), goyish, goyisha (adj.): a Gentile—anyone who is not a Jew

grauber yung: a coarse young man

gurnicht: a nothing, entirely worthless

Guten Appetit! Enjoy your meal!

Guten Welt! It's a good world!

gutte neshoma: a good soul

haimish: homey—warm, cozy, friendly, informal

kein: not any

kein Ainglish: "no English," i.e., "I don't speak any English."

Kiddush: the prayer that sanctifies the Sabbath and Jewish holidays

kikel: a circle

kind, kinder (pl.): child

kishka: intestine; a sausage stuffed and roasted

knish: dumplings filled with potatoes, onions, chopped liver, or cheese

kopf: head

kopfwetig: headache

kosher: ritually clean according to dietary laws

küchen: pastry

kugel: a pudding made of noodles or potatoes

latke(s): a pancake

Litvak: a Jew from Lithuania or neighboring regions

mama-loshen: the mother tongue, i.e., Yiddish

matzo: unleavened bread

mazel: luck

mazel tov: good luck

mechaieh: a pleasure, a great joy

megillah: a rigmarole; anything complicated or overextended

melamed: a teacher of elementary Hebrew

menorah: a candelabrum for religious functions

mensh, menshen (pl.): a human being; a decent person

meshugge (adj.): crazy

meshuggener: an absurd man, a homespun comic

mikvah: a ritual bath of purification which a Jewish bride took before her wedding; pious women also took it after the menstrual period and childbearing

minyan: the ten male Jews required for religious services

mishegoss: a silly or absurd state of affairs, a whim

mishpocheh: relatives

mitzva: a good work

mohel: the man who circumcises the male baby eight days after birth

mutchnik: one who tortures, torments, or harasses; a bully

narrish: foolish

neshoma: soul

nosh: a snack

Oy vay! an expression used to communicate anything from delight to misery, similar to "O My!"

perücke: wig

Pesach: Passover, the most cherished Jewish holiday, commemorating the Exodus from Egypt

pesachicha: anything set aside for Passover use, including pots and cookware

poritz: a count or nobleman

pulka: chicken thigh

pushke: a container usually nailed to the kitchen wall, for money to be donated to charity

Rosh Hashanah: the Jewish New Year which celebrates the creation of the world and inaugurates ten days of repentance

schön: lovely, beautiful

schönendank: a thank-you

schwach: weak

seder: a combination banquet and religious service held in a Jewish family to commemorate Passover

shana: pretty

shanda: shame

sheitel: a wig traditionally worn by Orthodox Jewish women in Eastern Europe to make them unattractive to other men after they are married

Shevuoth: a two-day holiday which commemorates the covenant between God and Israel on Mt. Sinai

shikker (adj.): drunk

shikseh: a young, female Gentile

shivah: seven days of solemn mourning for the dead after the funeral

shlemiel: a foolish person, an unfortunate person, a born loser

shlep: to drag or pull

shochet: a person licensed to slaughter animals according to kosher requirements

shofar: a ram's horn blown in the synagogue during the high holy days

shul: a house of prayer, a synagogue

shviger: mother-in-law

Svenska: a Swedish girl

taka: truly, indeed

tante: aunt

tochis: the posterior, the buttocks

trayf: unkosher, not prepared according to ritual laws

tsimmes: a side dish of mixed cooked fruits

tsuris: troubles, worries

vershtunkena: a slob

weib,weiber (pl.): woman, wife

weltschmerz: world-weariness

Yiddisheh frummeh baba: pious Jewish grandmother

Yiddisheh maidel, maidlach (pl.): Jewish unmarried girl

Yom Kippur: the Day of Atonement, the last of the annual ten days of penitence observed by prayer, fasting, and inner searching

yontif: a celebration, holiday

zayde: grandfather

zuker: sugar